practical
gardening

practical
gardening

The complete step-by-step guide to successful gardening,
from designing, planning and planting,
to year-round maintenance tasks

Peter McHoy

HERMES
HOUSE

This edition published byHermes House in 2002

© Anness Publishing Limited 1997, 2002

Hermes House is an imprint of Anness Publishing Limited
Hermes House, 88–89 Blackfriars Road, London SE1 8HA

Published in the USA by Hermes House, Anness Publishing Inc.
27 West 20th Street, New York, NY 10011

Publisher: Joanna Lorenz
Project Editors: Clare Nicholson and Judith Simons
Designers: Patrick McLeavey & Partners and Jo Brewer
Commissioned Photography: Peter Anderson and John Freeman
Illustrator: Michael Shoebridge

Previously published as *The Ultimate Practical Gardener*

1 3 5 7 9 10 8 6 4 2

CONTENTS

INTRODUCTION

ABOVE: *Spring is a good time to plant herbaceous plants ready for summer.*

Successful gardening requires a combination of thorough planning and skilled execution and this book tells you how to plan and furnish your garden and, just as importantly, when to do it. Whether you are confined to a tiny backyard or a balcony, or you have a fairly typical small town garden or larger plot, this book offers ideas and solutions.

Making the most of

ABOVE: *Adequate feeding is one of the keys to success for container plants.*

whatever space you have depends partly on design and partly on planting. If you want a low-maintenance garden the emphasis should be on hard landscaping and the use of ground cover and low-maintenance plants. If you are a plant collector,

ABOVE: *As soon as the summer display is over, replant containers for a spring display.*

a design with the emphasis on planting space will be important, but choosing the right plants in proportion to the available space is vital. You will find lots of ideas for redesigning a garden, from initial suggestions to execution.

That said, the most careful planning and preparation will count for little if it is not complemented by sound practical knowledge of when

ABOVE: *Christmas roses are hardy, but protection will prevent mud splashes.*

the vital tasks must be undertaken. In the second half of the book, jobs have been arranged by season rather than precise weeks, as gardening is very much dependent on the weather and exact dates can be misleading.

You cannot garden successfully by the calendar alone. Frosts can come early in autumn or occur unexpectedly in early summer. The ground may be frozen when you would like to be planting, or too dry when you would want to sow your summer seeds. Use the suggested timings as a guide, but be prepared to bring things forward or put them back to suit your own area and the particular season. The most time-critical jobs are likely to be in spring and autumn, the seasons when frost-tender plants are put outside or taken in. If in doubt about the best time, it is always worth making a note of when your local parks department does the job. Winter jobs, on the other hand, are usually less time-critical and in many cases it will not matter if you move a job backwards or forwards by as much as a month. This is fortunate as it gives you the opportunity to delay a job if the weather is harsh, and to make up for lost time during those brighter spells.

Whatever your experience and whatever your gardening environment, this book has been designed to provide the kind of down-to-earth practical help that every gardener needs from time to time.

LEFT: *Azaleas are popular shrubs, but they require an acid soil. You can use a simple kit to check the soil acidity.*

RIGHT: *Modern solidago hybrids are excellent border plants for late summer.*

LEFT: *Varieties of* Anemone x hybrida *and* A. hupehensis *come into their own when most border flowers are over.*

RIGHT: Sorbus aucuparia *will sometimes retain its berries into winter if birds don't eat them first.*

ELEMENTS *of* DESIGN

Attractive gardens seldom just happen, they are designed. And despite the apparent contradiction, design does not become easier with decreasing size: rather it becomes more difficult and demanding. A large garden tends to look good anyway, with the odd weedy bed going almost unnoticed among the overall impression of lawns, stately trees and shrubs. In a small garden long vistas are out of the question and the use of trees and shrubs is often severely limited. Keep the design simple, stick to a style, and follow the suggestions in this section for making a plan to scale. Then check the effect by marking out the shapes in the garden before you start work. This way you will be assured of success.

ABOVE: *Sometimes accommodating essentials, such as this tool shed, attractively can become a problem. Careful screening can help minimize their impact.*

OPPOSITE: *A small garden should not lack impact. Provided it is well planted and has some strong focal points, it becomes easy to ignore the limitations of size.*

PLANNING YOUR GARDEN

SOME SUCCESSFUL GARDENS ARE WORKED OUT on the ground, in the mind's eye, perhaps visualized during a walk around the garden, or conceived in stages as construction takes place. This approach is for the gifted or very experienced, and it is far better to make your mistakes on paper first.

A major redesign can be time-consuming and expensive, especially if it involves hard landscaping (paving, walls, steps, etc). However, simply moving a few plants is rarely enough to transform an uninspiring garden into something special. It is worth having a goal, a plan to work to, even if you have to compromise along the way. Bear in mind that you may be able to stagger the work and cost over several seasons,

but having a well thought out design ensures the garden evolves in a structured way.

Use the checklist opposite to clarify your 'needs', then decide in your own mind the *style* of garden you want. Make a note of mundane and practical considerations, like where to dry the clothes and put the refuse, plus objects that need to be screened, such as a compost area, or an unpleasant view.

Unattractive views, and necessary but unsightly objects within the garden, such as toolsheds, are a particular problem because they can dominate a small garden. Well-positioned shrubs and small trees can act as a screen. To improve the outlook instantly use a large plant in a tub.

ABOVE: *In this garden the bird table helps to draw the eye away from the practical corner of the garden.*

LEFT: *Make a small garden look larger than it really is by ensuring the sides are well planted and creating a striking focal point.*

OPPOSITE: *Shape and form can be as important as colour in creating a stylish garden.*

LABOUR-SAVING TIPS

• To minimize cost and labour, retain as many paths and areas of paving as possible, but only if they don't compromise the design.

• If you want to enlarge an area of paving, or improve its appearance, it may be possible to pave over the top and thus avoid the arduous task of removing the original.

• Modifying the shape of your lawn is easier than digging it up and relaying a new one. It is simple to trim it to a smaller shape if you want a lawn of the same area, and if you wish to change the angle or shape, it may be possible to leave most of it intact, and simply lift and relay some of the turf.

LEFT: *Strong lines and several changes of level give this small garden plenty of interest. In this kind of design, the hard landscaping is more important than the soft landscaping (the plants).*

CHOICES CHECKLIST

Before you draw up your design, make a list of requirements for your ideal garden. You will almost certainly have to abandon or defer some of them, but at least you will realize which features are most important to you.

Use this checklist at the rough plan stage, when decisions have to be made . . . and it is easy to change your mind!

Features

Barbecue	☐
Beds	☐
Borders, for herbaceous	☐
Borders, for shrubs	☐
Borders, mixed	☐
Birdbath	☐
Changes of level	☐
Fruit garden	☐
Gravelled area	☐
Greenhouse/conservatory	☐
Herb garden	☐
Lawn (mainly for decoration)	☐
Lawn (mainly for recreation)	☐
Ornaments	☐
Patio/terrace	☐
Pergola	☐
Pond	☐
Raised beds	☐
Summerhouse	☐
Sundial	☐
Vegetable plot	☐
Plus	☐

Functional features

Compost area	☐
Garage	☐
Toolshed	☐
Plus	☐

Necessities

Children's play area	☐
Climbing frame	☐
Sandpit	☐
Swing	☐
Clothes dryer	☐
Dustbin area	☐
Plus	☐

CHOOSING A STYLE

Before sitting down with pencil and paper to sketch out your garden, spend a little time thinking about the style that you want to achieve. In many gardens plants and features are used for no other reason than that they appeal; an excellent reason, perhaps, but not the way to create an overall design that will make your garden stand out from others in the street.

The styles shown in the following six pages are not exhaustive, and probably none will be exactly right for your own garden, but they will help you to clarify your thoughts. You should know roughly what you want from your garden before you start to design it.

FORMAL APPROACH

Formal gardens appeal to those who delight in crisp, neat edges, straight lines and a sense of order. Many traditional suburban gardens are formal in outline, with rectangular lawns flanked by straight flower borders, and perhaps rectangular or circular flower beds cut into them. Such rigid designs are often dictated by the drive for the car and straight paths laid by the house builder.

Although the gardens shown here are all very different, what they have in common is a structure as important as the plants contained within it. The designs are largely symmetrical, with no pretence at creating a natural-looking environment for the plants.

The very size and shape of most small gardens limits the opportunities for natural-looking landscapes, so a formal style is a popular choice.

Parterres and knot gardens

Parterres and knot gardens often appeal to those with a sense of garden history, though in a small garden the effect can only ever be a shadow of the grand designs used by sixteenth-century French and Italian gardeners.

Parterres are areas consisting of a series of shaped beds, or compart-

ABOVE: *A knot garden. This kind of garden is not colourful, but the strong lines and formal shape, backed by a variety of greens, make it a restful place to relax.*

LEFT: *This small, enclosed courtyard garden balances a central focal point with a boundary that features this dramatic entrance.*

ments, that fit together to form a pattern, often quite complex, on the ground. They were designed, often, to be viewed from the upper windows of grand houses.

Knot gardens, originally designed to be viewed from above, are similar but low-growing clipped hedges are used to form the geometric and often interwoven designs. The space between hedges can be filled with flowers or, more historically correct, coloured sands or gravel, or even crushed coal if black appeals.

These are expensive gardens to create, slow to establish, and labour-intensive to maintain, but the results can be stunning. This kind of garden is unsuitable for a young family.

Formal herb gardens

Herb gardens are popular features and are much easier to create than knot gardens. Illustrations of both old and new herb gardens in books will often give you ideas for designs.

Rose gardens

A formal rose garden is easy to create, and it will look good even in its first season. To provide interest throughout the year, edge the beds with seasonal flowers and underplant the roses with spring bulbs or low-growing summer flowers.

Paved gardens

A small garden lends itself to being paved throughout. By growing most plants in raised beds or in containers, less bending is involved and many of the smaller plants are more easily appreciated. Climbers can be used to make the most of vertical space, and if you plant in open areas left in the paving, the garden can still look green.

Courtyard gardens

Space can be at a real premium in the heart of a town, but you can turn your backyard into an oasis-like courtyard garden, with floor tiles and white walls that reflect the light. Add some lush green foliage, an 'architectural' tree or large shrub, and the sound of running water. Although the plants may be few, the impact is strong.

Traditional designs

A small formal garden, with a rectangular lawn, straight herbaceous border, and rose and flower beds is still a popular choice with gardeners looking for the opportunity to grow a wide variety of plants such as summer bedding, herbaceous plants, and popular favourites such as roses. The design element is less important than the plants.

LEFT: *The use of white masonry paint can help to lighten a dark basement garden or one enclosed by high walls.*

BELOW: *This long, narrow plot has been broken up by strong lines: a useful design technique.*

INFORMAL EFFECTS

The informality of the cottage garden and the 'wilderness' atmosphere of a wild garden are difficult to achieve in a small space, especially in a town. However, with fences well clothed with plants so that modern buildings do not intrude, an informal garden can work even here.

Cottage gardens

The cottage garden style is created partly by design and the use of suitable paving materials (bricks for paths instead of modern paving slabs), and also by the choice of plants.

Relatively little hard landscaping is necessary for a cottage garden – brick paths and perhaps stepping-stones through the beds may be enough. It is the juxtaposition of 'old-fashioned' plants and vegetables that creates the casual but colourful look associated with this type of garden.

Mix annuals with perennials – especially those that will self-seed such as calendulas and *Limnanthes douglasii*, which will grow everywhere and create a colourful chaos. If flowers self-sow at the edge of the path, or between other plants, leave most of them to grow where they have chosen to put down roots.

Plant some vegetables among the flowers, and perhaps grow decorative runner beans up canes at the back of the border.

Wildlife gardens

A small wildlife garden seems almost a contradiction in terms, but even a tiny plot can offer a refuge for all kinds of creatures if you design and plant with wildlife in mind.

Wildlife enthusiasts sometimes let their gardens 'go wild'. However, this is not necessary. A garden like this one looks well kept and pretty, yet it provides long vegetation where animals and insects can hide and find

RIGHT: *The house itself will inevitably dominate a small garden, especially when you look back towards it. Covering the walls with climbers will help it to blend in unobtrusively.*

food. There is water to attract aquatic life, and flowers and shrubs to bring the butterflies and seeds for the birds.

An orchard can also be a magnet for wildlife of many kinds.

Woodland gardens

A woodland effect is clearly impractical for a very tiny garden, but if you have a long, narrow back garden, trees and shrubs can be used very effectively. Choose quick-growing deciduous trees with a light canopy (birch trees, *Betula* species, are a good choice where there's space,

RIGHT: *The woodland effect can be delightfully refreshing on a warm spring or summer day, but works best with trees that have a tall canopy that allows plenty of light to filter through. Although a pond is attractive in this situation, care will have to be taken to remove leaves in the autumn.*
BELOW: *A pretty pond is a super way to attract wildlife, and looks especially good if well integrated into the garden like this one.*

but they can grow tall). Avoid evergreens, otherwise you will lose the benefit of the spring flowers and ferns that are so much a feature of the traditional woodland garden.

Use small-growing rhododendrons and azaleas to provide colour beneath the tree canopy, and fill in with ground cover plants, naturalized bulbs such as wood anemones and bluebells, and plant woodland plants such as ferns and primroses.

Use the woodland effect to block out an unattractive view or overlooking houses. As an added bonus it is low-maintenance too.

Rocks and streams

Rock or water features alone seldom work as a 'design'. They are usually most effective planned as part of a larger scheme. Combined, however, rocks and water can be used as the central theme of a design that attempts to create a natural style in an informal garden.

Meandering meadows

Instead of the rectangular lawn usually associated with small gardens, try broadening the borders with gentle sweeps, meandering to merge with an unobstructed boundary if there is an attractive view beyond. If the distant view is unappealing, take the border round so that the lawn curves to extend beyond the point of view. Use shrubs and lower-growing border plants to create the kind of border that you might find at the edge of a strip of woodland.

Bright beds and borders

If plants are more important than the elements of design, use plenty of sweeping beds and borders, and concentrate heavily on shrubs and herbaceous plants to give the garden shape. Allow plants to tumble over edges and let them grow informally among paving.

If you want to create a strong sense of design within such a plant-oriented small garden, use focal points such as ornaments, garden seats or birdbaths.

DISTANT INFLUENCES

Professional garden designers are frequently influenced by classic styles from other countries, especially Japan, but amateurs are often nervous of trying such designs themselves. Provided you start with the clear premise that what pleases you is the only real criterion of whether something works, creating a particular 'foreign' style can be great fun. Adapt the chosen style to suit climate, landscape and the availability of suitable plants and materials.

Japanese gardens

'Real' Japanese gardens are for the purist who is prepared to give the subject much study. Raked sand and grouped stones have special meaning for those briefed in the Japanese traditions, but can be enigmatic to untrained Western eyes.

Many elements from the Japanese style can be adapted for Western tastes, however, and many gardeners are happy to introduce the essential visual elements without concern for deeper meanings. This style is easily adapted to a small space, and the uncluttered appearance makes a confined area appear larger.

Stone and gravel gardens

Although stones and rocks are widely used in Japanese gardens, they can also be key components in creating a garden which is more reminiscent of a dry river bed in an arid region – the sort of garden that you might find in a rocky, semi-desert area.

This kind of garden needs minimal maintenance, and if you choose drought-tolerant plants it should look good even in a very dry summer.

Stone gardens appeal to those with a strong sense of design, and an adventurous spirit, rather than to plant-lovers. Although the plants play a vital role in the drama of the scene, opportunities for using a wide range of plants is limited.

Gravel gardens are also a practical choice where space is limited. You can add some large boulders or rocks as focal points, and plants can be used much more freely. It is easy to plant through the gravel, and a wide range of plants can be grown in groups or as isolated specimens.

LEFT: *You don't need a lot of plants to create a Japanese-style garden. Strong hard landscaping and the restrained use of plants is a hallmark of the Japanese garden style.*

OPPOSITE TOP: *The use of formal water, painted wall and patio overhead gives this garden a Mediterranean atmosphere.*

OPPOSITE: *The dry gravel slope and the use of plants like yuccas help to create the illusion of a garden in a warm, dry climate.*

Mediterranean gardens

The illusion of a Mediterranean garden is most easily achieved in a backyard or tiny walled garden. The effect is difficult to achieve if you view neighbouring homes and gardens over a low fence – guaranteed to kill any self-deception as to location!

Paint the walls white, or a pale colour, to reflect the light and create a bright, airy feeling. If possible include alcoves in which you can place plants, or build ledges on which you can stand pots.

Pave the area with bricks, terracotta-coloured pavers or tiles – but steer clear of paving slabs. Use plenty of decorative terracotta pots and tubs.

The illusion is completed by using plenty of appropriate plants, such as pelargoniums, oleanders, bougainvilleas, and daturas (brugmansias). Stand pots of large cacti and succulents outdoors too.

The success of this kind of garden owes less to its structural design than to the use of appropriate plants, ornaments, and garden furniture.

Exotic effects

You can give your garden an exotic appearance by concentrating on exotic-looking plants that are hardier than

their appearance might suggest. Grow them in pots on the patio (which will enable you to move the tender kinds to a greenhouse or conservatory, or just a sheltered position, if you garden in a cold area), or in a gravel garden.

Tough, spiky plants to consider for this kind of garden are many of the hardy yuccas, and phormiums if they grow in your area without protection. Add some agaves such as *A. americana* if you live in a very mild area.

Palms are associated with warm climates, but some are tough enough to withstand moderately severe winters. *Trachycarpus fortunei* is particularly reliable. Just a few well-chosen plants can create images of far-away places.

BASIC PATTERNS

Having decided on the *style* of garden that you want, and the *features* that you need to incorporate, it is time to tackle the much more difficult task of applying them to your own garden. The chances are that your garden will be the wrong size or shape, or the situation or outlook is inappropriate to the style of garden that you have admired. The way round this impasse is to keep in mind a style without attempting to recreate it closely.

If you can't visualize the whole of your back or front garden as, say, a stone or Japanese garden, it may be possible to include the feature as an element within a more general design.

STARTING POINTS
If you analyse successful garden designs, most fall into one of the three basic patterns described below, though clever planting and variations on the themes almost always result in individual designs.

Circular theme
Circular themes are very effective at disguising the predictable shape of a rectangular garden. Circular lawns, circular patios, and circular beds are all options, and you only need to overlap and interlock a few circles to create a stylish garden. Plants fill the gaps between the curved areas and the straight edges.

Using a compass, try various combinations of circles to see whether you can create an attractive pattern. Be prepared to vary the radii and to overlap the circles if necessary.

Diagonal theme
This device creates a sense of space by taking the eye along and across the garden. Start by drawing grid lines at 45 degrees to the house or main fence. Then draw in the design, using the grid as a guide.

Rectangular theme
Most people designing use a rectangular theme – even though they may not make a conscious effort to do so. The device is effective if you want to create a formal look, or wish to divide a long, narrow garden up into smaller sections.

Circular theme

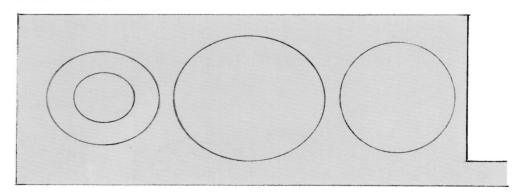

Diagonal theme

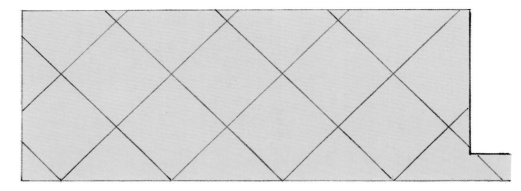

Rectangular theme

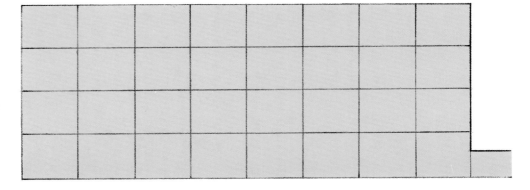

Circular theme

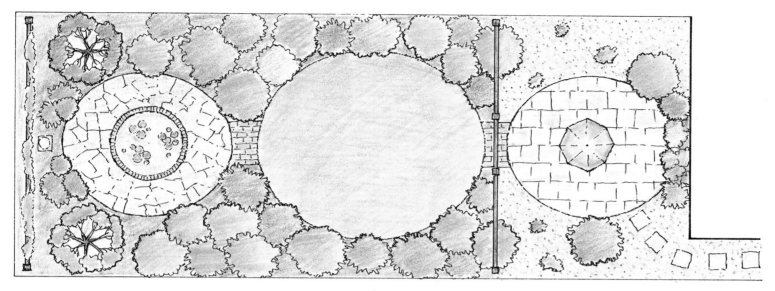

Diagonal theme

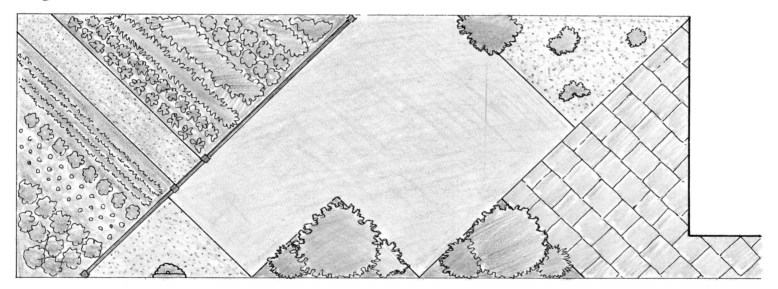

Rectangular theme

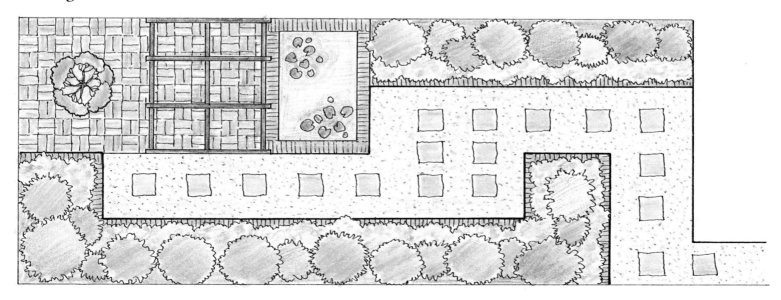

DIFFICULT SITES

Difficult sites and problem shapes are a challenge, but one that can be met with a little determination and a touch of inspiration. Some ways to tackle a selection of special areas are suggested in the following pages.

If your garden is little more than a roof or a balcony, or your house has been wedged in on a building plot that is perhaps L-shaped, or even triangular, traditional garden design techniques might seem difficult to apply.

Many of the design ideas outlined in the previous chapter can still be applied, however, although you may require an alternative design strategy for specific areas.

Patios usually feature as an element in a larger overall design, but in turn have to be designed themselves. Difficult sites like slopes, windy

ABOVE: *When your front garden is as tiny as this, compensate by making the most of vertical space with climbers and windowboxes.*

LEFT: *High walls, which would otherwise have dominated this garden, are balanced by strong vertical lines. Even the tops of the walls have been put to good use!*

alleys and passageways between houses demand thoughtful planning and appropriate plants.

Front gardens present a special problem, not because of size or shape, but because a large portion of the garden is usually dedicated to the car – often there is a broad drive to the garage or a hard standing area where the vehicle is left for long periods. Legal restrictions about what you can do with your front garden can be another potential problem – especially on estates where the developers or local authority want to maintain an 'open plan' style.

If conditions really are too inhospitable for permanent plants, or the space too limited for a 'proper' garden, containers can provide the answer. Use them creatively, and be prepared to replant or rotate frequently so that they always look good, whatever the time of year.

Unpromising backyards and basements can be transformed as much by a coat of masonry paint, a few choice plants, and some elegant garden furniture and tubs, as by an extensive – and expensive – redesign. Imagination and inspiration are the keynotes for this type of garden design.

In this chapter you will find many solutions to specific problems like these, and even if your particular difficulty is not covered exactly, you should be able to find useful ideas to adapt.

ABOVE: *This long, narrow plot has been broken up into sections, with an angled path so that you don't walk along the garden in a straight line.*

LEFT: *Roof gardens are always cramped, but by keeping most of the pots around the edge it is possible to create a sense of space in the centre.*

UNUSUAL SHAPES

Turn a problem shape to your advantage by using its unusual outline to create a garden that stands out from others in your street. What was once a difficult area to fill will soon become the object of other gardeners' envy because of its originality.

Long and narrow – based on a circular theme

This plan shows a design based on a circular theme. The paved area near the house can be used as a patio, and the one at the far end for drying the. washing, largely out of sight from the house. Alternatively, if the end of the garden receives more sun, change the roles of the patios.

Taking the connecting path across the garden at an angle, and using small trees or large shrubs to prevent the eye going straight along the sides, creates the impression of a garden to be explored.

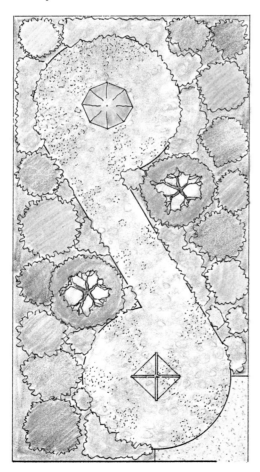

Long and narrow – based on diagonal lines

This garden uses diagonals to divide the garden into sections, but the objective is the same as the circular design. It avoids a straight path from one end of the garden to the other, and brings beds towards the centre to produce a series of mini-gardens.

Long and tapered to a point

If the garden is long as well as pointed, consider screening off the main area, leaving a gateway or arch to create the impression of more beyond while not revealing the actual shape. In this plan the narrowing area has been used as an orchard, but it could be a vegetable garden.

Staggering the three paved areas, with small changes of level too, adds interest and prevents the garden looking too long and boring. At the same time, a long view has been retained to give the impression of size.

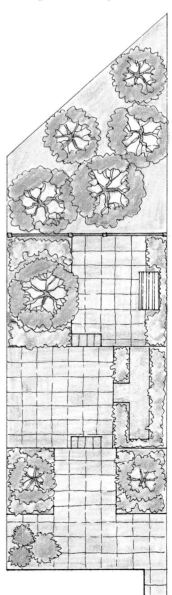

Corner sites

Corner sites are often larger than other plots in the road, and offer scope for some interesting designs. This one has been planned to make the most of the extra space at the side of the house, which has become the main feature rather than the more usual back or front areas.

Curved corner sites

Curved corner gardens are more difficult to design effectively. In this plan the house is surrounded by a patio on the left-hand side, and a low wall partitions the patio from the rest of the garden, making it more private. For additional interest, the drive is separated from the gravel garden by a path. Gravel and boulders, punctuated by striking plants such as phormiums and yuccas, effectively marry the straight edges with the bold curve created by the corner site.

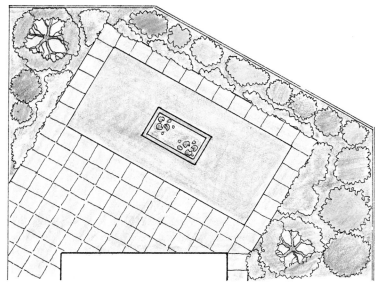

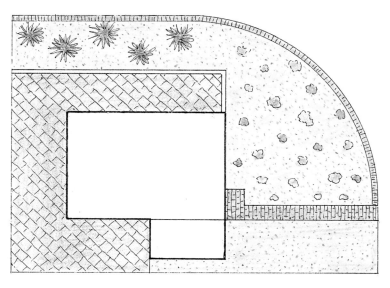

Square and squat

A small square site like this offers little scope for elaborate design, so keep to a few simple elements. To give the impression of greater space the viewpoint has been angled diagonally across the garden. For additional interest, the timber decking is slightly raised creating a change of level. In a tiny garden a small lawn can be difficult to cut, but you could try an alternative to grass, such as chamomile, which only needs mowing infrequently.

A variety of styles have been used in this plan, a combination of diagonals and circles – both of which counter the basic rectangle of the garden itself.

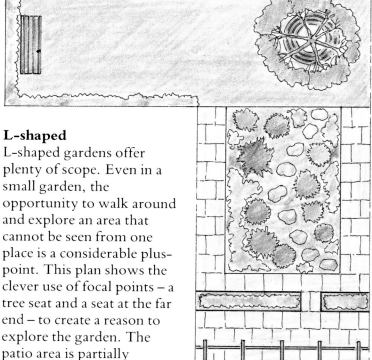

L-shaped

L-shaped gardens offer plenty of scope. Even in a small garden, the opportunity to walk around and explore an area that cannot be seen from one place is a considerable plus-point. This plan shows the clever use of focal points – a tree seat and a seat at the far end – to create a reason to explore the garden. The patio area is partially covered with overhead beams and separated from the rest of the garden by raised flowerbeds.

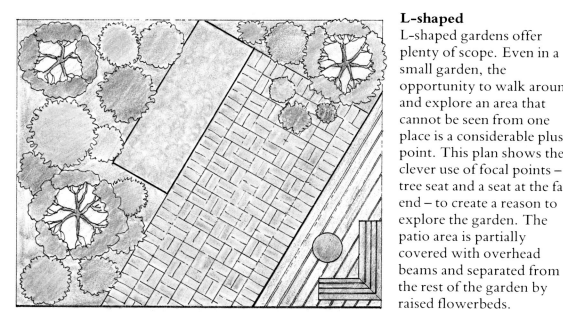

PLANNING PATIOS

The majority of small garden patios are little more than a paved area adjoining the back of the house, usually with little sense of design and often boring for most of the year. Your patio can be a key focal point that looks good in all seasons. A patio needs careful designing. It should be an attractive feature in its own right yet still form an integrated part of the total garden design.

Siting a patio

The natural choice for a sitting-out area is close to the house, especially if you plan a lot of outdoor eating. It's convenient, and forms an extra 'room', a kind of extension to the home, with a good view of the rest of the garden.

However, this spot may be shady for much of the day, in a wind tunnel created by adjacent buildings, or simply not fit in with your overall garden design.

Be prepared to move the patio away from the main building to gain

ABOVE: *Consider alternatives to paving slabs – bricks, clay and concrete pavers.*
BELOW: *The clever patio overhead makes this area function like an extra room.*

shelter or sun or if it suits your design. Using a position at one side of the garden, or even at the end, may give you more privacy from neighbours or a better view of the garden.

Choosing a shape

Most patios are rectangular – the logical shape for most gardens – but feel free to express yourself in a way that suits the overall design. A circular or semi-circular patio can form part of a circular theme. However, a round patio in a small garden designed around rectangles is likely to look incongruous.

Setting the patio at an angle to the house retains the convenience of straight lines, yet creates a strong sense of design. Consider using this shape on a corner of the house.

Patio boundaries

A clearly defined boundary will emphasize the lines of a design based on a rectangular grid. A low wall, designed with a planting cavity, will soften the hard line between paving and lawn.

High walls should be used with caution as a patio boundary, but occasionally they can be useful on one or perhaps two sides of the patio as a windbreak or privacy screen. A screen block wall will break up the space less than a solid wall, blocks or bricks. Planting suitable shrubs in front of the wall will soften the impact and help to filter the wind.

Changes of level

If the garden slopes towards the house a change of level helps to make a feature of a patio. Use a few shallow

LEFT: *Patios don't have to be by the house. A cosy corner of the garden can even be more appealing.*

BELOW: *A patio at its best where plants and people meet. The use of bricks instead of large slabs gives the illusion of size.*

steps to act like a 'doorway' to the rest of the garden.

A raised patio is a practical solution if your garden slopes away from the house. This creates a vantage point, a terrace from which you can overlook the rest of the garden. On a flat site, simply raising the level by perhaps 15cm (6in) can be enough to give the patio another dimension.

Paving materials

The choice of paving sets the tone of the patio: brash and colourful, muted but tasteful, integrated or otherwise. Do not be afraid to mix materials. Single rows of bricks will break up a large area of slabs. Choose any combination of materials that is appropriate for the setting.

If the patio is close to the house, choose bricks or pavers that match the house bricks closely. The facing bricks used for the house may be unsuitable for paving, but you should be able to achieve a close match.

FINISHING TOUCHES TO PATIO

It is the finishing touches that turn a patio from a hard, flat and uninteresting area into a spot where you can enjoy relaxing.

Patio pergola

The overhead beams of a pergola help to give the patio an enclosed, integrated appearance that effectively extends the home. They provide excellent support for climbers that can bring useful shade as well as beauty. Avoid covering the whole patio with a thick canopy of climbers, however, or you will be searching for the sun, and spattered in drips after a summer shower.

Grape vines are good climbers for an overhead, particularly as their leaves fall so you will get full winter sun. A relative with much larger leaves and gorgeous autumn colour is *Vitis coignettiae*.

You can attach overhead beams to a brick wall with joist hangers (remove some of the mortar, insert the hanger, and refill with mortar). Use ground anchors and supports for the posts to keep the timber out of contact with damp ground and prolong its life.

RIGHT: *If you position your patio away from the house, it may be necessary to construct a free-standing overhead feature.*

ABOVE: *Joist hangers are used to secure sawn timber to the house for a patio overhead.*

Built-in features

A built-in barbecue blends with the garden in a way that a free-standing one cannot, and it will probably be used more often. Built-in seats save space and, like the barbecue, give the patio a well-designed look. A few bright cushions give hard bench seats comfort and colour.

Planting spaces

Most people pack their patio with containers, but planting directly into the ground makes watering less of a chore. Permanent plants such as shrubs and small trees are best grown in the ground whenever possible. Some manufacturers make paving slabs that are designed to form a series of planting holes.

GETTING THE HEIGHT RIGHT

Patio beams should always be high enough to give plenty of clearance beneath them when clothed with plants. Even plants trained and tied in regularly may have shoots that cascade downwards, and this is especially hazardous with thorny plants such as climbing roses. If the beams are used as hanging basket supports in an area where you will be walking, make sure the bottom of the basket will be above head height. As a guide, a clearance of about 2.4m (8ft) should be the minimum in most instances.

ROOF GARDENS

Despite the handicaps, people manage to create verdant areas on top of tower blocks. If they are not overlooked, roof gardens can prove to be very private. However, there are potential structural limitations that must be checked out first. Never construct a roof garden without seeking professional advice from a structural engineer on whether the roof is able to take the weight.

You might be advised that it is safe, or told to keep the weight to certain areas, perhaps to the parapet wall, but you should abandon any idea of a roof garden if advised that it would be unsafe. Sometimes additional strengthening can be added, but this is a major and potentially expensive job.

The shape of the roof will largely determine your design. Usually raised beds are built in around the edge, with a sitting area in the centre. Pots can be used to provide variety within the paved area.

The roof is one place where artificial grass does have a place in the garden. Paving is heavy, artificial grass light. And it adds a touch of much-needed colour.

Suitable plants

Most plants simply won't stand the winds and cold winter temperatures on a roof. Choose a framework of wind- and cold-tolerant shrubs, which will provide shelter for the more vulnerable perennial plants and summer bedding.

Windbreak screens

Screens are useful windbreaks but also invaluable in masking many of the unattractive features that a rooftop presents. Use a trellis and cover it with tough climbers such as ivy.

Keeping weight down

Do everything possible to keep down the weight. Avoid thick, heavy paving stones – if you do use paving, choose the thinnest. Use lightweight, loam-free soil mixtures, and plastic or glass-fibre containers instead of terracotta or wood.

ABOVE: *A roof garden can be quite spectacular, especially if the building is strong enough to take structural features such as those shown in this picture.*

RIGHT: *Trellises provide privacy and shelter from the wind and can be fairly light which avoids increasing the weight.*

Watering

Plants in containers need frequent watering in warm weather. Carrying water to the rooftop in cans soon becomes unappealing, and getting out a hosepipe to connect to a tap indoors is also cumbersome. Give serious thought to installing an automatic watering system.

FRONT GARDENS

Front gardens greet visitors and can give delight to passers-by. Unfortunately they are difficult to design well if you have to accommodate a driveway for the car, and possibly a separate path to the front door. Even enthusiastic gardeners with delightful back gardens are often let down by an uninspired front garden. We have taken four typical front gardens and shown how they can be improved. Pick ideas from any of these that you think could enhance your own space.

EXAMPLE ONE

This is a typical design for a front garden: a rectangular lawn is edged with a flower border used mainly for seasonal bedding, and bordered by a hedge. The redesigned garden concentrates on softening the harsh demarcation between drive and ornamental section. Plants now play a more prominent role, and the emphasis is on informality instead of angular lines.

Problems

• The drive isn't part of the garden design, and this makes the area left for plants and grass look even smaller.
• The soil close to the base of a hedge is often dry and impoverished, so bedding plants don't thrive.

Solutions

• Most of the lawn has been dispensed with, and the flower beds enlarged and planted with low-maintenance shrubs. Plenty of evergreens have been used to provide year-round interest.
• Gravel has been used for the drive, and extended to form a broad and informal sweep to the front door. Not everyone likes gravel as a surface to walk on, however, and pavers could have been used instead. If plenty of plants cascade over the edge, the widening sweep would still look soft and attractive.

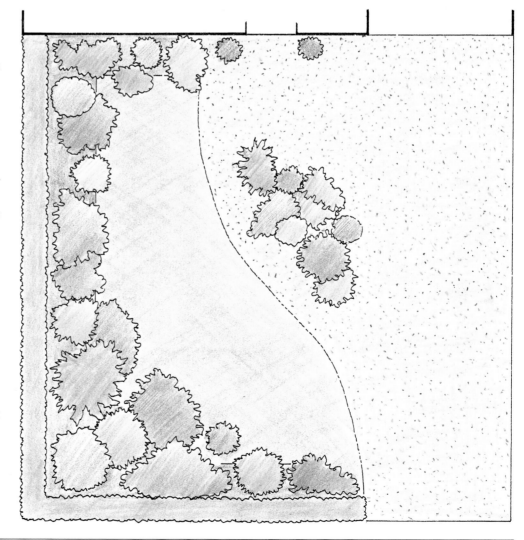

EXAMPLE TWO

Tall conifers along the drive dominate the garden and will continue to do so even after redesigning it. Remove trees that are too large rather than attempt to design around them.

Problems

- Tall hedges offer privacy, but here the scale is out of proportion, and depending on the aspect may keep out too much light.
- Rose beds are popular, but the small circular bed in the lawn looks incongruous with the rectangular design and can be difficult to mow around.
- Narrow, straight-edged beds around the edges make the lawn seem even smaller.

Solutions

- The concrete drive has been paved with bricks or brick-like pavers.
- A central planting strip has been left to break up the expanse of paving.
- The tall, dark hedge has been replaced with an attractive white ranch fence. The gravelled area beneath is planted with alpines.
- Climbing roses replace the central weeping rose. Trained against the house they provide a fragrant welcome in summer.
- Existing borders remain to minimize the reconstruction.
- Small shrubs such as hebes and lavenders have been used, along with low-growing perennials like *Stachys lanata* (syn. *S. byzantina* or *S. olympica*) and *Bergenia cordifolia*, instead of seasonal bedding plants.
- A small deciduous tree, a crab apple, replaces the large conifer in the bottom corner. The area beneath can be planted with spring-flowering bulbs such as crocuses and snowdrops.
- The small circular bed has been enlarged and filled with gravel, as a base on which to stand pots.
- The narrow bed has been filled in with grass removed when the new paving in front of the house was laid. Bricks or blocks form a crisp edge.

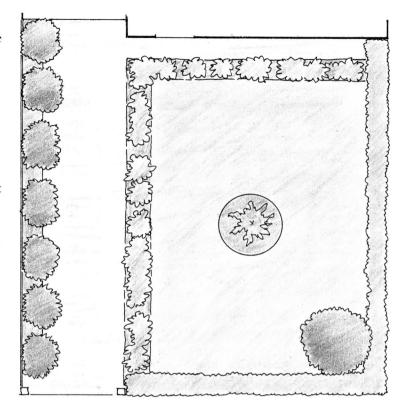

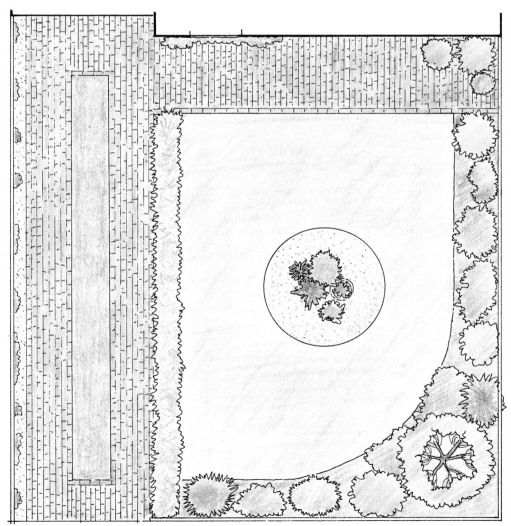

FRONT GARDENS

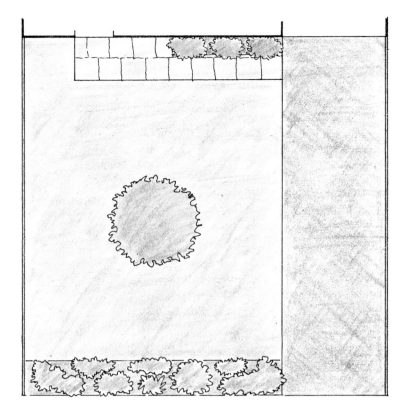

EXAMPLE THREE

Gardens don't come much more boring than this: a concrete drive, small narrow flower bed in front of the window and along the edge of the garden, and a single flowering cherry tree.

The solution for this garden was a simple one, as the redesigned garden shows. The cottage-garden style includes plants of all kinds which grow and mingle happily together with minimum intervention.

Besides being a short cut to the front door, the stepping stones encourage exploration of the garden and its plants. You actually walk through the planting, which cascades and tumbles around the paving slabs. The garden design has been reversed, with plants forming the heart of the garden rather than peripherals around the edge.

Problems

● Although the cherry is spectacular in flower, and provides a show of autumn colour, it is only attractive for a few weeks of the year. Its present position precludes any major redesign and so it is best removed.
● Unclothed wooden fences add to the drab appearance.
● Small flower beds like these lack impact, and are too small for the imaginative use of shrubs or herbaceous perennials.

Solutions

● The lawn and tree have been removed, and the whole area planted with a mixture of dwarf shrubs, herbaceous perennials, hardy annuals, and lots of bulbs for spring interest.
● Stepping-stones have been provided for those who want to take a short-cut (they also make access for weeding easier).
● The fences have been replaced with low walls so that the garden seems less confined.

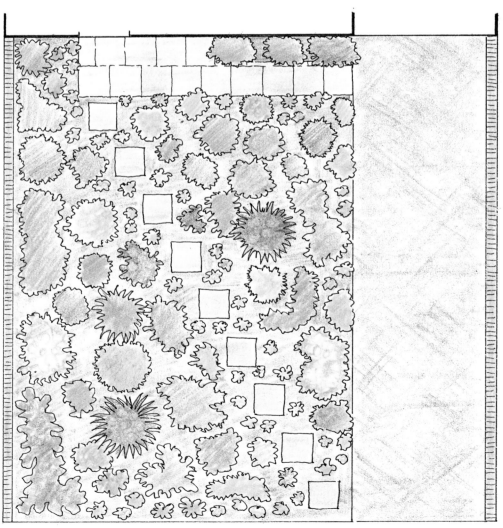

EXAMPLE FOUR

This garden is a jumble of shapes and angles, and lacks any sense of design. With its new look, the old curved path has been retained because its thick concrete base and the drain inspection covers within it would have made it difficult to move, but all the other lines have been simplified and more appropriate plants used.

Problems

• Rock gardens are seldom successful on a flat site, and although small rock beds in a lawn can be made to resemble a natural rock outcrop, in this position the rocks can never look convincing.

• The tree here is young but will grow large and eventually cast considerable shade and dominate the garden.

• Small beds like this, used for seasonal bedding, are colourful in summer but can lack interest in winter. This curve sits uneasily with the straight edge at one end and the curve of the path at the other.

Solutions

• The rock garden has been paved so that the cultivated area is not separated by the drive.

• Gravel replaces the lawn. This needs minimal maintenance and acts as a good foil for the plants.

• Dwarf and medium-sized conifers create height and cover. By using species and varieties in many shades of green and gold, and choosing a range of shapes, this part of the garden now looks interesting throughout the year.

• Stepping-stones add further interest. Because it isn't possible to see where the stepping stones lead to from either end (the conifers hide the route), a sense of mystery is added and this tempts the visitor to explore.

• The existing path has been retained but covered with slate crazy-paving it looks more interesting.

• A pond creates a water feature.

• The awkward, narrow curving strip has been turned into a 'stream', with circulating water flowing over a cascade into the pond at one end.

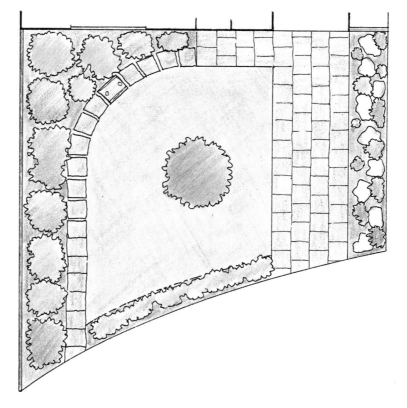

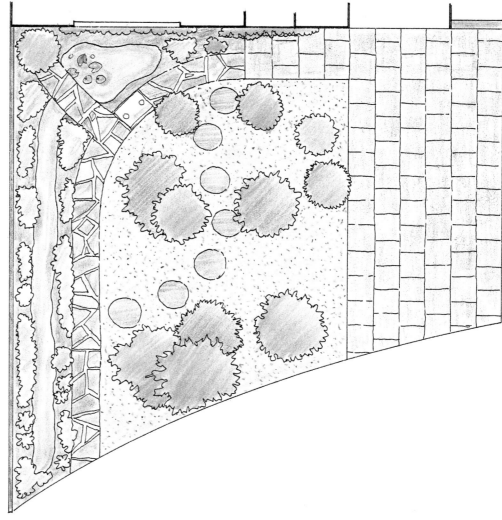

BASEMENT GARDENS AND BACKYARDS

Some gardens are not just small, they are gloomy too because they are below street level, or hemmed in by tall walls. Because there is little that can be done to alter this sort of garden structurally, it is best to direct any efforts towards improving the environment and devising a strategy that helps plants survive, or at least ensure lots of lush-looking plants to flourish despite the handicaps. Not all of the techniques shown here will be applicable to your own garden, but most of them can be adapted to suit even the most unpromising site.

Using lighting

Garden lights can extend the hours of enjoyment you derive from your garden, and you don't need many of them for a lot of impact in a small area. You can illuminate most of the space – useful if you often entertain in the evening – or use just one or two spotlights to pick out dramatic elements in the design. Some can be swivelled so that you can highlight different features. For subtle lighting, a cheaper and pretty option is to use lanterns which hold candles.

Painting the walls

In a garden enclosed by walls or fences, you need to do everything possible to reflect light and make the background bright and cheerful. Painting the walls a pale colour will improve things dramatically.

Using trellis

Trellis can be used as a decorative feature in its own right, or as a plant support. If you want to make a feature of it, paint it white, but if it is used primarily as a plant support, make sure it has been treated with a non-toxic preservative. Enclose unsightly downpipes in a trellis 'box' over which you can grow an evergreen climber such as ivy.

Adding water features

The sound of running water is refreshing on a summer's day, and in a small area you only need a trickle to do the job. A wall spout (with a tiny pool at ground level, from which the

ABOVE: *Ferns thrive in shady positions where many other plants would languish. If you can provide moisture from a water feature, so much the better.*
RIGHT: *Even the tiniest basement garden or backyard has space for a water feature.*

water is recirculated) or a self-contained wall fountain is ideal.

Introducing wind chimes

Wind chimes both look and sound good. Choose one primarily for the sound it makes.

Training wall shrubs

Cover some of the walls with climbers, but try espalier or fan-trained fruit trees or espalier pyracanthas too.

Furnishing in style

White-painted furniture looks bright in a small, enclosed garden, but don't add too much furniture or the area will look cluttered rather than elegant.

Using containers with character

If the area is small, make everything work for its space. Instead of plastic containers, use interesting old kitchen utensils, or other unexpected holders, but be sure to add drainage holes to prevent waterlogging.

Focal points in shade

Basement areas and enclosed backyards are often inhospitable for plants – the light is poor and the walls keep off much of the rain. If, in addition, you have a tree that casts shade, even the shade-loving plants will struggle. Use these positions for ornaments or make them into focal points.

Planting ferns

Ferns do well in a cool, shady spot, so use them freely in those areas too dull for bright summer flowers. Try a collection of hardy ferns – they won't look dull if you nestle an attractive ornament among them, or include white flowers, perhaps backed by a white wall. On a hot summer's day the space will be an oasis of coolness and tranquillity.

Growing white-flowered plants

Use pale flowers if the area lacks direct sun. You won't be able to use plants that need strong sun light, but fortunately some of the best white-flowering plants are shade-tolerant. Try white varieties of impatiens and white nicotianas, for example. White flowers will show up more brilliantly than coloured ones in a dull spot.

Introducing exotics

Gardens enclosed by walls can be hot and sunny too, and being sheltered provides the ideal environment for many exotic plants to grow successfully. Try a few bold houseplants to create a tropical effect.

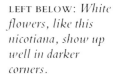

LEFT: *Use wall pots and half baskets to make a dominant wall more interesting. They will be more effective staggered rather than in straight rows.*

LEFT BELOW: *White flowers, like this nicotiana, show up well in darker corners.*

Making the most of steps

Open railings can be used as supports for attractive climbers, planted in pots at the base of the steps, but always keep them trimmed so that slippery leaves do not trail across the steps or obstruct the hand-rail. If the steps are very wide, place pots of bright flowers on the steps themselves to produce a ribbon of colour. Do not obstruct the steps. If there is no space on the steps, use a group of containers filled with flowers at the top and bottom of the stairway.

Fixing windowboxes and wall baskets

Use windowboxes lavishly – not only beneath windows but fixed to walls too. Windowboxes, wall pots and half-baskets can all bring cascades of colour to a bare wall. Stagger the rows instead of placing them in neat and tidy lines.

Capturing the scents

An enclosed garden is an ideal place in which to grow scented plants – the fragrances are held in the air instead of being carried off on the wind. Use plenty of aromatic plants, especially big and bold plants like daturas, and those with a heavy perfume such as evening-scented nicotianas and night-scented stocks.

BALCONIES AND VERANDAS

For someone without a garden, a balcony may be their entire 'outdoor room', and a 'garden' to enjoy from indoors when the weather is inclement. Even more than a patio, the balcony or veranda is an outdoor extension of the home.

The area is usually small, so the money you are prepared to spend on gardening will go a long way. Invest in high quality flooring and furniture, and ornate containers, which will create a classy setting for your plants.

Choosing flooring

The floor will help to set the tone and style, and it can make or mar a tiny 'garden' like this.

Paving slabs are best avoided: they are heavy, frequently lack the kind of refinement that you can achieve with tiles, and the size of individual slabs may be too large to look 'in scale' for the small area being covered.

Think of the veranda or balcony floor as you might the kitchen or conservatory floor – and use materials that you might use indoors. Quarry tiles and decorative ceramic tiles work well, and produce a good visual link with the house. Make sure ceramic tiles are frostproof however. Tiles are relatively light in weight, and their small size is in proportion to the area.

Wooden decking is another good choice for a veranda.

The problem of aspect

Aspect is an important consideration. Unlike a usual garden, or even a roof garden, the light may be strong and intense all day, or there may be constant shade, depending on position. Balconies above may also cast shade.

If the aspect is sunny, some shade from above can be helpful. Consider installing an adjustable awning that you can pull down to provide shade for a hot spot. Choose sun-loving plants adapted to dry conditions for this situation – your indoor cacti and

RIGHT: *Roof gardens and balconies are often improved if you lay a wooden floor and create a lattice overhead.*

succulents will be happy to go outside for the summer.

If the aspect is shady for most of the day a lot of flowering plants won't thrive. You may have to concentrate on foliage plants, though some bright flowers, such as impatiens and nicotiana, do well in shade.

Countering the wind

Like roof gardens, balconies are often exposed to cold and damaging winds. The higher a balcony the greater problem wind is likely to be.

To grow tender and exotic plants, provide a screen that will filter the wind without causing turbulent eddies. A trellis clothed with a tough evergreen such as an ivy is useful, or use screens of woven bamboo or reeds on the windiest side – these not only provide useful shelter and privacy, but make an attractive backdrop for plants in containers.

Adding colour round the year

Create a framework of tough evergreens to clothe the balcony or veranda throughout the year, and provide a backdrop for the more colourful seasonal flowers.

Use plenty of bright seasonal flowers in windowboxes or troughs along the edge, with trailers that cascade down over the edge.

In the more sheltered positions, grow lots of exotic-looking plants, and don't be afraid to give lots of your tough-leaved houseplants a summer holiday outside.

Pots of spring-flowering bulbs extend the season of bright flowers, but choose compact varieties – tall daffodils, for example, will almost certainly be bent forward as wind bounces back off the walls.

Add splashes of colour with cut flowers. In summer choose long-lasting 'exotics' such as strelitzias and anthuriums.

ABOVE: *In mild areas or a sheltered position, you can turn your balcony into a tropical garden.*

RIGHT: *Turn your balcony into an outdoor room where many indoor plants thrive in summer.*

FEATURES
and STRUCTURES

Overall garden design is important, but it is individual features that make a garden special. Major structural decisions, such as the type of paving to use, the shape of the lawn, or how to define the boundaries, have a significant impact, but even small details like ornaments and garden lights can lift a small garden above the ordinary. The use of containers is especially important in a small garden – on a tiny balcony they may be the garden. Use them imaginatively, choosing containers that are decorative, and grouping them for added interest.

ABOVE: *Create the urge to explore with small paths that lead to features such as seats and ornaments.*

OPPOSITE: *The garden floor is important, whether paving or a lawn, but it is features, like this arbour and its seat, that give the garden character.*

the GARDEN FLOOR

The GARDEN FLOOR – LAWN, PAVING, PATHS, even areas of gravel or ground cover plants – can make or mar your garden. These surfaces are likely to account for more area than the beds and borders. Although they recede in importance when the garden is in full bloom, for much of the year they probably hold centre stage.

Removing existing paths and paved areas presents a practical problem. If they are laid on a thick bed of concrete you will probably have to hire equipment to break up the surface. Provided these areas do not compromise your design too much, it is much easier to leave as many as you can in position. Consider paving over the top with a more sympathetic material. It should be relatively easy to extend the area if you want to.

Lawns are more easily modified than paths and paved areas. At worst you can dig them up and resow or relay them. If you simply want to change the shape, you can trim off surplus grass or lift and relay just part of the lawn.

ABOVE: *Paths can be both functional and attractive, often giving the garden shape and form.*

OPPOSITE: *Hard landscaping, such as bricks, combined with soft landscaping, such as lawns, can look very harmonious if designed with integration in mind.*

OPPOSITE ABOVE: *A brick edging marks the boundary between lawn and border, and serves the practical purpose of making mowing easier.*

LEFT: *Areas like this would soon become weedy if not densely planted. Here hostas suppress the weeds, and Soleirolia soleirolii spills over onto the path.*

Timber decking is very popular in some countries, seldom used in others. Much depends on the price of timber locally, and to some extent the climate, but decking should always be on your list of options.

There are useful alternatives to grass for areas that are not used for recreation or are seldom trodden on. Ground cover plants not only suppress weeds in flower beds, but can replace a lawn where the surface does not have to take the wear and tear of trampling feet. Inset stepping-stones to protect the plants. Where the garden is *very* small, low-growing ground cover may be much more practical than a lawn that is almost too tiny to cut with a mower.

LAWNS

The lawn is often the centrepiece of a garden, the canvas against which the rest of the garden is painted. For many gardeners this makes it worth all the mowing, feeding and grooming that a good lawn demands. If your lawn has to serve as a play area too, be realistic and sow tough grasses, and settle for a hard-wearing lawn rather than a showpiece. It can still look green and lush – the important consideration from a design viewpoint. Instead of aiming for a bowling-green finish, the shape of the lawn or a striking edging could be its strong visual message.

Working with circles

Circular lawns can be very effective. Several circular lawns, linked by areas of paving, such as cobbles, work well in a long, narrow garden.

If the garden is very small, all you will have space for is a single circular lawn. If you make it the centrepoint with beds around it that become deeper towards the corner of the garden, you will be able to combine small trees and tall shrubs at the back with smaller shrubs and herbaceous plants in front. To add interest, include a couple of stepping-stone paths that lead to a hidden corner.

Using rectangles

Rectangular lawns can look boring, but sometimes they can be made more interesting by extending another garden feature – such as a patio or flower bed – into them to produce an L-shaped lawn.

Alternatively, include an interesting feature such as a birdbath or sundial (often better towards one side or end of the lawn than in the middle). A water feature is another good way to break up a boring rectangle of grass.

An angled lawn

If you have chosen a diagonal theme for your design, you will probably want to set your lawn at an angle to the house so that it fits in with the

ABOVE RIGHT: *A sweeping lawn can help to create a sense of perspective.*
RIGHT: *This lawn would look boring with straight edges. The curves add style.*

other features. The same rectangle of lawn becomes much more interesting when set at an angle of about 45 degrees. By lifting and patching the lawn, you may be able to achieve this without having to start from scratch.

Creating curves

A sweeping lawn with bays and curves where the flower borders ebb and flow is very attractive. It is difficult to achieve in a small garden. However, you can bring out a border in a large curve so the grass disappears around the back. You may be able to do this by extending the border into an existing rectangular lawn.

Changing height

If you have to create an impression in a small space, try a raised or sunken lawn. The step does not have to be large – 15–23cm (6–9in) is often enough. If making a sunken lawn, always include a mowing edge so that you can use the mower right up to the edge of the grass.

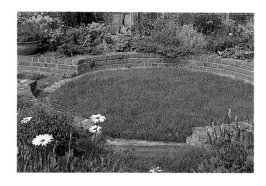

ABOVE: *Sunken lawns make a bold feature.*

KEEPING A TRIM EDGE

Circular lawns must be edged properly. Nothing looks worse than a circle that isn't circular, and of course constant trimming back will eat into the lawn over the years. To avoid this, incorporate a firm edging, such as bricks placed on end and mortared into position, when you make the lawn.

Where the edges are straight use proprietary lawn edging strips.

HOW TO CREATE A MOWING EDGE

If flowers tumble out of your borders, or there is a steep edge that makes mowing difficult, lay a mowing edge of bricks or paving slabs.

1 Mark out the area of grass to be lifted using the paving as a guide. Lift the grass where you want to lay the paved edge. To keep the new edge straight, use a half-moon edger against the paving slab. Then lift the grass to be removed by slicing it off with a spade.

2 Make a firm base by compacting gravel or a mixture of sand and gravel where the paving is to be laid. Use a plank of wood to ensure it is level. Allow for the thickness of the paving and a few blobs of mortar.

3 It is best to bed the edging on mortar for stability, but as it will not be taking a heavy weight just press the slabs onto blobs of mortar and tap level (use a spirit-level to double-check).

IMAGINATIVE PAVING

Most gardens have a patio or at least a paved area close to the house. Often it is the main feature around which the remainder of the back garden is arranged. It can be the link that integrates home and garden, creating an outdoor room. At its worst, paving can be boring and off-putting; at its best it can make a real contribution to the overall impact of the garden.

On the following pages you will find a selection of popular paving materials, with suggestions for use, and their advantanges and disadvantages. Always shop around because the availability and price of natural stones vary enormously, not only from country to country, but also from area to area.

Even the availability of man-made paving will vary from one area to another. Choosing the material is only part of the secret of successful paving – how you use it, alone or combined with other materials, is what can make an area of paving mundane or something special.

Colour combinations

Your liking for bright and brash colour combinations will depend on the effect you want to create. Be wary of bright colours though – they can detract from the plants, although they will mellow with age.

Sizing up the problem

In a small garden, large-sized paving units can destroy the sense of scale. Try small-sized paving slabs (which are also easier to handle), or go for bricks, pavers, or cobbles.

Mix and match

Mixing different paving materials can work well, even in a small space. Try areas or rows of bricks or clay pavers with paving slabs, railway sleepers with bricks, in fact any combination that looks good together and blends with the setting. Avoid using more than three different materials, however, as this can look too fussy in a small garden.

LEFT: *Bricks and pavers often look more attractive if laid to a pattern such as this herringbone style.*

Paving patterns

You can go for a completely random pattern – crazy-paving is a perfect example – but most paving is laid to a pre-planned pattern using rectangular paving slabs or bricks. Look at the brochures for paving slabs. These usually suggest a variety of ways in which the slabs can be laid.

Although a large area laid with slabs of the same size can look boring, avoid too many different sizes, or complex patterns in a small space. Simplicity is often more effective.

Bricks and clay pavers are often the best choice for a small area, because their small size is more likely to be in harmony with the scale of the garden. The way they are laid makes a significant visual difference, however, so choose carefully.

The stretcher bond is usually most effective for a small area, and for paths. The herringbone pattern is suitable for both large and small areas, but the basket weave needs a reasonably large expanse for the pattern to be appreciated.

Stretcher bond

Herringbone

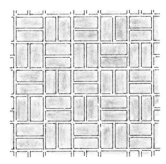

Basket weave

HOW TO LAY PAVING

1 Excavate the area to a depth that will allow for about 5cm (2in) of compacted hardcore topped with about 3–5cm (1–2in) of ballast, plus the thickness of the paving and mortar. As an alternative to hardcore topped with ballast, you can use 5cm (2in) of scalpings. Check the depth of the foundation before laying the paving. If adjoining the house, make sure that the paving will end up below the damp-proof course.

2 Put five blobs of mortar where the slab is to be placed – one at each corner, and the other in the middle.

3 Alternatively, cover the area where the paving is to be laid with mortar, then level.

4 Position the slab carefully, bedding it on the mortar.

5 Use a spirit-level to ensure that the slab is level, but use a small wedge of wood under one end to create a slight slope over a large area of paving so that rainwater runs off freely. Tap the slab down further, or raise it by lifting and packing in a little more mortar. Position the level over more than one slab (place it on a straight-edged piece of wood if necessary).

6 Use spacers of an even thickness to ensure regular spacing. Remove these later, before the joints are filled with mortar.

7 A day or two after laying the paving, go over it again to fill in the joints. Use a small pointing trowel and a dryish mortar mix to do this. Finish off with a smooth stroke that leaves the mortar slightly recessed. This produces an attractive, crisp look. Wash any surplus mortar off the slabs before it dries.

PAVING MATERIALS

There are plenty of paving materials from which to choose, so spend time looking through brochures and visit garden centres and builders' merchants before you come to a decision.

PAVING SLABS
Rectangular paving slabs

The majority of paving slabs are based on a full-sized slab 45 × 45cm (18 × 18in) or 45 × 60cm (18 × 24in). Half and quarter slabs may be a little smaller in proportion to allow for mortar joints. Thickness may vary according to make, but provided you mix only those made by the same manufacturer this won't matter.

A *smooth* surface can be boring, slippery, and a little too much like public paving, but many have a *textured* finish. Textures vary. A riven finish usually looks like natural stone, an exposed aggregate finish has exposed gravel to give a natural-looking non-slip finish.

Slabs imprinted with a section of a larger pattern are usually unsatisfactory in a small area. As quite a large area of paving is usually required to complete the pattern, they only emphasize the space limitations.

Shaped paving slabs

Use shaped slabs with caution. Circular slabs are useful for stepping-stones, but are difficult to design into a small patio. Hexagonal slabs also need a fairly large area to be appreciated. Special half-block edging pieces are usually available to produce a straight edge.

Paved and cobbled finish slabs

Some designs are stamped with an impression to resemble groups of pavers or bricks, some containing as many as eight basket-weave 'bricks' within the one slab. They create the illusion of smaller paving units, and are very effective in a small area.

RIGHT: *Bricks, unlike clay pavers, are laid with mortared joints. This can emphasize the design.*

TOP LEFT: *Slabs like this are particularly useful for a small area because they give the illusion of smaller paving units.*
TOP RIGHT: *Paving slabs with a riven finish look convincingly like real weathered stone.*
MIDDLE LEFT: *Paving slabs will always weather. Pale colours like this will soon look darker, while bright colours will become muted.*
MIDDLE RIGHT: *Hexagonal paving slabs can be attractive, but are not usually satisfactory in a very small area.*
BOTTOM: *Rectangular shapes like this can be used alone, or integrated with other sizes to build up an attractive design.*

Planting circles

A few manufacturers produce paving slabs with an arc taken out of one corner. Four of these placed together leave a circular planting area for a tree or other specimen plant.

BRICKS AND PAVERS

Bricks and pavers are especially useful for a small garden. You can create an attractive design even in a small area, and you may be able to obtain them in a colour and finish that matches your home, which will produce a more integrated effect.

Always check that the bricks are suitable for paving, however, as some intended for house building will not withstand the frequent saturation and freezing that paths and patios are subjected to. After a few seasons they will begin to crumble. Clay pavers, on the other hand, have been fired in a way that makes them suitable for paving. Concrete pavers and blocks are another option, though these are usually more suitable for a drive than a small patio.

Rectangular pavers

Clay pavers look superficially like bricks but are designed to lock together without mortar. They are also thinner than most bricks, though this is not obvious once they have been laid. Concrete pavers or paving blocks are laid in a similar way and are more attractive than concrete laid in-situ for a drive. They can look a little 'municipal'.

Interlocking pavers and blocks

Concrete pavers or blocks are often shaped so that they interlock. Interlocking clay pavers may also be available.

Bricks

Bricks require mortar joints – they won't interlock snugly like clay pavers. On the other hand you may be able to use the same bricks for raised beds and low walls, giving the whole design a more planned and well-integrated appearance.

To use bricks economically, lay them with their largest surface exposed, not on edge. This excludes the use of pierced bricks (which have holes through them). It does not matter if they have a frog (depression) on one side, provided this is placed face-down.

Setts and cobbles

Imitation granite setts, which are made from reconstituted stone, and cobbles, which are natural, large, rounded stones shaped by the sea or glaciers, are both excellent for small areas of irregular shape. Their size makes them much easier to lay to a curve. Bed them into a mortar mix on a firm base.

Tiles

Quarry and ceramic tiles are appropriate for small areas near the house, or to create a patio that looks just that little bit different. Always make sure ceramic tiles are frostproof. Lay them on a concrete base that has been allowed to set, and fix them with an adhesive recommended by the supplier or manufacturer.

LEFT: *Hard paving comes in many forms. The top row shows (from left to right) natural stone sett, clay paver, clay brick, artificial sett. The centre row shows a typical range of concrete paving blocks. The bottom row illustrates some of the colours available in concrete paving slabs.*

PATHS AND PATH MATERIALS

As with any other garden structure, paths should be designed to suit the purpose they are to serve. There are a wide range of materials on the market to suit every need so shop around before deciding which you require.

Practical paths should be functional first and attractive second. Drives for cars and paths to the front door must be firmly laid on proper foundations. And don't skimp on width – it is extremely frustrating for visitors if they have to approach your door in single file. It might be better for the route to take a detour, perhaps forming an L-shape with the drive, if there isn't enough space for a wide path directly to the door.

Internal paths, used to connect one part of the garden to another, can be more lightly constructed, and are softened with plants.

Casual paths, which often lead nowhere and are created for effect, such as stepping-stones through a flower bed, can be lightly constructed and much less formal in style.

RIGHT: *Although the gaps between these paving slabs have been filled with chipped bark in this example, you could also use gravel.*

BELOW: *Paving can reflect artistic ambitions.*
BELOW RIGHT: *Victorian-style rope edging.*

Bricks and pavers
These are ideal materials for internal garden paths that have to be both practical and pretty. Complex bonding patterns are best avoided unless the path is very wide.

Paving slabs
By mixing them with other materials the look of paving slabs can be much improved. A narrow gravel strip either side can look smart, and the gravel can be extended between the joints to space out the slabs. The slab-and-gravel combination is ideal if you need a curved path.

A straight path can be broken up with strips of beach pebbles mortared between the slabs. Tamp them in so that they are flush with the surrounding paving.

Crazy-paving
Use this with caution. In the right place, and using a natural stone, the effect can be mellow, and harmonize well with the plants. Be more wary of using broken paving slabs – even though they are cheap. Coloured ones can look garish, and even neutral slabs still look angular and lack the softness of natural stone.

Path edgings
Paths always make a smarter feature with a neat or interesting edging. If you have an older-style property, try a Victorian-style edging. If it is a country cottage, try something both subtle and unusual, like green glass bottles sunk into the ground so that just the bottoms are visible. Or use bricks: on their sides, on end, or set at an angle of about 45 degrees.

CREVICE PLANTS
Plants look attractive and soften the harsh outline of a rigid or straight path. They are easy to use with crazy-paving or any path edged with gravel. It may be necessary to excavate small holes. Fill them with a good potting mixture. Sow or plant into these prepared pockets.

Some of the best plants to use for areas likely to be trodden on are chamomile, *Thymus serpyllum* and *Cotula squalida*. For areas not likely to be trodden there are many more good candidates, such as *Ajuga reptans* and *Armeria maritima*.

HOW TO LAY CLAY OR CONCRETE PAVERS

The method of laying clay or concrete pavers described in the following steps can be used for a drive or a patio as well as a path.

1 Excavate the area and prepare a sub-base of about 5cm (2in) of compacted hardcore or sand and gravel mix. Set an edging along one end and side first, mortaring into position, before laying the pavers.

2 Lay a 5cm (2in) bed of sharp sand over the area, then use a straight-edged piece of wood stretched between two height gauges (battens fixed at the height of the sand bed) to strike off surplus sand and provide a level surface.

3 Position the pavers, laying 2m (6½ft) at a time. Make sure they butt up to each other, and are firm against the edging. Mortar further edging strips into place as you proceed.

5 Brush more sand into the joints, then vibrate or tamp again. It may be necessary to repeat this once more.

4 Hire a flat-plate vibrator to consolidate the sand. Alternatively, tamp the pavers down with a club hammer over a piece of wood. Do not go too close to an unsupported edge with the vibrator.

TIMBER DECKING

Timber decking creates a distinctive effect, and will make a refreshing change from ordinary paving for the patio area. As with paving, the material used should be in proportion to the size of the garden, so the width of the planks is important. Wide planks look best in a large garden, but in a small, enclosed area narrower planks are usually preferable.

Different designs can be achieved by using planks of different widths and fixing them in different directions, as illustrated here, but on the whole it is best to keep any pattern fairly simple. Leave a small gap between each plank, but not so large that high-heeled shoes can slip into it.

The construction method and timber sizes must reflect the size of the overall structure and its design – especially if built up over sloping ground. In some countries there are building codes and regulations that may have to be met. If in doubt, seek professional help with the design, even if you construct it yourself.

All timber used for decking must be thoroughly treated with a wood preservative. Some preservatives and wood stains are available in a range of colours, and this provides the opportunity for a little creativity. Dark browns and black always look good and weather well, but if you want to be more adventurous choose from reds, greens and greys.

If you want your decking to have a long life, special pressure-treated timber is the best choice. However, the range of colours available is bound to be less extensive.

Parquet decking

The easiest way to use timber as a surface is to make or buy parquet decking. Provided the ground is flat panels are easy to lay and can look very pleasing. Bed them on about 5cm (2in) of sand over a layer of gravel, to ensure free drainage beneath. If you already have a suitable concrete base to use, you can lay them directly onto this.

LEFT: *Timber decking makes a refreshing change from paving slabs or bricks, and can give the garden a touch of class.*

Patterns of Timber Decking

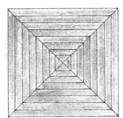
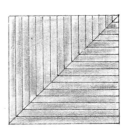

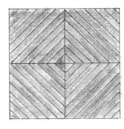

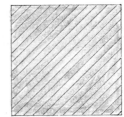

GROUND COVER WITH PLANTS

If you want to cover an area of ground with a living carpet simply for texture, and don't expect to walk on the area, suitable ground cover plants are the answer.

To use ground cover plants like this, rather than simply as a means to suppress weeds in a flower bed, they must be evergreen, compact, and grow to a low, even height.

HOW TO PLANT CLUMP-FORMING GROUND COVER

1 Clear the ground of weeds first, and be especially careful to remove any deep-rooted or difficult perennial weeds.

2 Add plenty of garden compost or rotted manure, then rake in a controlled-release fertilizer. Add these before laying a mulching sheet.

3 Cover the area with a weed-suppressing mulching sheet. You can use a polythene sheet, but a special woven mulching sheet is much better.

4 Make crossed slits through the sheet where you want to plant. Avoid making the slits too large.

5 Excavate planting holes and firm in the plants. If necessary tease a few of the roots apart first.

6 Water thoroughly, and keep well watered. Remove the sheet once the plants are well established.

GROUND COVER PLANTS

Some of the best plants for the job are *Armeria maritima*, bergenias, *Cotoneaster dammeri*, *Euonymus fortunei* varieties, *Hypericum calycinum*, and *Pachysandra terminalis*. If you want flowers as the main feature, heathers are difficult to better.

HOW TO PLANT CREEPING GROUND COVER

The mulching sheet method is a good way to get clump-forming plants such as heathers off to a good start, but don't use it for those that creep and root, such as ajugas and *Hypericum calycinum*. Plant these normally but apply a loose mulch about 5cm (2in) thick to cover the soil.

GRAVEL GARDENS

Gravel is an inexpensive and flexible alternative to paving or a lawn, although it is not suitable for a patio. It blends beautifully with plants, needs little maintenance, and can be used in both formal and informal designs. It is also a useful 'filler' material to use among other hard surfaces, or in irregularly shaped areas where paving will not easily fit and a lawn would be difficult to mow.

LEFT: *Gravels naturally vary considerably in colour.*

Types of gravel

Gravel comes in many different shapes, sizes and colours. Some types are angular, others rounded, some are white, others assorted shades of green or red. All of them will look different in sun or shade, when wet or dry. The subtle change of colour and mood is one of the appeals of gravel. The gravels available will depend on where you live, and which ones can be transported economically from further afield. Shop around first going to garden centres and builders merchants to see what is available in your area before making your choice.

Gravel paths

Gravel is often used for drives, but it is also a good choice for informal paths within the garden. It conforms to any shape so is useful for paths that meander. However, it is not a good choice for paths where you will have to wheel the mower.

HOW TO LAY A GRAVEL PATH

1 Excavate the area to a depth of about 15cm (6in), and ram the base firm.

2 Provide a stout edge to retain the gravel. For a straight path, battens secured by pegs about 1m (3ft) apart is an easy and inexpensive method.

3 First place a layer of compacted hardcore. Add a mixture of sand and coarse gravel (you can use sand and gravel mixture sold as ballast). Rake level and tamp or roll until firm.

4 Top up to the required height with the final grade of gravel. In small gardens, the size often known as pea gravel looks good and is easy to walk on. Rake and roll repeatedly until the surface is firm and stable.

If the path is wide, it is a good idea to build the gravel up towards the centre slightly so that puddles do not form after heavy rain.

Gravel beds

Gravel can be used as a straight substitute for grass and requires much less maintenance. You can even convert an existing lawn very simply by applying a weedkiller to the grass, laying edging blocks around the edge, then topping up with gravel.

Informal gravel beds still require some kind of edging restraint to prevent the gravel from spreading. If the bed is surrounded by a lawn, simply make sure that the gravelled area is about 5cm (2in) below the surrounding grass.

Other practical ways to prevent the gravel from scattering onto beds and other unwanted areas are to create a slightly sunken garden or to raise the surround slightly with a suitable edging.

Informal gravel areas often look especially effective if some plants are grown through the gravel – either in beds with seamless edges where the gravel goes over them, or as individual specimen plants.

HOW TO LAY A GRAVEL BED

1 Excavate the area to the required depth – about 5cm (2in) of gravel is sufficient in most cases.

2 Level the ground. Lay heavy-duty black polythene or a mulching sheet over the area. Overlap strips by about 5cm (2in).

3 Then tip the gravel on top and rake level.

4 To plant through the gravel, draw it back from the planting area and make a slit in the polythene. Plant normally, enriching the soil beneath if necessary.

5 Firm in and pull back the polythene before re-covering with gravel.

FORMING BOUNDARIES

MOST OF US HAVE AN INSTINCTIVE DESIRE TO mark our territory with a very visible boundary. It gives us a sense of privacy and the illusion of security, but above all it marks out our plot of land, the area in which we create our own very special paradise.

The problem with a small garden is that the boundary forms a large part of the garden, and the chances are that you will see it from whichever direction you look. In a large garden the boundary often merges into the background, but in a small one it can easily dominate.

Tall walls can be an asset – the walled town garden has many of the treasured attributes of an old walled country garden – but drab wooden fences and large overgrown hedges pose real problems if you want to make your garden look smart and stylish.

Don't take your boundary for granted, and never assume it can't be improved. Replacing a fence or grubbing up a long-established hedge are not projects to be tackled lightly – they can be expensive or labour-intensive. Never make changes until you have consulted neighbours that

LEFT: *This is an excellent example of a combination boundary – a wooden picket fence supported on a low wall, with an escallonia flowering hedge growing through it.*

OPPOSITE ABOVE: *Walls make secure boundaries, but to prevent them looking oppressive cover with climbers, and if possible create a view beyond, as this attractive gate has done.*

OPPOSITE: *A wall as tall as this can easily dominate a small garden, but by treating it boldly and using it as a feature it becomes an asset.*

are affected. The boundary may belong to them, in which case it is not yours to change unilaterally. Even if it is legally yours to replace, the courtesy of discussing changes with others affected will go a long way to helping you remain on good terms with your neighbours.

Although you are unlikely to want to exceed them in a small garden, there may be legal limitations on boundary height, perhaps laid down in the terms of the contract when you bought the property. In some countries there may be restrictions placed by the highways authority on road safety grounds.

Restrictions are most likely in front gardens – some 'open plan' estates, for example, may have limitations on anything that might infringe the integrated structure of the gardens.

None of these restrictions need inhibit good garden design, but it is always worth checking whether any restrictions exist before erecting or planting a new boundary.

HEDGES FOR GARDENS

Many of the classic hedges, like beech, yew, and tall conifers like × *Cupressocyparis leylandii*, and even the privet (*Ligustrum ovalifolium*) have strictly limited use in a small garden. In small gardens the emphasis should be on plants that have much to offer or compact growth. The hedges suggested here are just some of the plants that could be used to mark your boundary without being dull or oppressive. Be prepared to experiment with others.

Clipped formality

The classic box hedge (*Buxus sempervirens*) is still one of the best. It clips well and can be kept compact, but choose the variety 'Suffruticosa' if you want a really dwarf hedge like those seen in knot gardens. A quick-growing substitute is *Lonicera nitida*, and there's a golden form that always looks bright – but be prepared to cut frequently. Some of the dwarf berberis stand close clipping – try the red-leaved *Berberis thunbergii* 'Atropurpurea Nana'. Yew (*Taxus baccata*) is also excellent for formal clipping, and it can be kept compact enough for a small garden.

Colourful informal hedges

If you want to cut down on clipping, and want something brighter and more colourful than most foliage hedges, try the grey-leaved *Senecio* 'Sunshine' or the golden *Philadelphus coronarius* 'Aureus' (unfortunately sheds its leaves in winter). *Viburnum tinus* can also be kept to a reasonable height, and provided you avoid pruning out the new flowers it will bloom in winter. Many of the flowering and foliage berberis also make good 'shrubby' hedges. These will lack a neatly clipped profile, but pruning and shaping is normally only an annual job.

ABOVE: *Although* Lonicera nitida *needs frequent clipping, it makes a neat formal hedge.*

LEFT: *Many shrub roses can make an attractive flowering hedge in summer, but do not plant them too close to the edge of a path otherwise their thorny stems may be a nuisance.*

Using roses

Roses make delightful – and often fragrant – boundaries, but they have shortcomings. Their summer beauty is matched by winter ugliness, and they are not a good choice for a boundary where passers-by may be scratched by thorns. You can use a row of floribunda (cluster-flowered) roses, but the shrubby type are usually preferred for this job.

Old-fashioned lavender and rosemary dividers

Both these herbs make excellent informal flowering hedges, with the merit of being evergreen too. You could try the shorter lavender in front of the taller rosemary. Both become untidy with age, so replace the plants when it becomes necessary.

Other flowering hedges

Forsythia is one of the most popular flowering hedges, but careful pruning is required to achieve consistent flowering on a compact hedge. There are plenty of alternatives, including the shrubby potentillas, berberis like *B. × stenophylla*, with bold flowers, though this one can take up a lot of space, and even tall varieties of heathers if you just want a boundary marker rather than a barrier.

ABOVE: *Box is one of the classic plants to use for clipped formality. This is a glaucous form.*

HOW TO PLANT A NEW HEDGE

1 Prepare the ground very thoroughly. Excavate a trench – ideally about 60cm (2ft) wide – and fork in plenty of rotten manure or garden compost.

2 Add a balanced fertilizer at the rate recommended by the manufacturer. Use a controlled-release fertilizer if planting in the autumn.

3 Use a garden line, stretched along the centre of the trench, as a positioning guide. If the area is windy or you need a particularly dense hedge, plant a double row of trees. Bare-root plants are cheaper than container-grown plants, but only separate them and expose the roots once you are ready to plant. Only the most popular hedging plants are likely to be available bare-root, and for many of the plants suggested you will have to plant a single row of container-grown plants.

4 Use a piece of wood or a cane cut to the appropriate length as a guide for even spacing. Make sure the roots are well spread out. If planting container-grown plants, tease out some of the roots that are running around the edge of the root-ball.

5 Firm the plants in well and water thoroughly. Be prepared to water the hedge regularly in dry weather for the first season. Keep down weeds until the hedge is well established, then it should suppress the weeds naturally.

GARDEN WALLS

Except for special cases, such as basement flats and the need for privacy or screening in a difficult neighbourhood, high walls are inappropriate for a small garden. However, low walls up to about 1–1.2m (3–4ft) are a useful alternative to a hedge, particularly if you want to avoid regular trimming. Although the rain shadow and shade problems remain the same for a wall as a hedge, a wall will not impoverish the soil in the same way as a hedge.

Low walls

A low wall, say 30–60cm (1–2ft) tall, will serve the same demarcation function as a taller one, but in more appropriate scale for a small garden, and shrubs planted behind it are more likely to thrive. Modest garden walls like this are much easier to construct than tall ones, which may need substantial reinforcing piers, and are well within the scope of a competent garden handyman to build.

Brick walls

Plain brick walls can harmonize with the house, but generally look dull from a design viewpoint. A skilled bricklayer can often add interest by laying panels or strips to a different pattern. The choice of brick and the capping will also alter the appearance. Some are capped with bricks, others have special coping tiles. These all add to the subtle variety of brick walls.

Block walls

Many manufacturers of concrete paving slabs also produce walling blocks made from the same material. These are especially useful for internal garden walls and raised beds. They are often coloured to resemble natural stone, but brighter colours are available if you want to match the colour scheme used for the paving. Bear in mind that colours will weather and become much more muted within a couple of years.

ABOVE: *An interesting brick wall.*
RIGHT: *A wall like this makes a solid and secure boundary without making the garden appear too enclosed.*

Screen block walls

Screen block walls (sometimes called pierced block) are most frequently used for internal walls, perhaps around the patio or to divide one part of the garden from another, but they can also be used to create a striking boundary wall too.

These blocks have to be used with special piers and topped with the appropriate coping. They are useful if you want to create a modern image, or perhaps the atmosphere of a Mediterranean garden.

Mixing materials

Some of the smartest boundary walls are made from more than one material. Screen blocks look good as panels within a concrete walling block framework. Screen blocks can also be incorporated into a brick wall, and help to let light through and to filter some of the wind. Panels of flint or other stone can be set into an otherwise boring tall brick wall.

BELOW: *Walls can be colourful . . . if you create planting areas. The summer bedding plants used here are replaced at the end of the season with bulbs and spring bedding plants to use the planting areas to their full advantage.*

Cavity walls

Low cavity walls that can be lined with plants soon become an eye-catching feature. Pack them with colourful summer flowers, or plant with permanent perennials such as dwarf conifers, which maintain interest throughout the year (but be sure to choose truly dwarf conifers for this). If you plant cascading forms

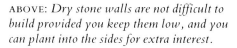

ABOVE: *Dry stone walls are not difficult to build provided you keep them low, and you can plant into the sides for extra interest.*

such as nasturtium or trailing lobelia, the effect can be really stunning. For a spring display, try aubrietia and the yellow *Alyssum saxatile*, with a few dwarf spring-flowering bulbs.

Dry stone walling

Dry stone walls are more often used for retaining banks or as internal dividers, but in an appropriate setting this kind of wall makes an attractive boundary. This type of wall looks best where dry stone walls are part of the natural landscape.

The great advantage of a dry stone wall – which is assembled without mortar – is the ability to plant in the sides. This can provide a home for many kinds of alpines.

Walls with a difference

The larger and taller the wall, the more imaginative you should be when designing it. Try incorporating an alcove for an ornament, or a panel into which you can set an artistic piece of wrought-iron that can be viewed against the green of a neighbouring field or garden.

WALL BUILDING MATERIALS

Most builders' merchants stock a good range of bricks, the majority are suitable for garden walls, but if you need a lot of bricks – enough to justify ordering direct – get in touch with a few brick companies. Their expertise can be invaluable, and most will be able to offer you a wide choice.

Buying bricks is something most of us do only rarely, so professional advise is especially useful. The author's experience, however, suggests that you can't always depend on the advise of a builder's merchant. Shop around until you find someone who really appears to have a knowledgeable passion for bricks – they will tell you about all the different finishes and colours available, and most importantly will know whether a particular brick is suitable for the job you have in mind. *Always* explain what you want your bricks for: a building, a garden wall, wall of a raised bed, or for paving. Some bricks which are perfectly suitable for house walls may be very unsuitable for paths or garden walls.

If you need a lot of bricks (many hundreds), it may be better, and cheaper, to buy direct from a brick manufacturer if they will deal with the general public.

ABOVE: *Bricks come in many colours and finishes, and these are just a small selection from the many kinds available. Names of* bricks vary from country to country, but whatever names are used you are likely to have a good choice.

MASONRY MORTAR

A suitable mortar for bricklaying can be made from 1 part cement to 3 parts soft sand. Parts are by volume and not weight. Cement dyes can be added to create special effects, but use coloured mortar cautiously.

Common bonds

Expert brick-layers may use more complicated bonds, but for ordinary garden walls – and especially those that you are likely to lay yourself, perhaps for a low boundary wall or for a raised bed within the garden – it is best to choose one of the three bonds illustrated below.

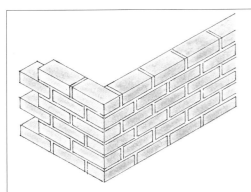

Running bond or stretcher bond This is the simplest form of bonding, and is used for walls a single brick wide – or where you want to create a cavity, such as a low wall with a planting space.

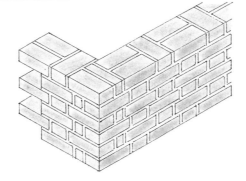

Flemish bond This is another way to create a strong bond in a wall two bricks wide. The bricks are laid both lengthways and across the wall within the same course.

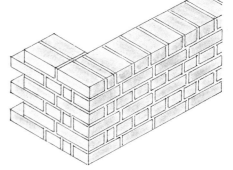

English bond This is used for a thick wall the width of two bricks laid side by side – useful where strength is needed for a high wall. Alternate courses are laid lengthways then across the wall.

HOW TO LAY BRICKS AND BLOCKS

Although bricks are being laid here, the same principles apply to laying walling blocks.

1 All walls require a footing. The one shown here is a for a low wall just one brick wide: for larger and thicker walls the dimensions of the footing will have to be increased.

Excavate a trench about 30cm (12in) deep, and place about 13cm (5in) of consolidated hardcore in the bottom. Drive pegs in so that the tops are at the final height of the base. Use a spirit-level to check levels.

2 Fill with a concrete mix of 1 part cement, 2½ parts sharp sand and 3½ parts 2cm(¾in) aggregate, and level it off with the peg tops.

3 When the concrete has hardened for a few days, lay the bricks on a bed of mortar, also place a wedge of mortar at one end of each brick to be laid. For stability, always make a pier at each end, and at intervals of about 1.8–2.4m (6–8ft) if the wall is long. Here two bricks have been laid crossways for this purpose.

4 For subsequent courses, lay a ribbon of mortar on top of the previous row, then 'butter' one end of the brick to be laid.

5 Tap level, checking constantly with a spirit-level.

6 The wall must be finished off with a coping of suitable bricks or with special coping sold for the purpose.

BOUNDARY FENCES

Fences have the great merit of being more instant than hedges and less expensive than walls. That is the reason they are so often chosen by builders for new properties, and why they are frequently chosen again when the original fences come to the end of their useful life.

Closeboard and panel fences are popular, but predictable and a little boring. There are plenty of styles to choose from, however, so select a fence appropriate to your garden design yet practical for the purposes you have in mind.

If you want privacy or animal-proofing, you will have to opt for one of the solid styles, but if it is just a boundary-marker that is needed there are many attractive fences that look stylish and won't appear oppressive in a small garden.

The names of particular fence types can vary from country to country. If you do not recognize any of the names here check with the illustrations.

Closeboard

Closeboard fencing is erected on site by nailing overlapping feather-edged boards to horizontal rails already secured to stout upright posts. It is a strong, secure fence, but not particularly attractive – especially viewed from the side with the rails.

Panels

Prefabricated panels are quick and easy to erect and a popular choice for that reason. Panels are usually about 1.8m (6ft) long and range in height from about 60cm (2ft) to 1.8m (6ft), generally in 30cm (1ft) steps. The interwoven or overlapping boards are sandwiched between a frame of sawn timber. The woven style is not as peep-proof as overlapping boards.

Interlap or hit-and-miss

This combines strength and a solid appearance with better wind-filtering than a solid fence (which can create turbulent eddies that can be damaging

ABOVE: *Closeboard fencing well covered with climbing roses.*

ABOVE: *Wattle or woven fences make an attractive background for plants.*

ABOVE: *A low wooden fence is not obtrusive and can look very attractive.*

to plants). It is constructed from square-edged boards that are nailed to the horizontal rails on alternate sides. Overlapping the edges gives more privacy, while spacing them further apart can look more decorative.

Picket

Picket fences look good in country gardens, but can also be a smart choice for a small town garden. Narrow, vertical pales are nailed to horizontal timbers, spaced about 5cm (2in) apart. You can make them yourself or buy kits with some of the laborious work done for you. The simplest shape for the top of each pale is a point, but you can make them rounded or choose a more ornate finial shape. A picket fence can be left in natural wood colour, but they look particularly smart painted white. Because they are usually relatively low, and you can see plenty of garden through the well-spaced pales, they don't dominate the garden in the same way as a tall, solid fence.

Ranch-style

Ranch-style fences consist of broad horizontal rails fixed to stout upright posts. They are usually quite low, and frequently consist of just two or three rails. White-painted wood is a popular material, but wipe-down plastic equivalents are very convincing and easy to maintain. For a small garden they provide a clear boundary without becoming a visual obstruction. Also, rain and sun shadows are not created in the way that occurs with more solid fences.

Post and chain

This is the least obtrusive of all fences. Purely a boundary marker, it will do nothing to deter animals or children, or keep balls out of the garden, but it is a good choice if you want a fence that is hardly noticeable. You can use wooden, concrete or plastic posts and metal or plastic chains. Choose a white plastic chain if you want to make a feature of the fence, black if you want the chain to recede and blend into the background.

Chain link

Chain link is not an aesthetic choice, but it is highly practical and an effective barrier for animals. It is probably best to have a contractor erect a chain link fence, as it needs to be tensioned properly. You may like the fact that you can see through it, especially if the view beyond is attractive, but you may prefer to plant climbers beside it to provide a better screen. Choose tough evergreens such as ivy if you want year-round screening.

Bamboo

Bamboo is a natural choice if you've created an oriental-style garden, but don't be afraid to use this type of fence for any garden style if it looks right. Bamboo fences come in many shapes and sizes, and the one you adopt will depend partly on the availability and cost of the material and partly on your creativity and skill in building this kind of fence.

ABOVE: *A fence like this just needs a supply of bamboo and skill at tying knots!*

LEFT: *A white picket fence can make the boundary a feature of the garden.*

HOW TO ERECT A FENCE

Many gardeners prefer to employ a contractor to erect or replace a fence. They will certainly make lighter work of it with their professional tools for excavating post holes, and a speed that comes with expertise, but some fences are very easy to erect yourself. Two of the easiest are panel and ranch-type fences, which are illustrated in simple steps below.

HOW TO ERECT A PANEL FANCE

1 Post spikes are an easier option than excavating holes and concreting the post in position. The cost saving on using a shorter post and no concrete will go some way towards the cost of the spike.

Use a special tool to protect the spike top, then drive it in with a sledge-hammer. Check periodically with a spirit-level to ensure it is absolutely vertical.

2 Once the spike has been driven in, insert the post and check the vertical again.

3 Lay the panel in position on the ground and mark the position of the next post. Drive in the next spike, testing for the vertical again.

4 There are various ways to fix the panels to the posts, but panel brackets are easy to use.

5 Insert the panel and nail in position, through the brackets. Insert the post at the other end and nail the panel in position at that end.

6 Check the horizontal level both before and after nailing, and make any necessary adjustments before moving on to the next panel.

7 Finish off by nailing a post cap to the top of each post. This will keep water out of the end grain of the timber and extend its life.

HOW TO ERECT A RANCH-STYLE FENCE

1 Although ranch-style fences are easy to erect the posts must be well secured in the ground. For a wooden fence, use 12.5 × 10cm (5 × 4in) posts, set at about 2m (6½ft) intervals. For additional strength add intermediate posts. A size of 9cm (3½in) square is adequate for these.

Make sure the posts go at least 45cm (18in) into the ground.

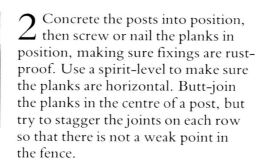

2 Concrete the posts into position, then screw or nail the planks in position, making sure fixings are rust-proof. Use a spirit-level to make sure the planks are horizontal. Butt-join the planks in the centre of a post, but try to stagger the joints on each row so that there is not a weak point in the fence.

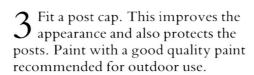

3 Fit a post cap. This improves the appearance and also protects the posts. Paint with a good quality paint recommended for outdoor use.

ABOVE LEFT: *Panel fences are easily erected and provide a peep-proof barrier, but are best clothed with plants to soften the effect.*
ABOVE: *Ranch-style fences make an unobtrusive barrier – ideal where the garden merges into the countryside.*

THE PLASTIC ALTERNATIVE

There are many plastic ranch-style fences. They will vary slightly in the way they are assembled. Detailed instructions should come with them, however, and you should have no difficulty.

The 'planks' are sometimes available in different widths – 10cm (4in) and 15cm (6in) for example – and these help to create different visual appearances. Gates made from the same material are also available from some manufacturers.

Posts are usually concreted into the ground, and the cellular plastic planks are push-fitted into slots or special fittings. Special union pieces are used to join lengths, and post caps are usually glued and pushed into position.

White ranch fencing needs to be kept clean to look good, and plastic can simply be washed when it looks grubby.

FINISHING TOUCHES

EVERY GARDEN SHOULD BE FULL OF SURPRISES, packed with finishing touches that complete the overall effect.

Many of the focal point techniques used in large gardens can be scaled down and applied on a small scale, and even in a small space the garden can express the owner's sense of fun and personality in the little extras that are grafted onto the basic design.

The whole area can be made to work, every corner can be exploited with devices if not plants, and a degree of flexibility can be built in that makes variety a real possibility.

ABOVE: *A seat like this suggests a gardener with a strong sense of design.*

OPPOSITE ABOVE: *Ornaments have been used to excellent effect here. A sundial commands centre stage and the eye is taken across the garden to a figure which adds light and life.*

OPPOSITE BELOW: *Figures usually look best framed by plants.*

LEFT: *This quiet corner has been transformed by white-painted trellis and seat.*

In a large garden most ornaments, furniture and fixtures like garden lights are a static part of the design. In a small garden a slight rearrangement of the furniture, the changed position of a light, or the simple exchange of one ornament for another according to mood and season means that the garden need never be predictable despite limitations of size.

Ornaments in particular can set a tone for the garden: serious or frivolous, classic or modern. They suggest the owner's taste . . . and even sense of humour. Just as the painting on the living-room wall or the ornaments on the sideboard can tell you a lot about the occupier, so garden ornaments reveal the personality of the garden maker.

Garden lighting can be practical and even a useful security measure, but it also offers scope for artistic interpretation. Experiment with spotlights in various positions and discover the dramatically different effects created by the use of light and shadows from different angles.

Arches and pergolas are a more permanent element of the garden's design, but they don't have to be planned in at the design stage and are easily added to an existing garden.

PERGOLAS AND ARCHES

A sense of height is important even in a small garden. Unless there is vertical use of plants or upright garden features, the centre of the garden will be flat. Attention will pass over the centre and go instead to the edges of the garden: exactly the lifeless effect you want to avoid.

Small trees, wall shrubs and climbers can provide the necessary verticals, but if these are in short supply an arch or pergola may be the answer.

Traditionally, and especially in cottage gardens, they have been made from rustic poles, but where they adjoin the house or link home with patio, sawn timber is a better choice. The various constructions described here are free-standing, and usually used as plant supports. Their visual effect is to take the eye to further down the garden.

If a pergola or arch seems inappropriate, similar construction techniques can be used to create an intimate arbour.

HOW TO ASSEMBLE AN ARCH

The simplest way to make an arch is to use a kit, which only needs assembling.

1 First establish the post positions, allowing 30cm (1ft) between the edge of the path and post, so that plants do not obstruct the path.

2 Fence spikes are the easiest way to fix the posts. Drive them in using a protective dolly. Check frequently with a spirit-level. Insert the posts and tighten the spikes around them. Alternatively, excavate four holes, each to the depth of 60cm (2ft).

3 Position the legs of the arch in the holes. Fill in with the excavated earth, and compact.

4 Lay the halves of the overhead beams on a flat surface, and carefully screw the joint together with rust-proof screws.

5 Fit the overhead beams to the posts – in this example they slot into the tops of the posts and are nailed in place.

HOW TO JOIN RUSTIC POLES

Rustic arches and pergolas look particularly attractive covered with roses or other climbers. You can be creative with the designs, but the same few basic joints shown here are all that you will need.

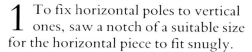

1 To fix horizontal poles to vertical ones, saw a notch of a suitable size for the horizontal piece to fit snugly.

2 If you have to join two horizontal pieces, saw two opposing and matching notches so that one sits over the other, and secure them.

3 To fix cross-pieces to horizontals or uprights, remove a V-shaped notch using a chisel if necessary to achieve a snug fit, then nail into place with rust-proof nails.

4 Use halving joints where two pieces cross. Make two saw cuts half way through the pole, then remove the waste timber with a chisel.

5 Secure the joint with a nail. For extra strength, paint the joint with woodworking adhesive first.

6 Bird's mouth joints are useful for connecting horizontal or diagonal pieces to uprights. Cut out a V-shaped notch about 3cm (1in) deep, and saw the other piece to match. Use a chisel to achieve a good fit.

7 Try out the assembly on the ground, then insert the uprights in prepared holes and make sure these are secure before adding any horizontal or top pieces. Most pieces can be nailed together, but screw any sections subject to stress.

ABOVE: *Rustic poles are an appropriate choice for a feature such as this.*

GARDEN LIGHTING

Garden lights not only make your garden look more dramatic as dusk falls, they also extend the hours during which you can enjoy it. If you like entertaining in the garden on summer evenings, or just want to sit and relax, lights will add another dimension to the space.

When illuminating your garden you are not attempting to fill the garden with floodlights, but rather to use spotlights to pick out a particular tree, highlight an ornament, or bring to life the droplets of a cascade or fountain.

You don't even need elaborate mains lighting. Low-voltage lighting supplied from a transformer indoors is perfectly adequate for most lighting jobs in a small garden.

Lighting beds
Summer bedding looks good with pools of light thrown downwards onto the beds. If you find the lights obtrusive during the day, choose a low-voltage type that is easy to move around. Simply push the spiked supports into the bed when you want to use the garden in the evening.

Picking out plants
Use a spotlight to pick out one or two striking plants that will form focal points in the evening. The white bark of a birch tree, perhaps underplanted with white impatiens, the tall ramrod spikes of red hot pokers (kniphofias), or a spiky yucca, make excellent focal points picked out in a spotlight. Tall feathery plants, such as fennel, also illuminate well.

Spotlighting ornaments
Ornaments and containers full of plants also make striking features to pick out in a spotlight.

Before highlighting an ornament, try moving the beam around. Quite different effects can be achieved by directing it upwards or downwards, and side lighting creates a very different effect to straight-on illumination.

ABOVE: *An illuminated garden can become magical as dusk falls, and you will derive many more hours of pleasure from being able to sit out in the evening.*

Illuminating water
Underwater lighting is popular and you can buy special sealed lamps designed to be submerged or to float, but the effect can be disappointing if the water is murky or if algae grows thickly on the lenses. A simple white spotlight playing on moving water is often the most effective.

THINKING OF THE NEIGHBOURS

There is a problem with using garden lights in a small garden: you have to consider neighbours. It is unsociable to fix a spotlight where the beam not only illuminates your favourite tree but also falls on the windows of your neighbour's house. If you direct beams downwards rather than upwards, the pools of light should not obtrude.

WHEN PROFESSIONAL ADVICE IS NEEDED . . .

Low voltage lighting is designed for DIY installation, but mains voltage demands special care. If you know how to wire up your garden, using special outdoor fittings, and are aware of any regulations concerning the depth cables have to be buried and the protection required, you may be able to do the wiring yourself. But if in the slightest doubt use a professional electrician. If you want to keep the cost down, offer to do the labouring, such as digging trenches, yourself.

LEFT: *The best garden lighting is not obtrusive or unattractive during the day, and throws off white light when illuminated.*

HOW TO INSTALL LOW-VOLTAGE LIGHTING

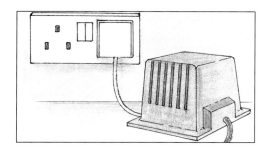

1 A low-voltage lighting kit will come with a transformer. This must always be positioned in a dry place indoors or in a garage or outbuilding.

2 Drill a hole through the window frame or wall, just wide enough to take the cable. Fill in any gaps afterwards, using a mastic or other waterproof filler.

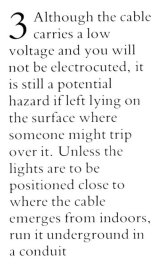

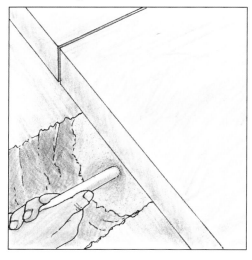

3 Although the cable carries a low voltage and you will not be electrocuted, it is still a potential hazard if left lying on the surface where someone might trip over it. Unless the lights are to be positioned close to where the cable emerges from indoors, run it underground in a conduit

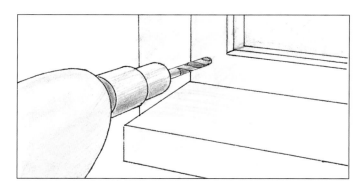

4 Most low-voltage lighting systems are designed so that the lamps are easy to position and to move around. Many of them can just be pushed into the ground wherever you choose to place them.

FURNISHING THE GARDEN

A few seats and a table make the garden an inviting place to eat, or to sit and relax. Unfortunately where space is at a premium every item has to be chosen and placed with care. Built-in seats, and especially tree seats, are a good choice for a small garden.

Portable furniture

Furniture that can be moved is useful for a quick scene change and helps to prevent your garden becoming predictable. It is surprising how effective a canvas 'director's chair' can look on a summer's day, and it is quick and easy to fold up and store when not in use.

Built-in

Built-in furniture saves space and helps prevent a small garden looking cluttered. The best place for built-in seating is the patio, where it can often be designed along with the rest of the structure. White-painted planks look smart, and can quickly be transformed with cushions to look elegant as well as feel comfortable.

Built-round

A tree seat makes an eye-catching garden feature, and this is one occasion when the advice not to have a seat beneath a tree can be ignored! White paint will help the seat to stand out in the shade of its branches.

Wrought and cast iron

Genuine cast and wrought iron furniture is expensive and very heavy, but alloy imitations are available with all the charm of the original but at a more manageable price and weight. White is again a popular colour, but bear in mind that although this type of furniture can stand outside throughout the year, it will soon become dirty. Cleaning the intricate patterns isn't easy. Colours such as green look smart yet don't show the dirt.

Use cushions to add patches of colour, and to make the chairs less uncomfortable to sit on!

LEFT: *White-painted metal furniture looks tasteful and can help enliven a dull corner of the garden.*

BELOW: *A charming wooden seat.*

BELOW LEFT: *A reconstituted stone seat has a timeless appeal that beckons you to sit and rest.*

Wooden seats and benches

Timber seats can be left in natural wood colour to blend with the background or painted so that they become a focal point. White is popular, but green and even red can look very smart. Yacht paint is weather-resistant.

Plastic

Don't dismiss plastic. Certainly there are plenty of cheap and nasty pieces of garden furniture made from this material, but the better pieces can look very stylish for a patio in the setting of a modern garden.

HOW TO MAKE A TREE SEAT

1 Start by securing the legs in position. Use 3.8cm × 7.5cm (1½in × 3in) softwood, treated with a preservative. You will need eight lengths about 68cm (27in) long. Concrete them into position.

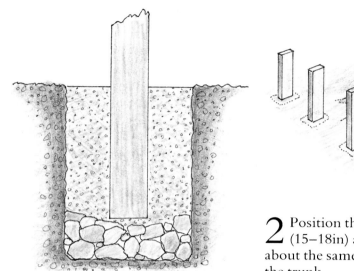

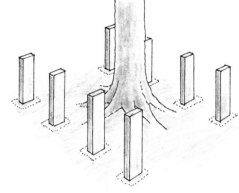

2 Position the legs about 38–45cm (15–18in) apart in two rows about the same distance either side of the trunk.

3 Cut four pieces of 2.5cm × 5cm (1in × 2in) softwood for the cross-bars. Allow 7.5cm (3in) overhang at each end.

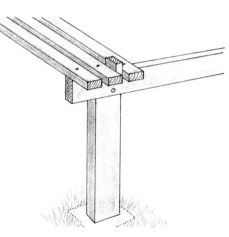

4 Drill and screw these to the posts. Then, cut slats to the required length (the number will depend on the size of your seat). Allow for a 2.5cm (1in) space between each slat. Paint the slats and cross-bars with white paint (or a wood preservative or stain if you prefer), and allow to dry before final assembly. Test the spacing, using an offcut of wood as a guide, and when satisfied that they are evenly spaced on the cross-bars, mark the positions with a pencil. Then glue and nail into position.

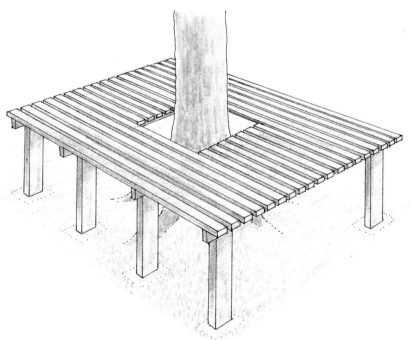

CONTAINER CHOICES

MANY PLANT CONTAINERS ARE PURELY practical: plain clay pots, unadorned plastic windowboxes, wooden troughs that are functional but not inspiring. There is nothing wrong with any of these if they are to be covered with trailers and cascading blooms, but most plants have an upright habit and an interesting container forms part of the display and becomes an important feature.

Containers are especially useful in a small garden because they bring life and colour, or just subtle shades of green, to corners that might otherwise remain bare. By hanging interesting or colourful containers on bleak walls, by using them alongside the steps to a basement garden, or simply using tubs by the front door, containers make the most of all the available space.

LEFT: *Don't discard the old metal watering-can. It can be painted and pressed into use for plants such as ivies.*

FAR LEFT: *This old copper boiler has found new life as a container for tulips and pansies.*

OPPOSITE ABOVE: *Although a clematis seems an unlikely choice for these old chimney pots, it will eventually cascade down over the edge.*

OPPOSITE BELOW: *Containers are invaluable in a small garden as they can be used to take advantage of any spare space.*

BELOW: *It is surprising how much you can do with a roof garden, by growing a wide range of plants in containers.*

Don't confine your choice of container plants to summer bedding and spring bulbs, however. If you do, your containers will look like monuments to past glories for many months of the year. Plant evergreen shrubs, or groups of evergreen border plants. Use short-term pot plants in the winter and don't be afraid to discard them after a few weeks.

Houseplants can be used in summer to add a touch of the exotic to your patio. Provided they are carefully acclimatized first (placed in a sheltered position, and protected from winds and strong sun, perhaps with a covering of horticultural fleece for the first week), you can use them to create tropical corners. It's best to use only those plants with thick or fleshy leaves.

Be bold. Use kitchen utensils such as pots and pans as containers, old chimney pots, drainpipes, boots and shoes, but always make sure that there are drainage holes.

You can even make large clay pots more interesting by painting on an attractive design with masonry paint. Use a stencil if you are not artistically inclined.

POTS FOR DOORWAY DECORATION

Always choose an imposing plant in an attractive container to go by the front door, and if possible one that looks good for a long period.

This is the place for a clipped bay in an ornate pot or Versailles tub, or an attractive bamboo in an oriental-style container.

If you have chosen imposing plants to go by the front door supplement these with a group of smaller containers that add seasonal colour, and perhaps scent. Don't be afraid to move pots around to maintain interest. Keep a small lilac in a tub or grow pots of hyacinths to move them to the front door as they come into flower to add a heady perfume.

Formal shrubs

If space really is limited and the rest of the garden has a formal style, a couple of clipped or trained evergreens can look elegant throughout the year. Clipped bays are good, but in cold areas are likely to suffer from damaged leaves in winter, but many conifers have a naturally formal outline and remain attractive throughout the year with minimal attention. Box can be bought clipped into topiary shapes, and though expensive to buy will add instant impact. You can easily buy a box plant and clip it into a ball or pyramid

shape over the course of a couple of years, if you are happy with a simple geometric shape.

Scented delights

Scent always arouses comment from visitors to the door. In winter you will have to rely on bulbs like hyacinths and *Iris danfordiae*. In spring follow these with daphne and then lilac (both indifferent for the rest of the year, so be prepared to move them to a less conspicuous part of the garden after flowering).

Summer brings the opportunity to use scented bedding plants such as flowering tobacco plants and stocks.

Climbers in pots

A climber round the door always looks attractive, and you can usually erect a trellis for support. If there is a choice, plant directly into the ground, but if that is not possible, pot a climber in a tub. Large-flowered

LEFT: *Remember to appeal to the sense of smell as well as sight. Here lavender not only colour co-ordinates, it adds a touch of fragrance as well.*

BELOW LEFT: *Formally clipped box can be expensive to buy, but with patience you can train your own. They are ideal for a formal setting.*

BELOW: *Don't forget that pots can always be used to grow well-trained shrubs.*

clematis will do well, and even a honeysuckle. You can try a climbing or rambling rose, but these are more demanding in pots.

GROUPING POTS AND PLANTS

If isolated pots seem to lack impact, try grouping them together – the mutual support they lend each other gives them a strength that they lack individually. If the pots are rather plain, placing smaller ones in front will mask those behind and bring the display almost to ground level.

Groups in the porch

Make a bold display in a porch by using tall plants, especially evergreen shrubs, at the back and smaller flowering plants in front.

If space is limited, instead of going for a lush effect with lots of foliage and flowers, concentrate on the containers rather than the plants. Decorative pots are often available as matching sets. Grouping these together looks good even if the plants they contain are only mediocre.

Groups in corners

Difficult corners are an ideal place in which to use containers to create colour, filling in a spare piece of ground where nothing much seems to do well. Patios usually have corners that would otherwise remain unused. Group shrubs or tall houseplants at the back and colourful summer bedding plants in front, along with bright-leaved indoor plants for the warmest months.

Alternatively, choose a small group of elegant containers and use the plants in a more restrained way. A trailer growing from a pedestal container with a cluster of distinctive small pots around the base can be as eye-catching as a large group.

In a dull corner, perhaps formed where two wooden fences join, or where house joins fence in a sunless position, try making a bed of small-sized gravel on which to place a group of terracotta pots. Red gravel will help to bring colour. Fill the pots with bright annuals for the summer, and winter-flowering pansies and bulbs for winter and spring. Try spacing the pots out and adding a few interesting pieces of rock among them.

ABOVE LEFT: *Grouping plants in a porch makes a high-impact feature. Replace plants when they have passed their best, to keep it looking good.*

ABOVE: *Feature groups of plants in containers where the garden needs an uplift. The beach pebbles add an individual touch.*

LEFT: *Individually, these containers would not look special, but grouping them makes a focal point.*

Groups on the lawn

Clusters of pots are an ideal means to breaking up a large expanse of lawn. Don't stand them directly on the grass, but use a bed of sand or gravel – this will stand out well from the grass, and make mowing round the containers easier.

PERMANENT PLANTS FOR TUBS

It is easy to have colourful tubs and troughs in summer, but to get the best from containers you need some year-round interest. Sometimes it is worth thinking beyond the traditional summer annuals, and to reserve a few containers for permanent plants.

Small trees and shrubs give height to your patio display, and plantings that provide winter interest mean that your garden never becomes boring. Use small containers and window-boxes to add splashes of seasonal colour, but include a few large tubs or troughs planted up with shrubs and perennials for a more permanent display.

Many shrubs used in troughs and tubs eventually outgrow their containers. Plant these in the border and start off with new ones.

ABOVE: *This Japanese maple will eventually make an attractive small tree. In the meantime the container is an eye-catching feature.*

LEFT: *Few gardeners bother to grow herbaceous perennials in containers, but some, like this Lychnis coronaria, are brilliant in flower. If you dead-head the lychnis regularly it will remain colourful for many months.*

RIGHT: *The silver-grey cineraria in this container cannot be permanently planted in cold areas, but is easily replaced each year. Plants like this are useful for filling in the gap around the base of trees and shrubs grown as standards.*

Trees for tubs

Trees are unlikely candidates for containers, and certainly for small gardens. Fortunately the restricted root-run usually keeps them compact and they never reach the proportions of trees planted in the ground. Even in a small garden some height is useful.

Choose trees that are naturally small if possible. Laburnums, crab apples (and some of the upright-growing and compact eating apples on dwarfing roots too), *Prunus* 'Amanogawa' (a flowering cherry with narrow, upright growth), and even trees as potentially large as *Acer platanoides* 'Drummondii' (a varie-gated maple) will be happy in a large pot or tub for a number of years. Small weeping trees also look good. Try *Salix caprea* 'Pendula', *Cotoneaster* 'Hybridus Pendulus' (cascades of red berries in autumn). Even the pretty

dome-shaped grey-leaved *Pyrus salicifolia* 'Pendula' is a possibility.

These must have a heavy pot with a minimum inside diameter of 38cm (15in), and a loam-based compost. Even then they are liable to blow over in very strong winds unless you pack some other hefty pots around them, at least in bad weather.

Good shrubs for tubs

Camellias are perfect shrubs for tubs, combining attractive, glossy evergreen foliage with beautiful spring flowers. *Camellia x williamsii* and *C. japonica* hybrids are a good choice. Many rhododendrons and azaleas are also a practical proposition, and if you have a chalky soil this is the best way to grow these plants . . . provided you fill the container with an ericaceous compost.

Many hebes make good container plants (but not for very cold or exposed areas), and there are many attractively variegated varieties. The yellow-leaved *Choisya ternata* 'Sundance' and variegated yuccas such as *Yucca filamentosa* 'Variegata' and *Y. gloriosa* 'Variegata' are also striking shrubs in containers.

For some winter interest, try *Viburnum tinus*.

Border perennials

Few people bother to grow border perennials in containers, but if you have a paved garden, or would like to introduce them to the patio, don't be afraid to experiment. Dicentras, agapanthus, and many ornamental grasses are among the plants that you might want to try, but there are very many more that you should be able to succeed with – and they will cost you nothing if you divide a plant already in the border.

Evergreen perennials

Evergreen non-woody perennials such as ajugas, bergenias and *Carex morrowii* 'Evergold' are always useful for providing colour and foliage cover in the winter, but look best as part of a mixed planting.

HOW TO PLANT A TREE OR SHRUB IN A TUB

1 Choose a large tub or pot with an inside diameter of at least 38cm (15in), except for very small shrubs. Make sure it is heavy (clay or ceramic for instance, not plastic) and place pieces of broken clay pots or chipped bark over the drainage hole.

2 Part-fill with a loam-based potting soil. Do not use lightweight alternatives as the weight is required for stability.

3 Knock the plant from its pot, and if the roots are tightly wound round the root-ball, carefully tease out some of the roots so that they will grow into the surrounding potting soil more readily.

4 Test the plant for size and position. Add or remove soil as necessary, so that the top of the root-ball and soil level will be 2.5–5cm (1–2in) below the rim of the pot to allow for watering.

5 Firm the compost around the roots, as trees and shrubs offer a great deal of wind resistance. Water thoroughly after planting, and never forget to water regularly in dry weather.

ROCK AND WATER GARDENS

ROCK AND WATER FEATURES ADD AN EXTRA dimension to any garden, but imagination is needed to get the best from them in a small area. The vast majority of rock and water plants thrive best in a sunny position, and it may be difficult to find a suitable site in a small garden. If you can't find a spot that is in the sun for at least half the day – and preferably longer – it might be better to choose a water feature that depends less on plants for its effect, and to grow your rock plants in other ways, such as between paving and in raised beds or a gravel garden.

Very small ponds are much more difficult to 'balance' biologically than large ones, and green water is often a problem for much of the year. If the garden is very tiny choose a bubble fountain, wall spout, or container pond instead.

Rock gardens look best on a natural slope or built to look like a natural outcrop of rocks in a large lawn. Most small gardens offer neither opportunity. Combining a rock feature with the pond is often the most satisfactory solution. You can create the raised ground from the soil excavated for the pond.

Rock plants – or alpines if you prefer the label – offer huge scope for an enthusiastic gardener with a passion for plants but without the space to grow many. You can plant dozens in the space taken by just one medium-sized shrub, and even the tiniest garden can be home for hundreds of plants.

Be careful with the choice of water plants. Some irises and rushes are compact, others are rampant and will soon make a take-over bid. There are waterlilies that need deep water and a large surface area, others that will be happy in 23cm (9in) of water and will make do with a much smaller surface area.

TOP: Sedum spurium '*Atropurpureum*'.

ABOVE: *Campanulas – here growing through* Asplenium scolopendrium – *are popular rock plants.*

RIGHT: *This sink garden contains more than half a dozen different plants in less space than a single shrub would normally occupy.*

OPPOSITE: *Raising the edges of this pond has emphasized its role as the centre of attention.*

OPPOSITE ABOVE: *Various species of dianthus do well in a rock garden and always have a special appeal.*

PONDS AND WATER FEATURES

Making a pond is very easy nowadays – most flexible liners are strong and long-lasting, and pre-formed pools are as near as you can get to buying an instant pond off the shelf. If you don't have space for a 'proper' pond, make one in a barrel or shrub tub.

If you want to grow plants and keep fish, choose a bright position for your pond, one that receives sun for at least half the day. Avoid overhanging trees, they not only cast shade but shed leaves too, which can pollute the water.

Fountains and cascades

Introduce a cascade if you build a rock garden with your pond. A simple low-voltage submersible pump linking the head of the cascade with a hose is usually adequate for a small cascade with a modest flow of water.

Fountains need a large area of water, otherwise drift will cause a gradual drop in the water level. Be aware that the disturbed surface does not suit waterlilies and some other aquatic plants. A simple bubble or geyser type of jet is often more appropriate than a high, ornate jet in a small garden.

ABOVE: *You don't need a large garden to enjoy the sight and sound of moving water, as this attractive feature shows.*

Wall features

In a courtyard or a basement garden enclosed by walls, a wall fountain is often the best choice. You don't need a great gush of water.

You can fix a spout that pours water into a reservoir at the base of the wall to be recirculated through a hidden pump; alternatively buy one that is self-contained with water simply trickling into an integrated dish beneath the spout.

Miniature ponds

If you've no room for a proper pond, make one in a half-barrel or even a plastic shrub tub. Sink it into the ground, half-sink it into the soil, or have it free-standing, perhaps on a paved area such as the patio. Container ponds are not suitable for fish, but you can grow an interesting small collection of aquatic plants in them, including miniature waterlilies.

HOW TO MAKE A POND USING A LINER

1 Mark out the shape of your pond with a piece of rope, hosepipe or by sprinkling sand. Then remove the grass and excavate the soil to the required depth, leaving a shallow ledge about 23cm (9in) wide at about that depth from the top.

2 Remove the grass or soil around the edge if you plan to pave it. Allow for the thickness of the paving plus a bed of mortar. Check levels and remove extra soil from one side if necessary. The water surface needs to be level to the sides of the pond.

3 Remove sharp stones and large roots, then line the pool with about 1cm (½in) of damp sand – it should stick to the sides if they slope slightly. Use a polyester mat (from water garden specialists) or old carpet instead of sand if the soil is stony.

HOW TO INSTALL A PRE-FORMED POND

1 Transfer the shape of your pool to the ground by inserting canes around the edge. Use a hosepipe or rope to define the shape.

2 Excavate the hole to approximately the right depth, and following the profile of the shelves as accurately as possible.

3 Place a straight-edged piece of wood across the top and check that the edges are level. Measure down to check the depths.

4 Place the pool in the hole and add or remove more soil if it does not sit snugly. Also remove any sharp stones. Check that it is absolutely straight with a spirit-level.

5 Remove the pond and line the shape with sand. Backfill so that the pond shape fits the hole snugly.

6 Run water in from a hose, and backfill and firm again as the water rises. Check the levels frequently as the backfilling often tends to lift the pool slightly.

4 Drape the liner over the hole, anchoring the edges with bricks. Run water into the pool from a hose. As the weight of water takes the liner into the hole, release the bricks occasionally. Some creases will form but are not usually noticeable.

5 Trim the liner, leaving an overlap around the edge of about 15cm (6in), to be covered by the paving.

6 Bed the paving on mortar, covering the edge of the liner. The paving should overlap the edge of the pool by about 3cm (1in). Finish off by pointing the joints with mortar.

WAYS TO GROW ROCK PLANTS

If you have a sunny corner, a rock garden could be an attractive way to fill it. Alternatively, introduce rocks with a pond. A steeply sloped rock garden provides an opportunity to include a series of cascades that run through the rock garden to the pool beneath. It also solves the problem of what to do with the soil excavated during pond construction!

If your interests lie more with the exquisite beauty of the plants than with the landscaping aspects of a rock garden, there are plenty of ways to include alpines in areas other than a rock garden.

Combined with water
Rock gardens and ponds both require a sunny position to do well, and they associate well together. It is often possible to introduce a series of cascades linking a small pool at the top with the main pool below. Bury the connecting hose when constructing the rock garden, and use plenty of rocks to make the cascades look as natural as possible.

Very pleasing combined rock and water gardens can also be constructed without running water.

Island rock beds
Provided the lawn is reasonably large, and informal in shape, small rock outcrops can be created. You don't need many rocks for this kind of rock garden, just a few bold ones, carefully positioned so that they look as though they are protruding through the ground. For rocks to look convincing it is important to slope them into the ground, and for the strata to lie in one direction.

Rock plants in gravel gardens
Rock plants look good in gravel, so include them in a gravel garden or create a small flat gravel bed just for rock plants. Provide the same soil conditions as for a raised rockery, but on the flat. In addition, you can include a few rocks to create the impression of a scree.

Sink gardens
Alpines are perfect for sink gardens. Genuine stone sinks are ideal, but these are scarce and expensive. Perfectly attractive gardens can be created in imitation stone sinks.

Although you can simply plant 'on the flat' within the trough or sink, much more effective are 'landscaped' displays in which a section of rock face is created.

ABOVE: *If you like alpines but don't want a rock garden, why not have a whole collection of sink gardens?*

LEFT: *A low rock bank is another easy way to grow rock plants, and is very simple to construct.*

Raised beds
The great advantage of a raised bed for alpines is that you are better able to appreciate their beauty in miniature. You can build the beds with bricks or walling blocks, but natural stone is much better, especially if you can leave plenty of planting holes in the sides.

Peat beds
The vast majority of alpines grow happily in ordinary or alkaline soil, but a few require acid conditions. If these plants appeal, build a peat bed from peat blocks, bonding the blocks like bricks. Fill with a peaty mixture or an ericaceous potting soil and plant the alpines in your chosen arrangement.

HOW TO MAKE A ROCK GARDEN

1 The base is a good place to dispose of rubble, which you can then cover with garden soil – the ideal place for soil excavated from the pond.

2 It is best to use a special soil mixture for the top 15–23cm (6–9in), especially if soil excavated from the pond is used. Mix together equal parts soil, coarse grit and peat (or peat substitute), and spread this evenly over the mound.

3 Lay the first rocks at the base, trying to keep the strata running in the same direction.

4 Lever the next row of rocks into position. Use rollers and levers to move them.

5 As each layer is built up, add more of the soil mixture, and consolidate it around the rocks.

6 Ensure that the sides all slope inwards, and make the top reasonably flat rather than building it into a pinnacle. Position the plants, then cover the exposed soil with a thin layer of horticultural grit.

CHOOSING AND PLANTING

A visit to any garden centre will reveal a huge selection of plants for your rock garden. One of the delights of collecting alpines is the constant surprises as new treasures are encountered, and the ability to indulge in a wide range of plants that won't take up much space.

The plants suggested here can only be an arbitrary selection of some of the best, with the emphasis on plants that are fairly widely available.

Useful for a wall
- *Acaena microphylla* (top or face)
- *Achillea tomentosa* (top)
- *Alyssum montanum* (top)
- *Alyssum saxatile* (top or face)
- *Arabis caucasica* (top or face)
- *Arenaria balearica* (top or face)
- *Aubrietia* (face)
- *Campanula garganica* (face)
- *Cerastium tomentosum* (face)
- *Corydalis lutea* (face)
- *Dianthus deltoides* (top or face)
- *Erinus alpinus* (top or face)
- *Gypsophila repens* (top or face)
- *Sedum*, many (face)
- *Sempervivum*, many (face)

Try these in a trough
- *Arabis ferdinandi-coburgi* 'Variegata'
- *Aster alpinus*
- *Gentiana acaulis*
- *Hypericum olympicum*
- *Phlox douglasii*
- *Potentilla tabernaemontani*
- *Raoulia australis*
- *Rhodohypoxis baurii*
- *Sedum lydium*
- *Sempervivum* (various)

Good starter plants for a rock garden
Some of these plants are quite rampant or large – *Alyssum saxatile* and helianthemums, for example. If you are not familiar with particular plants, look them up in an encyclopedia.

- *Acaena microphylla*
- *Alyssum saxatile*

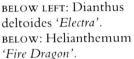

LEFT: Alyssum saxatile.

BELOW LEFT: Dianthus deltoides *'Electra'*.
BELOW: Helianthemum *'Fire Dragon'*.

- *Antennaria dioica* 'Rosea'
- *Arabis ferdinandi-coburgi* 'Variegata'
- *Armeria maritima*
- *Campanula carpatica*
- *Campanula cochleariifolia*
- *Dianthus deltoides*
- *Dryas octopetala*

- *Erinus alpinus*
- *Gentiana acaulis*
- *Gentiana septemfida*
- *Gentiana sino-ornata*
- *Geranium subcaulescens* 'Splendens'
- *Gypsophila repens*
- *Helianthemum*

- *Hypericum olypicum*
- *Iberis sempervirens* 'Snowflake'
- *Oxalis adenophylla*
- *Phlox douglasii*
- *Phlox subulata*
- *Pulsatilla vulgaris*
- *Raoulia australis*
- *Saxifraga* (mossy type)
- *Sedum spathulifolium* 'Cape Blanco'
- *Sedum spurium*
- *Sempervivums* (various)
- *Silene schafta*
- *Thymus serpyllum* (various)
- *Veronica prostrata*

LEFT: Sempervivum ballsii.

HOW TO PLANT ALPINES

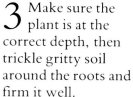

1 Position the plants while still in their pots so that you can see how they look and can move them around easily if necessary.

2 Use a trowel to take out a hole a little larger than the root-ball. You can buy narrow trowels that are particularly useful for planting in the crevices between rocks.

3 Make sure the plant is at the correct depth, then trickle gritty soil around the roots and firm it well.

4 Finish off by covering the exposed surface with more grit.

CHOOSING PLANTS

*Hard landscaping (paving, walls, fences, pergolas, and so on)
is what gives a garden a strong sense of design, and provides the skeleton
that gives the garden its shape. But it is the soft landscaping — the plants —
that provides the flesh, shape and texture of the garden.
The same basic design can look very different in the hands of
gardeners with different ideas on the use of plants.*

ABOVE: *Mixing different types of plant can
be very effective. This border contains shrubs,
herbaceous plants, bulbs, and grasses.*

OPPOSITE: *No matter how attractive the
design of a garden, it is the plants
that make it pretty.*

BEDS AND BORDERS

BEDS AND BORDERS NEED TO BE PLANNED. THE shape will affect the overall appearance, of course, but there are also practical considerations such as the amount of maintenance required, the theme to be created, as well as the crucial question of the actual plants to be used.

Formal beds and borders are normally dictated by the basic design concept, which will often determine the type of plants you can use. A formal rose garden will clearly feature roses, and only the 'filler' plants might have to be debated. A classic style with neat asymmetrical beds cut

into the lawn, or edged by clipped box, demands the type of formal bedding associated with this type of garden.

Herbaceous and shrub borders are much more open to interpretation, and the actual plants used will have as much affect on the overall impression created as the shape or size of the border.

In traditional large gardens there is a clear distinction between herbaceous borders and shrub borders, but few small gardens can afford this luxury and the inclusion of a 'mixed border' is the usual compromise. Here shrubs jostle for

LEFT: *By curving the corners of borders in a small garden you can generate extra planting space that helps to make the garden more interesting.*

OPPOSITE ABOVE: *A garden like this, with plenty of shrubs such as roses, require little maintenance and because the hard landscaping is minimal is relatively inexpensive to create.*

OPPOSITE BELOW: *Single-sided herbaceous borders can look right in a rural setting if you have enough space. A border like this can be colourful for many months.*

position with herbaceous plants and annuals, while summer bedding plants and spring bulbs make bids for any areas of inhabitable space left. There is nothing wrong with this type of gardening: the border looks clothed long after the herbaceous plants have died down, and there will be flowers and pockets of changing interest for a much longer period than could be achieved with shrubs alone.

Colour themes are also difficult to achieve in a small garden, and although single-colour borders can be planted in a small garden, it is best to be a little more flexible. Settle for a 'golden corner' rather than a golden border, or a blue-and-silver theme for just part of a border rather than a more extensive area.

Small beds cut into the lawn do not have to be filled with summer bedding and then replaced by spring bulbs and spring bedding. Instead plant them with blocks of perennial ground cover, or use a perennial edging and plant seasonal flowers within it.

ISLAND BEDS

Traditionally, low-growing seasonal plants have been grown in beds cut into the lawn – island beds – and taller herbaceous plants and shrubs placed in long borders designed to be viewed from one side. Island beds planted with herbaceous plants and shrubs bridge this divide, and provide planting opportunities that can be put to good use in a small garden.

Planting principles

Island beds are intended to be viewed from all sides, so the tallest plants usually go in the centre and the smaller ones around the edge. Don't be too rigid, however. Concentrate on creating a bed that you have to walk around to see the other side, rather than simply planting tall summer flowers like delphiniums in the centre. Shrubby plants, even medium-sized evergreens, might be better for the centre of the bed, with other lower-growing shrubs creating bays that can be filled with plants that die down for the winter. Your bed will then retain its function of breaking up a lawn and creating a diversion that has to be explored.

Don't be afraid to plant a small tree, such as *Malus floribunda*, in an island bed, to create much-needed height.

If seasonal bedding appeals more than shrubs and border perennials, then island beds can still be used creatively for these.

The question of shape

Most people think of island beds as informal in outline, but you can introduce rectangular beds if this suits the style of your garden.

Curved beds generally look much more pleasing, however, especially if you introduce broad and narrow areas so that there are gentle bays.

Design considerations

Use an island bed to break the line of sight. By taking it across the garden, an island bed may distract attention from an uninspiring view – whether beyond the garden or simply the fence itself. Attention is directed to the sides, and as you walk around the bed, the eye is taken into the bed rather than to the perimeters.

A series of island beds can be used to divide up a long, narrow garden. Instead of the eye being taken in a straight line to the end, the beds become a series of diversions.

BELOW: *Island beds help to break up a large lawn, and create a sense of height.*

ONE-SIDED BORDERS

Single-sided borders are useful if you want to create flowery boundaries around the perimeter and emphasize an open space within the garden, turning the garden in on itself. These borders are also useful for taking the eye to a distant focal point, and, by varying the width of the border, you can create a false sense of perspective that can appear to alter the size of the garden.

Straight and narrow beds

Most gardens have at least some straight and narrow borders around the edge of the lawn, a favourite spot for roses or seasonal bedding. If you want to cut down on the regular replanting work, plant with dwarf shrubs as backbone plants then include flowering ground cover herbaceous plants such as hardy geraniums and spring bulbs to provide flowers over a long period.

Make a border look wider by laying a mowing edge. Then use plants that will sprawl over the edge, softening the hard line and giving the impression of a wider border.

The advantages of curved borders

Straight edges are easier to mow and trim, but unless the border is wide and variation is created with the use of shrubs of various sizes, they can appear unimaginative and may take the eye too quickly along the garden, making it seem smaller. Gentle curves that create bays enable the plants to be brought further out into the garden and provide much more adventurous planting scope.

It may be possible to modify an existing straight border by cutting into the lawn. Bear in mind that mowing time is likely to be increased rather than decreased, however.

ABOVE: *Single-sided borders are the best choice for small town gardens that have high enclosing walls, especially if you can use climbers or tall plants to hide the wall.*
LEFT: *A single-sided mixed border.*

Turning corners

Don't forget that borders can turn corners. Right-angled turns seldom look satisfactory, however, so add a curve to the corner. This will give it greater depth at that point.

You can even take the border right round the garden in a continuous strip. A small square garden with a circular central lawn surrounded by border can look quite spectacular if well planted with a wide range of plants that hold interest throughout the seasons.

HOW TO MAKE BEDS AND BORDERS

If you are making a garden from scratch, areas allocated to lawns, beds and borders will be laid out accordingly, but you can often improve an existing garden by altering the shape of a border, or creating beds in what is currently a large and uninspiring lawn.

HOW TO MAKE A CURVED BORDER

1 If you want a quick and easy method, and can trust your eye for an even curve, lay hosepipe where you think the new edge should be. Run warm water through it first if the weather is cold, otherwise it may not be flexible enough to lie on the ground without awkward kinks.

2 The best way to judge whether the curves are satisfactory is to view the garden from an upstairs window, and have someone on the ground who can make further adjustments if necessary.

3 When the profile is satisfactory, run sand along the marker (dry sand in a wine bottle is a convenient method). Use an edging iron to cut the new edge, then lift the surplus grass and dig the soil thoroughly before attempting to replant.

4 An alternative and a more accurate way to achieve smooth curves is to use a stick or bottle fixed to a string attached to a peg. Use this as a pivot. By adjusting the length of the string and the position of the pivot, a series of curves can be achieved. Cut the edge as before.

HOW TO MARK OUT AN OVAL BED

For small formal beds, such as ovals and circles, it is best to sow or lay the grass over the whole area first, then cut out the beds once the grass has become established.

Start by marking out a rectangle that will contain the oval. Afterwards you can check that it is square by measuring across the diagonals, which should be the same length.

Place a peg half way along each side, and stretch a string between them. The two strings will cross at the centre point. Then cut a piece of string half the *length* of the oval and using a side peg as a pivot, insert pegs where it intersects the long string along the centre.

Make a loop from a piece of string twice the distance between one of these two pegs and the top or bottom of the oval (whichever is the furthest away).

With the loop draped over the inner pegs, scribe a line in the grass while keeping the string taut. You can make the line more visible by using a narrow-necked bottle filled with dry sand instead of a stick.

Use an edging iron to cut out the shape, then lift the grass with a spade.

HOW TO GET A NEAT EDGE

Emphasize the profile of your beds and borders, as well as your paths, by giving them a crisp or interesting edge. A mowing edge is a practical solution for a straight-edged border. Curved beds and borders usually have to be edged in other ways.

Some methods, like the corrugated edging strip and the wooden edge shown below are not particularly elegant, but they help to prevent the gradual erosion of the lawn through constant trimming and cutting back, and they maintain a crisp profile.

Using ornate or unusual edgings
For a period garden, choose a suitable edging. Victorian-style rope edging tiles are appropriate. If you live in a coastal area, consider using large seashells. If you enjoy your wine as well as your garden, why not put the empty bottles to use by forming an edging with them? Bury them neck-down in a single or double row, with just a portion showing.

TOP: *It is possible to buy a modern version of Victorian rope-edging.*
ABOVE: *Edgings such as this are useful if you want to create a formal or old-fashioned effect.*

HOW TO FIT EDGING STRIPS

Edging strips like this are available in a thin metal, soft enough to cut with old scissors, or in plastic. These strips help stop erosion of the grass through frequent edge clipping and cutting back. Although these may not be the most decorative edging strips, they are quick and easy to fit.

1 Make a slit trench along the lawn edge with a spade, then lay the strip alongside the trench and cut to length. Place the edging strip loosely into it.

2 Backfill with soil for a firm fit. Press the strip in gently as you proceed. Finish off by tapping it level with a hammer over a straight-edged piece of wood.

HOW TO FIT WOODEN EDGING ROLL

Wired rolls of sawn logs can make a strong and attractive edging where you want the bed to be raised slightly above the lawn, but bear in mind that it may be difficult to mow right up to the edge.

1 Cut the roll to length using wire-cutters or strong pliers to cut through the wires, and insert the edging in a shallow trench. Join pieces by wiring them together. Backfill with soil for a firm fit. Make sure that the edging is level, first by eye. Use a hammer over a straight-edged piece of wood to tap it down. Then check the height with a spirit-level. Adjust as necessary.

PLANTING FOR TEXTURE

Quite dramatic plantings can be achieved simply by planting blocks of the same plant – whether summer bedding, herbaceous perennials or shrubs. If the garden is seen as an area of voids and masses, blocks of colours and textures, the overall impression can be as important as individual plants. Ground cover plants are ideal for this purpose.

ABOVE: *Thyme is a useful ground cover for a sunny position, and will even tolerate being walked upon occasionally.*

HOW TO PLANT GROUND COVER

If planting ground cover plants as a 'texture block', or perhaps to cover an area of ground that is difficult to cultivate, such as a steep slope, it is best to plant through a mulching sheet. You can use black polythene, but a proper mulching sheet is better as it allows water to penetrate. However, do not use the sheet method for plants that colonize by spreading shoots that send up new plants, as the sheet will prevent growth by suppressing the shoots as effectively as the weeds.

1 Prepare the ground well, eliminating weeds. Add rotted manure or garden compost, and rake in fertilizer if the soil is impoverished.
Secure the sheet around each edge. Tuck the edges firmly into the ground and cover with soil. Make two slits in the form of a cross where you want to plant.

CONVENTIONAL PLANTING

Many ground cover plants spread by sideways growth, sending up new plants a short distance from the parent. These are best planted like normal herbaceous or shrubby plants. Suppress weeds initially with a 5cm (2in) layer of a mulch such as chipped bark. This is also the best way to plant any kind of ground cover that forms part of a mixed border.

2 Plant through the sheet as you would normally, firming the soil around the roots.
If you use small plants, planting with a trowel will not be a problem. Water thoroughly.

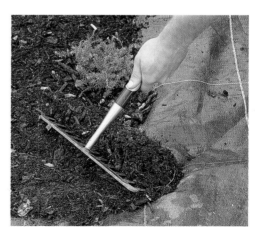

3 Although the mulching sheet will suppress weeds very effectively while the ground cover is still young and not able to do the job itself, it does not look attractive, so cover it with an ornamental mulch, such as chipped bark.

HOW TO PLANT SHRUBS

1 Most shrubs are sold in pots, and can be planted at any time of the year when the ground is not frozen or waterlogged. Space them out in their pots first, then adjust if the spacing does not look even.

2 Prepare the ground thoroughly, making sure it is free of weeds. Dig in plenty of organic material such as well-rotted manure or garden compost. Otherwise use a proprietary planting mix.

3 Excavate the hole and try the plant for size. Use a garden cane or piece of wood across the hole to make sure the plant is at its original depth. Add or remove soil as necessary.

4 Remove the plant from the pot. If the roots are tightly wound around the root-ball, carefully tease some of them free, to encourage rapid rooting.

5 Firm the plant in well to eliminate large air pockets. Gentle pressure with the heel is an efficient way to do this, or alternatively you can do this by hand.

6 Rake or hoe in a balanced fertilizer to get the plant off to a good start. In autumn use one that is slow acting or has controlled release, to avoid stimulating growth during the cold months. If planting in winter, wait until spring before adding the fertilizer. Water well, then mulch with a 5cm (2in) layer of organic material such as garden compost, cocoa shells, or chipped bark.

COLOUR THEMES

Colour themes can be very effective, and although it may not be practical to plant whole borders like this in a small garden, you can often use a colour theme in part of a border, devote an island bed to shades of one or two colours, or perhaps cheer up a dull corner with yellow and gold.

Mixed borders

The plants suggested here will form the foundation of a colour theme for a mixed border, but you can add to them and broaden the scope by using bulbs and annuals in appropriate colours too.

Red borders are best avoided in a small garden. They need space and the relief of contrasting colours to be at their most affective.

Blue and silver

Agapanthus hybrids
Deciduous to evergreen perennial. Light to deep blue ball-shaped flower heads mid and late summer *45 × 75cm (18 × 30in)*.

Artemisia absinthium
Deciduous sub-shrub. Deeply divided silvery-grey leaves. Yellow flowers in mid and late summer *1m × 60cm (3 × 2ft)*.

Artemisia ludoviciana
Herbaceous perennial. Silver-grey foliage *1m × 45cm (3ft × 18in)*.

Ceanothus x *burkwoodii*
Evergreen shrub. Clusters of bright blue flowers mid summer to mid autumn *2.4 × 2.1m (8 × 7ft)*.

Delphinium hybrids
Herbaceous perennial. Tall flower spikes in various shades of blue *1.8m × 60cm (6 × 2ft)*.

Festuca glauca
Grass. Dense tufts of blue-grey leaves *23 × 23cm (9 × 9in)*.

Hibiscus syriacus 'Blue Bird'
Deciduous shrub. Lilac-blue flowers late summer to mid autumn *2.4 × 2.4m (8 × 8ft)*.

Nepeta x *faassenii*
Herbaceous perennial. Spike-like heads of lavender-blue flowers all summer. Grey-green leaves *45 × 45cm (18 × 18in)*.

Perovskia atriplicifolia
Shrubby perennial. Feathery sprays of violet-blue flowers in late summer and early autumn. Grey-green leaves *1.2m × 45cm (4ft × 18in)*.

LEFT: *Many ceanothus grow tall, so use them where you need bold plants for the back of a blue border. There are both evergreen and deciduous kinds of ceanothus.*

BELOW LEFT: *Grey-leaved plants are useful for filling in between blue flowers. This one is Artemisia ludoviciana.*

ABOVE: *Delphiniums are some of the best blue herbaceous border plants.*

Santolina chamaecyparissus
Evergreen shrub. Silvery, woolly leaves on mound-forming plant. Small yellow flowers in mid summer *45 × 45cm (18 × 18in).*

Senecio 'Sunshine' (syn. *Brachyglottis* 'Sunshine')
Evergreen shrub. Silver-grey foliage. Yellow daisy-type flowers in mid and late summer *1 × 1.2m (3 × 4ft).*

Stachys lanata (syn. *S. byzantina* or *S. olympica*)
Almost evergreen herbaceous perennial. Bold silvery leaves. Spikes of purple flowers in mid summer *30 × 30cm (12 × 12in).*

Yellow and gold

Achillea filipendulina
Herbaceous perennial. Flat heads of lemon-yellow flowers in mid and late summer *1 × 1m (3 × 3ft).*

Alyssum saxatile
Evergreen shrubby perennial. Golden-yellow flowers in mid and late spring. Grey-green leaves *30 × 45cm (12 × 18in).*

Anthemis tinctoria
Herbaceous perennial. Yellow daisy-like flowers early to late summer. 'E. C. Buxton' is lemon-yellow, 'Grallagh Gold' is deep golden-yellow *75 × 45cm (2½ft × 18in).*

ABOVE: Achillea filipendulina *'Gold Plate', one of the essential plants for a yellow border.*

LEFT: Hypericum calycinum *can be a rampant partner for other plants, but use it wherever you need to create a bold splash of yellow in an unpromising position.*

BELOW: *Hemerocallis come in a range of colours, but there are many good yellow varieties, such as 'Dutch Beauty'.*

Berberis thunbergii 'Aurea'
Deciduous shrub. Yellow foliage, pale yellow flowers in mid spring. Red berries in autumn *1.2 × 1.2m (4 × 4ft).*

Choisya ternata 'Sundance'
Evergreen shrub that is generally planted in a somewhat sheltered position. Yellow foliage. White flowers in mid and late spring *1.5 × 1.5m (5 × 5ft).*

Forsythia x *intermedia*
Deciduous shrub. Covered with yellow flowers in early and mid spring *2.4 × 2.1m (8 × 7ft).*

Hemerocallis hybrids
Herbaceous perennial. There are many yellow varieties, flowering throughout summer *1m × 75cm (3 × 2½ft).*

Hypericum 'Hidcote'
Evergreen or semi-evergreen shrub. Large yellow flowers from mid summer to early autumn *1.5 × 1.5m (5 × 5ft).*

Ligustrum ovalifolium 'Aureum'
Evergreen or semi-evergreen shrub. Green and gold foliage *2.4 × 2.4m (8 × 8ft),* but can be clipped to keep it more compact.

Lonicera nitida 'Baggesen's Gold'
Evergreen shrub. Golden foliage *1.2 × 1.8m (4 × 6ft).*

Philadelphus coronarius 'Aureus'
Deciduous shrub. Yellow leaves (can become scorched in strong sun; turn green by late summer). White flowers in late spring and early summer *2.4 × 1.8m (8 × 6ft).*

Potentilla fruticosa
Deciduous shrub. Many varieties with yellow flowers all summer *1.2 × 1.2m (4 × 4ft).*

Solidago hybrids
Herbaceous perennial. Sprays of bright yellow flowers in late summer and early autumn *30cm–1.5m × 30–60cm (12in–5ft × 12in–2ft),* according to variety.

EVERBRIGHT EVERGREENS

Evergreens alone can make a dull garden. They need to be relieved by plants that renew themselves, otherwise you miss the variety that comes with fresh green leaves newly emerged from their buds or the final fling of many shrubs as they go out in a blaze of colourful glory in the autumn. But a garden without evergreens is equally dull, and the clever use of them will ensure that your garden always looks good, whatever the season.

Use a few evergreens in mixed borders and beds, so that there is some height and texture in winter, or devote an area of the garden to evergreens – a heather and dwarf conifer garden can look superb. Try evergreens for focal points and specimen trees in the lawn.

When creating an evergreen bed or border, use plants in many different shades of green, and use variegated plants between plain ones.

Aucuba japonica
Large, glossy leaves. Flowers insignificant, but red berries sometimes a bonus. Choose one of the variegated varieties *1.8 × 1.8m (6 × 6ft)*.

Berberis darwinii
Small, holly-shaped leaves. Masses of attractive small orange-yellow flowers in mid and late spring *2.4 × 2.4m (8 × 8ft)*.

Bergenia hybrids
Evergreen non-woody perennial, useful as ground cover in front of shrubs. Large, rounded leaves, often tinged red or purple in winter. Pink, red or white flowers in spring *30 × 60cm (1 × 2ft)*.

Camellia hybrids
Glossy leaves and large single or double flowers, usually in shades of pink, red or white, in spring *2.4 × 1.8m (8 × 6ft)*.

Ceanothus x *'burkwoodii'*
See *Colour themes*.

Choisya ternata 'Sundance'
See *Colour themes*.

ABOVE: Erica carnea *'Myretoun Ruby' is just one of many attractive winter-flowering plants.*

OPPOSITE: *Hebes are excellent compact, rounded plants (though some are tall). This is* Hebe × franciscana *'Variegata', suitable for even the tiniest plot.*

LEFT: *Evergreens have the advantage of looking good all year, like this combination of* Elaeagnus pungens *'Maculata' with* Hebe pinguifolia *'Pagei' in front.*

Cotoneaster dammeri
Prostrate ground cover to use in front of other shrubs. Small leaves. White flowers in early summer, red berries in autumn and winter *5–8cm × 1.5m (2–3in × 5ft)*.

Elaeagnus pungens 'Maculata'
Green leaves boldly splashed with gold in the centre. Very striking in winter sun *2.4 × 2.4m (8 × 8ft)*.

Erica
There are many species and varieties – look especially for varieties of *Erica carnea* (syn. *E. herbacea*) and *E. x darleyensis*, both winter-flowering and lime-tolerant *30 × 60cm (1 × 2ft)*.

Escallonia macrantha
Small leaves, clusters of pink or red flowers in summer *1.8 × 1.8m (6 × 6ft)*.

Euonymus fortunei
Will grow along the ground or up against a wall. Choose one of the variegated varieties, such as 'Emerald 'n' Gold' (green and gold) *30cm × 1.2m (12in × 4ft)* on the ground.

Hebe
Hebes make nicely shaped, usually rounded, plants and often have attractive flowers and sometimes colourful or variegated foliage. Heights can range from *30cm–1.2m (12in–4ft)*, with similar spreads, depending on species. Many are of borderline hardiness where frosts can be severe, so check with your local garden centre to see which ones are reliable enough for your area.

Ilex
The holly needs little introduction, but for a small garden choose one trained as a bush and a variegated variety such as 'Golden King' or 'Golden Queen' (the King is female and has berries, the Queen's male and doesn't!) *3 × 2.4m (10 × 8ft)*.

Lonicera nitida 'Baggesen's Gold'
See *Colour themes*.

Mahonia 'Charity'
Fragrant clusters of yellow flowers in early and mid winter *2.4 × 1.8m (8 × 6ft)*.

Phormium hybrids
Tall, sword-shaped leaves arising from ground level. Usually variegated cream or shades of pink or purple, according to variety. Of borderline hardiness in areas where frosts can be severe, so check with your local garden centre about which ones are suitable for your garden *1.2–1.8m × 1–1.2m (4–6ft × 3–4ft)*.

Rosmarinus officinalis
Grey-green, aromatic leaves. Small blue flowers in spring *1.8 × 1.5m (6 × 5ft)*.

Santolina chamaecyparissus
See *Colour themes*.

Senecio 'Sunshine'
See *Colour themes*.

Viburnum tinus
Deep to mid green leaves on tidy bush. White flowers (tinged pink in some varieties) from late autumn to early spring *2.4 × 1.8m (8 × 6ft)*.

Yucca filamentosa 'Variegata'
Sword-like leaves with broad cream and yellow margins. Large bell-shaped flowers on tall spikes in mid and late summer *1.2 × 1m (4 × 3ft)*.

DWARF CONIFERS

A good garden centre will have hundreds of dwarf conifers, in a huge range of shades, shapes, and sizes. The permutations are enormous, and the best way to choose them is to go along armed with a book or catalogue that will give you likely sizes after, say, 15 years, then choose combinations that will make a pleasing group.

COLOUR FOR THE COLD MONTHS

Evergreens provide winter clothes for the garden, but they don't look very dressy and they are best interspersed with plants that renew themselves. There is no substitute for flowers and fruits, which, though more transient, are all the more appreciated.

Autumn leaf colour can be as bold and bright as many flowers, but it is worth including some autumn blooms too. A few well-placed pools of late flowers will prolong summer and keep autumn at bay.

Don't overlook colourful barks and twigs in winter, which can become focal points on a sunny day.

Chimonanthus praecox
Deciduous shrub. Scented yellow flowers on bare stems in winter *2.4 × 2.4m (8 × 8ft)*.

Chrysanthemum
Look for varieties that flower late. Some flower well into late autumn and even early winter. Height varies with variety. Consult a specialist book or ask your garden centre for suitable varieties.

Colchicum speciosum and hybrids
Corms with large crocus-like flowers, mainly in shades of pink and mauve, single or double, in autumn. The foliage does not appear until spring *15 × 23cm (6 × 9in)*. The leaves can double the height.

Cornus mas
Deciduous shrub or small tree. Masses of tiny yellow flowers on bare branches in late winter and early spring *3 × 2.4m (10 × 8ft)*.

Crocus speciosus
Corm. Lilac-blue typical crocus flowers in mid autumn *10 × 8cm (4 × 3in)*.

Crocus tommasinianus
Corm, flowering between mid winter and early spring. Typical crocus flowers, usually lilac or purple in colour *8 × 8cm (3 × 3in)*.

Cyclamen coum
Corm. Miniature cyclamen-shaped flowers with reflexed petals. Mainly shades of pink, but also white. Flowers early winter to early spring. Leaves often marbled silver *8 × 15cm (3 × 6in)*.

Cyclamen hederifolium (syn. *C. neapolitanum*).
Similar to above but flowers from late summer to late autumn.

Erica
See *Everbright evergreens*.

Hamamelis mollis
Fragrant spidery yellow flowers on bare branches in mid and late winter *2.4 × 2.4m (8 × 8ft)*.

ABOVE:
Chrysanthemum
'Ruby Mound'.

LEFT: *Long before spring crocuses are in flower, the blooms of* C. tommasinianus *will be putting in an appearance. These were photographed in late winter.*

Helleborus niger
Evergreen perennial border plant.
Large white flowers in mid winter
30 × 45cm (12 × 18in).

Helleborus orientalis
Evergreen perennial border plant.
Large white, pink, or purple flowers
in late winter and early spring *45 ×
60cm (18in × 2ft).*

Iris unguicularis (syn. *I. stylosa*)
Evergreen perennial border plant.
Large blue iris flowers in winter and
early spring *30 × 45cm (12 × 18in).*

Jasminum nudiflorum
Sprawling shrub, usually grown
against a wall or trellis. Bright yellow
flowers from late autumn to early
spring *2.4 × 2.4m (8 × 8ft).*

Mahonia 'Charity'
See *Everbright evergreens.*

Nerine bowdenii
Heads of pretty pink, spidery flowers
on leafless stems from late summer to
early winter. The foliage appears in
spring *60 × 30cm (2 × 1ft).*

Prunus subhirtella 'Pendula' (syn.
'Autumnalis Pendula')
Small to medium-sized drooping
deciduous tree. White flowers,
sometimes tinged pink, from late
autumn and throughout the winter in
mild spells *3 × 3m (10 × 10ft).*

Sternbergia lutea
Bulb. Crocus-like yellow flowers in
mid and late autumn *10 × 10cm
(4 × 4in).*

Viburnum x *bodnantense* 'Dawn'
Deciduous shrub. Small clusters of
white to pink flowers on bare stems
from late autumn to early spring
2.4 × 1.5m (8 × 5ft).

Viburnum tinus
See *Everbright evergreens.*

LEFT ABOVE: *The hellebores span winter and
spring. This is* H. orientalis guttatus.
LEFT: Iris unguicularis *can be in bloom in
mild spells right through the winter. The
plants take a few years to settle down before
flowering prolifically.*
BELOW: Nerine bowdenii *flowers in autumn,
but will sometimes continue into winter.*

COLOURFUL STEMS

A specimen tree with attractive
bark, perhaps placed in a lawn or
in an open position and
surrounded by winter-flowering
heathers, can be a winter focal
point. One of the white-bark
birches such as *Betula jacquemontii*
always looks good. If you need a
really small tree, however, try
B. pendula 'Youngii', a small
weeping tree.

In a small garden, shrubs are
more likely to be a practical
proposition, and two of the best
are *Cornus alba* 'Sibirica' (red
stems) and *C. stolonifera*
'Flaviramea' (green stems).

As a half-way house between
tree and shrub, pollard *Salix alba*
'Chermesina', a willow with
scarlet shoots. Cut the stems
hard back to a stump perhaps
1.2m/4ft tall; do this every
second year.

AUTUMN LEAVES AND BERRIES

Autumn tints will provide a few extra weeks of border colour at a time when every bit of interest in the garden is appreciated. Berries also add a dash of spice, and some of them will remain for many months, even through to spring in a mild winter when the birds leave them alone.

Amelanchier laevis
A small deciduous tree or large shrub. Masses of white flowers in spring, sometimes black berries in summer, rich autumn foliage colour. *A. lamarckii* is very similar *3 × 2.4m (10 × 8ft).*

Berberis thunbergii
Deciduous shrub. Yellow flowers in spring, scarlet berries and brilliant red autumn foliage *1.2 × 1.5m (4 × 5ft).*

Berberis wilsoniae
Deciduous shrub. Small yellow flowers in mid summer, coral red berries and red and orange foliage in autumn *1 × 1.2m (3 × 4ft).*

Ceratostigma plumbaginoides
Deciduous sub-shrub. Clusters of small blue flowers appear from mid summer to late autumn. Leaves turn red in autumn *30 × 45cm (12 × 18in).*

Clerodendrum trichotomum
Large deciduous shrub. Starry white fragrant flowers in late summer, followed by blue berries in crimson calyces in early and mid autumn *2.4 × 2.1m (8 × 7ft).*

Cornus alba
Deciduous suckering shrub. Attractive autumn foliage colouring, red stems in winter *2.1 × 2.1m (7 × 7ft).*

Cotoneaster horizontalis
Deciduous, ground-hugging shrub for front of border (can also be used against a fence or wall). Small pink flowers in early summer, followed by red berries later. Bright red foliage tints in autumn *60cm × 1.8m (2 × 6ft).*

ABOVE: *The amelanchiers are usually grown for their white flowers in spring, but they have a second burst of colour when the leaves turn. This species is* A. laevis.

LEFT: Cornus alba *is an excellent shrub. After the brief spell of glory as the leaves colour before they fall, there is the winter-long attraction of red stems.*

Fothergilla major
Deciduous shrub. Dark green leaves, orange-yellow or red before they fall. Scented white flowers in late spring *1.8 × 1.5m (6 × 5ft)*.

Ilex
See *Everbright evergreens*.

Malus 'John Downie'
Small to medium-sized deciduous tree. White apple blossom in late spring. Conical yellow and crimson crab apples in autumn *6 × 2.4m (20 × 8ft)*.

Malus tschonoskii
Deciduous tree, which though tall is a candidate for a small garden by virtue of its slender, pencil-like profile. White blossom tinged pink in late spring. Dull red fruits flushed yellow (not a feature). Red and yellow autumn foliage *6 × 2.1m (20 × 7ft)*.

Pernettya mucronata
Evergreen shrub. Small, sharply pointed glossy leaves. Insignificant white flowers in late spring. Clusters of berries – shades of pink, red, purple and white, according to variety – in autumn and winter. Male and female plants must be grown together to ensure fruiting *1 × 1.2m (3 × 4ft)*.

LEFT: *Most sorbus are grown for their red or orange berries, but some also have white or yellow berries, and there is the bonus of spectacular leaf colour just before they fall. This is* Sorbus *'Joseph Rock'.*

Pyracantha 'Orange Glow'
Evergreen shrub, usually grown against a wall but also an attractive free-standing plant. White flowers in early summer, orange-red berries in autumn and winter. There are other suitable species and varieties *2.4 × 2.4m (8 × 8ft)*.

Rhus typhina (syn. *R. hirta*)
Deciduous small tree or large shrub. Large, divided leaves, colouring orange-red and yellow before they fall *3 × 3.5m (10 × 12ft)*.

Skimmia japonica
Evergreen shrub. Fragrant creamy-white flowers in spring, red berries in late summer and early autumn. Male plant needed to pollinate female *1 × 1m (3 × 3ft)*.

Sorbus
Many species and hybrids make small or medium-sized trees with red or yellow berries and good autumn foliage colour. Good ones are S. *aucuparia* and hybrids, S. 'Embley', and S. 'Joseph Rock'.

ABOVE: Pernettya mucronata *is available with pink and red berries as well as white ones. This variety is 'Mulberry Wine'.*
RIGHT: *Skimmias have long-lasting red berries. This one is* S. japonica *'Nymans'.*

VARIETY WITH VARIEGATION

Variegated plants make a border look lighter and more interesting when flowers are scarce, and variegated evergreens are particularly useful at times when little is flowering.

Avoid planting too many variegated plants close together. Use them between other plants with plain foliage where the leaf colouring will be shown off to advantage.

Aralia elata 'Variegata'
Deciduous shrub or small tree. Leaflets margined and marked creamy-white ('Aureovariegata' has a broad, irregular gold margin). White flowers in late summer and early autumn *3 × 2.1m (10 × 7ft)*.

Arundinaria viridistriata (syn. *Pleioblastus auricomus, Pleioblastus viridistriatus*)
Bamboo. Dark green leaves broadly striped yellow. Purplish-green canes *1m × 60cm (3 × 2ft)*.

ABOVE: Hosta fortunei albopicta.
BELOW: *Only a few variegated trees are suitable. This is* Aralia elata *'Variegata'*.

Aucuba japonica (variegated varieties)
See *Everbright evergreens*.

Buxus sempervirens 'Aureovariegata'
Evergreen shrub with small leaves striped, splashed and mottled pale yellow. 'Elegantissima' has irregular creamy-white margins *1.2 × 1m (4 × 3ft)*.

Carex morrowii 'Evergold'
Sedge
Clump-forming with grass-like leaves striped yellow along the centre *25 × 30cm (10 × 12in)*.

Cornus alba 'Elegantissima'
Deciduous suckering shrub with red stems and leaves margined and mottled with white. 'Spaethii' is similar but has gold variegation *2.1 × 1.8m (7 × 6ft)*.

Elaeagnus x *ebbingei* 'Limelight'
Evergreen shrub. Large green leaves with a central splash of deep yellow *2.4 × 2.1m (8 × 7ft)*.

Elaeagnus pungens 'Maculata'
See *Everbright evergreens*.

Euonymus fortunei (variegated varieties)
See *Everbright evergreens*.

Fuchsia magellanica 'Versicolor'
Deciduous shrub. Small fuchsia-type flower in summer and into autumn. Grey-green, white, yellow, and pink variegation. Hardy except in cold areas *1.2 × 1m (4 × 3ft)*.

Hebe x *franciscana* 'Variegata'
Evergreen shrub, not suitable for very cold areas. Small rounded leaves edged cream. Mauve-blue flowers in summer *60 × 60cm (2 × 2ft)*.

ABOVE: Pachysandra terminalis *is an excellent ground cover for shade, but the plain green form looks rather boring. 'Variegata' is much more interesting.*

LEFT: Houttuynia cordata *'Chameleon'.*

BELOW: Vinca minor *'Variegata'.*

Hostas (many variegated varieties)
Herbaceous perennial *30–60cm × 30–75cm (12in–2ft × 12in–2½ft).*

Houttuynia cordata 'Chameleon'
Herbaceous perennial. Outstandingly striking, heart-shaped foliage, variegated with shades of yellow, green, bronze and red. Small white flowers in summer *30 × 45cm (12 × 18in).*

Hypericum x moseranum 'Tricolor'
Evergreen shrub. Yellow flowers about 5cm (2in) across from mid summer to mid autumn. Green and white leaves edged pink *60 × 60cm (2 × 2ft).*

Ilex (variegated varieties)
See *Everbright evergreens.*

Iris pallida 'Variegata'
Sword-like leaves, striped creamy-white and green. Blue flowers in early summer *60 × 60cm (2 × 2ft).*

Iris pseudacorus 'Variegatus'
Sword-like leaves striped green and yellow while young, turning greener with age. Blue flowers in early summer. Although associated with water, it will grow in an ordinary border though it does best in damp soil *1m × 60cm (3 × 2ft).*

Ligustrum (variegated varieties)
See *Colour themes.*

Pachysandra terminalis 'Variegata'
Evergreen sub-shrub. Green and white leaves. Insignificant white flowers in late spring *30 × 45cm (12 × 18in).*

ABOVE: *Variegation is important in the herbaceous border. This is* Iris pallida *'Variegata'.*

Phormium hybrids
See *Everbright evergreens.*

Salvia officinalis 'Icterina'
Evergreen shrub. Grey-green leaves splashed with yellow *60 × 60cm (2 × 2ft).*

Vinca minor 'Variegata'
Evergreen prostrate shrub. Green and creamy-white leaves. Pale mauve flowers *20 × 60cm (8in × 2ft).*

Weigela florida 'Variegata'
Deciduous shrub. Leaves edged creamy-white. Pink flowers in early summer *1.5 × 1.2m (5 × 4ft).*

Yucca gloriosa 'Variegata'
See *Everbright evergreens.*

PLANTING FOR QUICK RESULTS

Annuals are almost instant – many are already in flower when you buy them – border perennials are respectable after a year, but shrubs can seem infuriatingly slow to mature.

Not all shrubs are slow-growers, however, so if you want your border to look well established in three years instead of five or even ten, try those suggested here.

Even those plants that grow quickly will leave gaps in the early years. In a mixed border, fill these gaps with the quicker-growing border perennials; in a shrub border add a few bushy annuals.

Bear in mind that some shrubs that grow quickly while young may continue to grow (over-enthusiastically) once they've reached what you consider a modest size. The height and spread estimates below are based on three years (though much depends on soil and climate), but the ones listed are only likely to grow a little more than this even by 10 years. Those that grow taller can be pruned back hard to restrict their size. *Buddleia davidii*, for example, will be much better if you cut it back hard each spring.

There are many more quick-growers, however, so don't assume that your scope for an almost instant border is limited solely to those listed below.

Aucuba japonica
See *Everbright evergreens*.

Buddleia davidii
Deciduous shrub. Fragrant, usually lilac-blue flower clusters at ends of arching branches, from mid summer to mid autumn. Other colours include shades of red, purple, and white *2.4 × 1.5m (8 × 5ft)*.

Caryopteris x *clandonensis*
Deciduous shrub. Narrow, grey-green leaves. Clusters of bright blue flowers in late summer and early autumn *1m × 60cm (3 × 2ft)*.

Choisya ternata
See *Colour themes*.

LEFT: *Tough, low-growing, quick to mature, and very bright in flower are qualities that make* Genista tinctoria *well worth considering. This variety is 'Royal Gold'.*

BELOW: Hypericum calycinum *grows and spreads rapidly, so don't plant it where these characteristics can become an embarrassment. The flowers are bold and beautiful.*

Cistus x *corbariensis*
Evergreen shrub. Dull green leaves wavy at the edge. Bold white flowers with a yellow mark at the base of each petal, in late spring and early summer *75 × 60cm (2½ × 2ft)*.

Cytisus x *kewensis*
Deciduous shrub. Pale yellow, pea-like flowers, in profusion in late spring. Spreading shape *45cm × 1m (18in × 3ft)*.

ABOVE: Leycesteria formosa *is quick-growing, and highly popular with birds. They love the dark purple berries.*
RIGHT: *Weigelas come in a range of colours, but mainly pinks and reds. They grow quickly and flower young and so make an excellent choice if you want fast results.*

Erica carnea
See *Everbright evergreens.*

Fuchsia magallanica
See *Variety with variegation.*

Genista tinctoria
Deciduous shrub. Deep yellow pea-type flowers all summer *75 × 60cm (2½ × 2ft)*, but height tends to be very variable.

Hebe 'Midsummer Beauty'
Evergreen shrub. Pale green leaves, slightly reddish beneath. Sprays of lavender-purple flowers from mid summer to mid autumn. Not reliably hardy in cold areas *1 × 1m (3 × 3ft)*.

Hypericum calycinum
Evergreen shrub. Large yellow, cup-shaped flowers all summer. Can be invasive *45 × 60cm (18in × 2ft)*.

Lavandula (various)
Evergreen shrub. The popular lavender. Grey-green leaves and flowers in shades of blue or purple *60 × 60cm (2 × 2ft)*.

Leycesteria formosa
Deciduous shrub. Cane-like stems forming a bamboo-like clump. Drooping flower tassels containing white flowers with claret bracts, followed by purple-black fruits *1.5 × 1m (5 × 3ft)*.

Lupinus arboreus
Short-lived deciduous shrub. Foliage and flower spikes resemble the herbaceous lupin, but the lightly fragrant flowers are much sparser. Usually yellow, but can be lilac to purple or blue. Good for a hot, dry site *1.2 × 1m (4 × 3ft)*.

Mahonia 'Charity'
See *Everbright evergreens.*

Philadelphus coronarius 'Aureus'
See *Colour themes.*

Potentilla fruticosa
See *Colour themes.*

Senecio 'Sunshine'
See *Colour themes.*

Spiraea x *bumalda* (various varieties)
Twiggy deciduous shrub. Flat flower heads, usually crimson, in late summer. Some varieties have variegated foliage *75 × 45cm (2½ft × 18in)*.

Weigela hybrids
Deciduous shrub. Funnel-shaped flowers in late spring and early summer. Mainly shades of red and pink *1.8 × 1.5m (6 × 5ft)*.

BELOW: Spiraea × bumalda (syn. S. japonica). *This is 'Anthony Waterer'.*

NO FUSS, LOW-MAINTENANCE PLANTS

There are plenty of people who do not have a lot of time to tend to their gardens. If you want to save the cost and time involved in regularly replanting with seasonal plants, grow hardy perennials and shrubs. But if you really want to cut down on maintenance, grow only those that are undemanding, with no need to prune regularly, or to keep lifting, dividing, or hacking back.

Most shrubs will require very occasional pruning, perhaps to cut out a dead or diseased shoot, or to improve the shape if growth is not symmetrical, and sooner or later border perennials will benefit from being lifted and divided, but the plants suggested here can be left for many years without attention. They will almost thrive on neglect, yet will not get out of control.

Aucuba japonica
See *Everbright evergreens.*

Berberis thunbergii
There are many varieties, including variegated, purple-leaved and gold-leaved. Shape and height also vary with variety: *B.t. atropurpurea* 'Bagatelle', for example, makes a dwarf rounded ball of growth covered with coppery-red leaves, usually less than *45cm (18in)* tall and broad, 'Helmond Pillar' is dark purple but grows into a narrow column *1.2m (4ft)* or so high but only about *30cm (12in)* wide.

Bergenia hybrids
See *Everbright evergreens.*

ABOVE: Cotoneaster horizontalis *can be grown as ground cover or as a climber.*

ABOVE: Cotinus coggygria *is sometimes called the smoke bush because of its flower heads. It can make quite a large shrub in time, but requires minimal attention.*

Choisya ternata
Both green and golden forms (see *Colour themes*) are trouble-free plants if protected from cold winds in winter.

Cornus stolonifera 'Flaviramea'
Deciduous shrub. Green leaves turn yellow before falling. Yellowish-green winter stems *1.8 × 1.8m (6 × 6ft)*.

Cotinus coggygria
Deciduous shrub. Rounded shape with pale green leaves (there are also purple-leaved varieties) that have brilliant autumn colours. Feathery sprays of purple or pink flowers in mid summer *2.4 × 2.4m (8 × 8ft)*.

Cotoneaster
There are many cotoneasters, from ground-huggers to shrubs *3m (10ft)* or more tall. *C. horizontalis* (see *Autumn leaves and berries*) and *C. dammeri* (see *Everbright evergreens*), are popular ground-huggers, but many others are suitable for a small garden.

Elaeagnus pungens 'Maculata'
See *Everbright evergreens.*

Erica carnea
See *Everbright evergreens.*

Fatsia japonica
Evergreen shrub. Large, hand-shaped glossy green leaves (there is a variegated variety). White, ball-shaped flower heads that appear on mature plants in mid autumn *2.4 × 2.4m (8 × 8ft)*.

Griselinia littoralis
Evergreen shrub. Pale green leaves (there are variegated varieties). Not suitable for cold areas. Slow-growing *3 × 3m (10 × 10ft)*.

Hebes
See *Everbright evergreens*.

Hemerocallis hybrids
See *Colour themes*.

Hibiscus syriacus
See *Colour themes*, but there are other varieties in different shades of blue, pink, and white.

Ilex
See *Everbright evergreens*.

Kniphofia hybrids
Herbaceous perennial. Large, stiff, poker-like orange or yellow flower spikes. Flowering season extends from early summer to mid autumn, according to variety *60cm–1.2m × 60cm–1.2m (2–4 × 2–4ft)*.

Liriope muscari
Evergreen perennial. Clumps of broad, grassy leaves, and spikes of mauve-lilac flowers from late summer to mid autumn *45 × 30cm (18 × 12in)*.

Mahonia japonica
Evergreen shrub. Glossy, dark green leaves divided into leaflets. Fragrant, lemon-yellow flowers from early winter to early spring *2.4 × 2.4m (8 × 8ft)*.

Pernettya
See *Autumn leaves and berries*.

Potentilla fruticosa
See *Colour themes*.

Ribes sanguineum
Deciduous shrub. Drooping clusters of small pink or red flowers in spring *1.8 × 1.8m (6 × 6ft)*.

Ulex europaeus
Evergreen shrub. Spiny growth, covered with deep yellow single or double flowers in spring. Flowers may also appear intermittently in winter *1.5 × 1.5m (5 × 5ft)*.

Viburnum davidii
Evergreen shrub. White flowers in early summer. Turquoise-blue berries later if both male and female plants are planted *1 × 1.2m (3 × 4ft)*.

Viburnum tinus
See *Everbright evergreens*.

Yucca
See *Everbright evergreens*, but the non-variegated form is equally suitable for a border or as a specimen plant.

ABOVE: *The kniphofias, sometimes called red-hot-pokers, are bold herbaceous border plants. Once well established they make large clumps. Some species are quite small, however, and different varieties flower at different times. Many kniphofias are unhappy in very cold areas and may need protection in some areas.*

DON'T FORGET THE DWARF CONIFERS

Conifers need negligible care, and if you choose dwarf species and varieties they will remain compact enough for a small garden. Be cautious about using them in a mixed border, however, as they seldom blend in as satisfactorily as ordinary shrubs.

PLANTS THAT PREFER SHADE

Shade is perhaps the universal problem in small gardens. It is difficult to find a significantly large growing area that is not within the shade of a building or a boundary fence, wall or hedge, for at least part of the day . . . and sometimes there are areas in shade for most or all of the day. Such positions are also often very dry, for obstructions that cast shade also cast a rain shadow.

With the exception of some really difficult areas, there are nearly always some plants that will establish themselves and thrive. In these difficult spots you must be prepared to give the plants a little extra help for the first year. The soil should be enriched with organic material, such as garden compost or rotted manure and fertilizer, but above all the ground must be kept moist. Regular watering in dry spells will be almost essential for the first season. After that, all the plants mentioned here will be able to look after themselves under normal conditions.

Those plants with an asterisk are suitable for dry shade. The others are unsuitable for dry sites, and some prefer moist ground.

ABOVE: Astrantia major *is not an eye-catching plant from afar, but does well in shade.*

Ajuga reptans
Almost evergreen perennial. There are several good varieties with variegated and coloured leaves. Short spikes of blue flowers in early and mid summer *15 × 23cm (6 × 9in)*.

ABOVE: Ajuga reptans *is one of those accommodating plants that will thrive in sun or shade, and it will even grow in crevices between paving. There are many varieties that are attractively variegated.*

Astilbe hybrids
Herbaceous perennial. Fern-like divided foliage. Feathery plumes of pink, white, or red flowers *60–90 × 45cm (2–3ft × 18in)*.

Astrantia major
Herbaceous perennial. Star-like papery-looking white or greenish-pink flowers in early and mid summer *60 × 45cm (2ft × 18in)*.

★Aucuba japonica
See *Everbright evergreens*.

★Bergenia hybrids
See *Everbright evergreens*.

★Brunnera macrophylla
Herbaceous perennial. Rough, heart-shaped leaves. Sprays of blue flowers like forget-me-nots, in late spring and early summer *45 × 45cm (18 × 18in)*.

★Buxus sempervirens
See *Variety with variegation*.

Camellia
See *Everbright evergreens*.

Dicentra spectabilis
Herbaceous perennial. Ferny foliage. Pink, red or white heart-shaped flowers on arching stems in late spring and early summer *45 × 45cm (18 × 18in)*.

★Epimedium perralderianum
Evergreen perennial. Young leaves bright green marked bronze-red, changing to copper-bronze in winter. Small yellow flowers in early summer *30 × 30cm (12 × 12in)*.

Sarcococca hookeriana humilis
Evergreen shrub. Slender, lance-shaped leaves. Very fragrant small white flowers in winter *60 × 60cm (2 × 2ft)*.

Saxifraga x umbrosa
Evergreen perennial. Rosettes of green leaves from which sprays of pink flowers appear in late spring and early summer *30 × 30cm (12 × 12in)*.

Skimmia japonica
See *Autumn leaves and berries.*

Symphoricarpos albus
Deciduous shrub. Small, urn-shaped pink flowers from mid summer to early autumn. White berries like marbles from mid autumn to mid winter *1.8 × 1.8m (6 × 6ft)*.

Tiarella cordifolia
Evergreen perennial. Maple-shaped leaves, turning bronze in winter. Feathery spikes of white fluffy flowers in late spring and early summer *23 × 30cm (9 × 12in)*.

Viburnum davidii
See *No fuss, low maintenance plants.*

Vinca minor
See *Variety with variegation.*

Helleborus
See *Colour for the cold months.*

Hosta
See *Variety with variegation.*

Hypericum calycinum
See *Planting for quick results.*

★Liriope muscari
See *No fuss low maintenance plants.*

Lonicera nitida
See *Colour themes.* The all-green species can be used, but the yellow 'Baggesen's Gold' looks brighter in a sunless position.

★Mahonia aquifolium
Evergreen shrub. Large, leathery divided leaves. Fragrant yellow flowers in early and mid spring *1.2 × 1.2m (4 × 4ft)*.

★Pachysandra terminalis
See *Variety with variegation.*

★Ruscus aculeatus
Evergreen sub-shrub. Strong erect stems covered with tough green 'leaves' (actually modified stalk). Inconspicuous flowers in early and mid spring, bright red berries in autumn if male and female plants are present *1 × 1m (3 × 3ft)*.

ABOVE LEFT: *Here the blue flowers of* Brunnera macrophylla *show up well against a golden conifer.*

RIGHT: Sarcococca hookeriana, *a winter-flowering plant that has unspectacular flowers but an arresting fragrance.*

LEFT: Symphoricarpos albus *is a vigorous, spreading shrub, which is best not planted among choice plants because of its rampant growth pattern, but it is very satisfactory for a difficult shady position.*

SUN LOVERS

Sunny spots where the ground is moist, or where the sun is intense for just part of the day before it moves around, present no problem for the majority of plants. All except the shade-loving plants are likely to thrive. But if the position is sunny nearly all day, and the soil tends to be free-draining and dry, you need plants adapted to such bright and arid conditions.

Fortunately, those plants that do well in these positions are often bright, floriferous, and very colourful. As a general rule, grey-leaved plants are well suited to these conditions, but if in doubt check.

Most of the plants suggested here tolerate dry soil well. However, give perennials and shrubs extra attention for the first season. Once they get their roots down they should be able to survive happily in a normal year.

Achillea filipendulina
See *Colour themes*.

Agapanthus hybrids
See *Colour themes*.

Alyssum saxatile
See *Colour themes*.

Artemisia arborescens
Semi-evergreen shrub. Silvery-white, much divided leaves. Yellow flowers in early and mid summer. Not reliably hardy in cold areas *1.2 × 1.2m (4 × 4ft)*.

Buddleia davidii
See *Planting for quick results*.

Caryopteris x *clandonensis*
See *Planting for quick results*.

Colutea arborescens
Deciduous shrub. Divided, pale green leaves, and yellow pea-like flowers in summer. These are followed by inflated seed pods, flushed coppery-red *2.4 × 2.4m (8 × 8ft)*.

Convolvulus cneorum
Evergreen shrub. Silvery foliage. Funnel-shaped white flowers, flushed pink beneath the petals, all summer *60 × 60cm (2 × 2ft)*.

Cytisus scoparius hybrids
Deciduous shrub. Green branches make it look evergreen. Pea-type flowers, in shades of yellow, red and pink, many multicoloured, in late spring and early summer *2.4 × 1.8m (8 × 6ft)*.

Echinops ritro
Herbaceous perennial. Divided, prickly grey-green foliage, spherical steel blue flower heads in mid and late summer *1m × 60cm (3 × 2ft)*.

ABOVE: *Osteospermums thrive in a hot, sunny situation. This one is* O. jacundum.

ABOVE LEFT: Colutea arborescens *has the bonus of interesting inflated seed pods as well as pretty yellow flowers.*

ABOVE RIGHT: Helianthemum nummularium *hybrids thrive in hot, sunny situations. They come in a variety of colours, mainly reds, pinks and yellows.*

OPPOSITE BELOW: Phlomis fruticosa *can be a rather coarse-looking plant, but it thrives in hot, dry soils.*

Eryngium variifolium
Evergreen perennial. Dark green leaves marbled white. Grey-blue flower heads with white collars, in mid and late summer *60 × 45cm (2ft × 18in)*.

Genista tinctoria
See *Planting for quick results*.

Hebe
See *Everbright evergreens*.

Helianthemum nummularium hybrids
Evergreen sub-shrub. Green or grey leaves. Masses of small flowers in shades of red, orange, yellow, pink, and white, in late spring and early summer, with a second flush later in the year if the dead flowers are trimmed off *15–23 × 60cm (6–9in × 2ft)*.

Kniphofia hybrids
See *No fuss, low maintenance plants*.

Lavandula
See *Planting for quick results*.

Nepeta x *faassenii*
See *Colour themes*.

Osteospermum hybrids
Evergreen sub-shrub. Still sometimes called *Dimorphothecas*. Large daisy-shaped flowers mainly in shades of purple, pink, and white, all summer. Not hardy in cold areas, but will tolerate frosts where the winters are not severe *30 × 60cm (12in × 2ft)*.

LEFT: Sedum spectabile *has fleshy, succulent leaves, enabling it to grow well even in a hot, sunny position.*

Perovskia atriplicifolia
See *Colour themes*.

Phlomis fruticosa
Semi-evergreen shrub. Grey-green foliage. Clusters of quaint, bright yellow flowers at the tips of shoots, in early and mid summer *75cm × 1.2m (2½ × 4ft)*.

Phormium
See *Everbright evergreens*.

Romneya coulteri
Sub-shrubby perennial. Large fragrant white flowers, *10–15cm* *(4–6in)* across from mid summer to mid autumn. Not recommended for cold areas *1.2 × 1.2m (4 × 4ft)*.

Rosmarinus officinalis
See *Everbright evergreens*.

Santolina chamaecyparissus
See *Colour themes*.

Sedum spectabile
Herbaceous perennial. Succulent leaves. Large, flat pink flower heads in early and mid autumn *45 × 45cm (18 × 18in)*.

Stachys lanata
See *Colour themes*.

Ulex europaeus
See *No fuss, low-maintenance plants*.

Yucca
See *Everbright evergreens*.

ANNUALS THAT LOVE THE SUN

Most hardy annuals thrive in hot, bright conditions, and especially those with daisy-like flowers that only open when it's warm and sunny. Be generous with the annuals, especially those native to sunny climates such as South Africa.

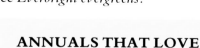

113

PLANTS FOR THE TROPICAL LOOK

If you are trying to create a garden based on Mediterranean influences with white-painted walls and with the emphasis on hot climate flora, you will need to use plenty of plants that give the impression that they are exotic or tender when in fact they are quite frost-tolerant.

Some of the plants suggested here are only hardy enough for warm areas where frosts are light and seldom prolonged, others are really tough.

You can of course use many of them in an ordinary border, but the ones suggested here are primarily effective as part of an area reserved for the more striking plants.

If you live in a cold area and have a greenhouse, conservatory, or even a porch, grow the more vulnerable plants in large pots and move them to this protected area for winter.

Arundinaria viridistriata
See *Variety with variegation*.

Clianthus puniceus
Evergreen climbing shrub. Divided, feathery leaves, crimson-scarlet claw-shaped flowers in early summer. Will only survive outdoors in mild districts. Can reach about *3m (10ft)*.

Cordyline australis
Palm-like plant with strap-like leaves at top of plant. *C. a. purpurea* has brownish-purple leaves. Where winters are mild and frost not severe it can be left in the ground and may grow into a tall tree. Elsewhere grow in a pot, where it will remain much smaller. Protect for the winter.

Fatsia japonica
See *No fuss, low-maintenance plants*.

Gunnera manicata
Huge leaves, like a giant rhubarb. In the ground it is large even for a big garden, but you can grow it in a tub or a patio pot to restrict its size. Keep very moist, and protect during the winter.

Kniphofia hybrids
See *No fuss, low-maintenance plants*.

ABOVE: Cordyline australis *'Alberti'*.

Lilium hybrids
You can buy bulbs and pot up your own lilies, or buy them when they are about to bloom. These may have been dwarfed chemically and will probably make better container plants. Heights vary.

Osteospermum hybrids
See *Sun lovers*.

Phormium hybrids
See *Everbright evergreens*.

Rheum palmatum
An ornamental rhubarb that reaches 2.4m (8ft) tall in flower, but the leaves are less than half this height. White or red flowers in early summer.

ABOVE: *For the cost of a packet of seeds you can have a show like this* Ipomoea tricolor *'Heavenly Blue'*.

ABOVE: *Where winters are mild* Zantedeschia aethiopica *can be overwintered outside.*
TOP: *The big, bold leaves of* Rheum palmatum *look very exotic.*
LEFT: *Lilies are quite easy to grow in pots provided you choose suitable varieties.*

Yucca
See *Everbright evergreens*, but the green form can be just as effective as a variegated variety.

Zantedeschia aethiopica
Well-known white arum flowers, popular with florists. Can be kept outdoors where winters are mild, but is usually best grown in a pot and given winter protection. The growth dies down in winter.

Exotic annuals
Some annuals that are regarded as indoor plants can be grown in the garden for the summer.

Among the flowering plants, celosias are always eye-catching, whether you grow the plume-shaped varieties or those shaped like a cock's comb. A mixture will usually include shades of yellow, red, and pink. The coleus is one of the best foliage pot-plants to try outdoors *en-masse* – plants are very easy to raise cheaply from seed. The multi-coloured foliage matches the exotic croton in boldness and colour combinations. Make sure they are carefully acclimatized, and don't put them out too early.

Many half-hardy bedding plants are easily raised from seed – try large daisy-like flowers such as arctotis, with flowers in shades of red, orange and pink. Salpiglossis are always eye-catching, and with their velvety, funnel-shaped flowers in shades of red, purple, and yellow, usually prominently veined and marked, certainly have that 'exotic' look.

Portulacas and cleomes (with spidery-looking flower heads) are among the other half-hardy annuals to include. But be sure to make space for *Ipomoea tricolor*, with its big blue flowers often *10cm (4in)* or so across, which are bound to make a real feature climbing up a trellis.

Disposable houseplants
Use flowering pot-plants to add short-term colour to your patio. Plants like gerberas, and dwarfed chrysanthemums, are inexpensive and generally treated as disposable plants if used indoors. Sink the pot into the soil so that the plant is easily removed after flowering.

ARCHITECTURAL PLANTS

Architectural plants may seem a contradiction in terms, for one implies the rigidity of buildings and structures, the other the informality and fluidity of plant life. The term is often a puzzle to non-gardeners, yet a plant enthusiast will know instantly when he sees an 'architectural' plant.

'Sculptural' plants

'Sculptural' is perhaps a better way to describe those plants, which, though clearly possessing all the natural beauty of any first-rate plant, also have structure and stature, and above all a shape – and perhaps texture – that an architect might be pleased to use to enhance his buildings and structures in the same way as a piece of sculpture might be used.

Some herbaceous plants, such as the acanthus, have assumed architectural status – in this case because the acanthus leaf occurs so often as a pattern in classical architecture, but also because the plant has the bold stance and distinctive profile that makes it stand out from the ordinary. Most architectural plants are trees and shrubs, however, with height as well as a distinctive outline. Use architectural plants sparingly and with careful consideration, not as part of a mixed planting but rather as you would large ornaments, as punctuation points within the garden.

Use architectural plants to make a bold statement in paved and gravel gardens, or to break up an otherwise boring area of lawn.

Acanthus spinosus
Statuesque plant with large, deeply divided leaves that are both erect and arching. Mauve and white, hooded flowers on stiff spikes in mid and late summer *1 × 1m (3 × 3ft)*.

Angelica archangelica
Biennial or short-lived perennial. Large, deeply divided, aromatic leaves on stiff, upright plant. Ball-like head of smaller clusters of yellowish-green flowers in mid and late summer *2.4 × 1m (8 × 3ft)*.

LEFT: Acanthus spinosus *is one of those plants with dramatic leaves and equally imposing flowers, and not one that will be ignored.*

BELOW: Angelica archangelica *makes a bold plant about 1.8m (6ft) tall, with large leaves and striking globular flower heads. Use it as a focal-point plant in the herb garden.*

Catalpa bignonioides 'Aurea'
Deciduous tree. The green species is far too large for a small garden, but 'Aurea' is more compact, and can be bought trained as a shrub-like multi-stemmed tree. The golden leaves are very large and handsome *4.5 × 4.5m (15 × 15ft)*.

Cordyline australis
See *Plants for the tropical look*.

Cornus controversa 'Variegata'
A small tree with wide-spreading branches spaced out to give it a layered effect. Leaves have striking silver margins *4.5 × 4.5m (15 × 15ft)*.

LEFT: *Daturas (now more correctly called brugmansias) are ideal for the summer patio but they have to be taken indoors for winter frost protection.*

RIGHT: *'Charity' is one of the most imposing hybrid mahonias, with bold sprays of yellow flowers blooming through the coldest months of the year.*

Crambe cordifolia
Herbaceous perennial. Normally a plant for a large garden, but sparsely planted it will make a bold statement. Enormous leaves and huge clouds of gypsophila-like small white flowers in early and mid-summer *1.8 × 1.8m (6 × 6ft)*.

Datura (syn. Brugmansia)
Tender shrub. Must be overwintered in frost-proof place, but often grown on patio in a large tub for summer. Large drooping leaves, big bell-shaped very fragrant flowers – usually white or cream, but there are also red and pink kinds *1.8 × 1.2m (6 × 4ft)* in tub.

Fatsia japonica
See *No fuss, low maintenance plants.*

Gunnera manicata
See *Plants for the tropical look.*

Juniperus scopulorum 'Skyrocket'
Conifer. You may also find it sold under the name of *J. virginiana* 'Skyrocket'. Very narrow, pencil-like growth. Typical conifer foliage *4.5m × 75cm (15 × 2½ft)*.

Kniphofia
See *No fuss, low maintenance plants.*

Mahonia 'Charity'
See *Everbright evergreens.*

RIGHT: *Salix matsudana 'Tortuosa' is a small tree that can be as fascinating in winter as it is in summer.*

Paulownia tomentosa
A large tree totally unsuitable for a small garden. It can be grown as a large shrub, however, by annual hard pruning close to ground level, when the leaves become huge. Treated like this height will be about *2.4–3m (8–10ft)* and spread about *1.8m (6ft)*.

Phormium hybrids
See *Everbright evergreens.*

Salix matsudana 'Tortuosa'
A small to medium-sized tree with spiralling and twisted stems as well as contorted leaves. Seen at its best in winter when the stems are bare *4.5 × 4.5m (15 × 15ft)*.

Yucca
See *Everbright evergreens*, but a green form is just as useful as a variegated variety as an architectural plant.

LIVING SCREENS

The screening plants described here are not rows of tall conifers or large windbreaks along the boundary, which are inappropriate in a small garden, but plants that you can use to screen objects within the garden and plants that you would be happy to grow as ornamentals too.

Generally, something that requires screening will need it the year round, so evergreens naturally predominate in any list of screening plants. But sometimes a summer-only screen is acceptable. For a summer screen within the vegetable plot consider Jerusalem artichokes, which provide excellent summer cover and a crop to harvest at the end of the season!

When looking for a good screening shrub, check that it is well clothed at the base. If you are prepared to erect a trellis or internal fence, many of the plants described under *Climbers and wall shrubs* will also make excellent internal screens. A trellis covered with sweet-smelling honeysuckle will make a summer screen that is pleasing to the eye and the nose. The most popular – and best – honeysuckles are deciduous, so don't expect winter cover, but some fragrant climbing honeysuckles, such as *Lonicera japonica*, are evergreen or semi-evergreen so you will have winter cover as well as summer scent – though at the price of less spectacular flowers.

Trellises and screen block walls
Sometimes it is possible to screen an unsightly object, such as a storage tank with just two or three well-chosen shrubs. Alternatively, erect a trellis or screen wall, carefully integrated as part of the garden design, then use climbers, wall shrubs or ordinary shrubs against these. This double-masking is often the most effective because you have a whole range of climbers that can be used on a trellis, including the ubiquitous but very practical and evergreen ivy, and wall shrubs such as pyracanthas.

Garage walls
Detached garages can dominate a small garden, so you probably need to soften the impact of the walls. Climbers are a natural choice, as are wall shrubs. But you could use a garage as an ideal backdrop for espalier or fan trained fruit trees.

Many evergreen shrubs will do an excellent masking job in front of a garage wall. Let hedging plants such

ABOVE: Griselinia littoralis *'Dixon's Cream'*.
LEFT: Griselinia littoralis.

as *Lonicera nitida* 'Baggesen's Gold' or a golden privet (such as *Ligustrum ovalifolium* 'Aureum') grow up untrimmed until the required height has been reached. Don't attempt to clip these like a formal hedge, but prune over-enthusiastic growth occasionally, and leave them with a natural shape.

LEFT: *For a fast-growing shrubby screen the climbing* Polygonum baldschuanicum *(syn.* Fallopia baldschuanica*) is difficult to beat.*

BELOW: Ligustrum ovalifolium *'Aureo-marginatum' (syn. 'Aureum') is a fast-growing hedging plant, much more attractive than the form with plain green leaves.*

Arundo donax
Grass. Forms tall, almost bamboo-like clump, with drooping blue-green leaves. There is also a variegated form 2.4 × 1.2m (8 × 4ft).

Buxus
Be careful not to choose a dwarf form if you want a taller screen. This is a classic shrub to clip to shape, and is much used for topiary as well as hedges. You could clip your screen to shape.

Griselinia littoralis
See *No fuss, low maintenance plants.*

Ilex
See *Everbright evergreens.*

Ligustrum ovalifolium 'Aureum'
See *Colour themes.*

Lonicera nitida 'Baggesen's Gold'
See *Colour themes.*

Miscanthus sacchariflorus
A large grass. Narrow, arching leaves, forming a dense clump 2.4 × 1m (8 × 3ft).

Polygonum baldschuanicum
Now more correctly *Fallopia baldschuanica.* Deciduous climbing shrub. A vigorous climber, but instead of using it as a screen up a trellis, try letting it grow over the eyesore itself, if it is an old shed, for example. Within a few years it will almost cover it. Profusion of small white or pale pink flowers in conspicuous sprays from mid summer to early autumn. Height and spread is usually dictated by its support.

PERMANENT PLANTS FOR CONTAINERS

The choices and permutations for summer bedding plants to use in containers are almost endless. Every year there are new varieties of seed-raised plants, and growers re-introduce some of the old and neglected tender perennials to keep up the supply of novelties.

On this page you will find ideas for permanent plants to try – those that will form part of the framework of the garden, summer and winter. Use them alongside, and not instead of, seasonal flowers. You might even be able to plant spring bulbs and summer annuals around the base of some of the shrubs suggested.

Agapanthus
See *Colour themes*.

Camellia
See *Everbright evergreens*.

Ceratostigma willmottianum
See *Autumn leaves and berries*.

Choisya ternata 'Sundance'
See *Colour themes*.

Clematis, large-flowered
Deciduous climbing shrub. Large flowers in a wide range of colours. Avoid the rampant species in a container. Try growing them in a half-tub, as described opposite.

Cotoneaster 'Hybridus Pendulus'
Deciduous shrub, grafted to form a small weeping tree. Small white flowers in early summer. Red berries in autumn *1.8 × 1m (6 × 3ft)*.

Laburnum
Small deciduous tree. Produces long tassels of yellow pea-like flowers in late spring and early summer *2.4 × 1.6m (8 × 6ft)*.

Laurus nobilis
Evergreen shrub. The popular kitchen herb, sweet bay. Sometimes attractively trained and clipped into a formal shape. About *1.8m (6ft)*.

Mahonia 'Charity'
See *Everbright evergreens*.

ABOVE: Choisya ternata *'Sundance', an excellent garden plant and attractive in a large container.*
TOP: *Agapanthus are excellent tub plants, but need winter protection in cold areas. This variety is* 'Delft'.

RIGHT: Clematis *'Nelly Moser' (top) and 'Lasurstern'.*

Miscanthus sinensis 'Zebrinus'
Grass. Forms a dense clump of vertical stems that unfurl at the top into narrow, reflexed leaves, with distinctive yellow bands. Grows to an approximate height of *1.2m (4ft)* when contained in a large tub or half-barrel.

Rhododendron
Evergreen shrub (some azaleas are deciduous). There are many rhododendrons and azaleas

(botanically types of rhododendron) dwarf enough to be grown in a container. An ericaceous compost is essential for good results. Colour and size depend on variety.

Rosmarinus officinalis
See *Everbright evergreens*.

Salix caprea 'Pendula'
Deciduous weeping tree. Also known as *Salix* 'Kilmarnock'. Small, umbrella-shaped tree with stiffly pendulous branches. Attractive catkins in spring.

Taxus baccata
Conifer. The popular yew, but choose a golden form such as 'Aurea'. This makes an irregular cone in outline. If you prefer a slimmer, more pencil-shaped profile, try *T. b.* 'Fastigiata Aurea'.

Viburnum tinus
See *Everbright evergreens*.

Yucca
See *Everbright evergreens*.

LEFT:
Rhododendron *'Loder's White'* in a clay pot decorated with masonry paint.

HOW TO PLANT A CLEMATIS BARREL

A clematis barrel can look really stunning when well established. You can choose several varieties to flower at the same time, or different ones that will flower at different times and so extend the period of interest, but bear in mind that this could make pruning more difficult.

1 Fill a half barrel or other large container with a loam-based compost. You need a large, deep container and heavy potting mixture which will support the canes as well as the plants.

2 Plant about three to four clematis in a barrel of this size. Angle the root-ball so that the plants point slightly inwards.

3 Secure the canes at the top. Tie them with string or use a proprietary plastic cane holder. Don't worry if the growth reaches the tops of the canes, it will just tumble down again and make the planting look even more dense.

CLIMBERS AND WALL SHRUBS

Small gardens almost inevitably have a lot of potential space for climbers and wall shrubs. Often there are external fences or walls that can be covered, interior surfaces, such as trellises, which can be used as screens, and nearly always there are all the walls of the house. Some will be in sun for most of the day, others will remain mainly in shade, but there are plants to suit every aspect.

Where space is at a premium, the vertical space provides a wonderful opportunity to grow more plants. Climbers and wall shrubs have a small 'footprint', and if pruned or trained so that they do not encroach too far out from the support, it is usually possible to grow other plants in front of them.

The climbers suggested here are all shrubs that will form a permanent part of the garden framework, but supplement them with annual climbers for a little extra variety and colour. Most annuals can be grown up a trellis – and they should be happy in a container if there is no soil in which they can be planted.

The heights given in the following list are an indication of how tall they are likely to grow in a small garden. Many climbers grow as high and wide as their support. Some clematis will grow to more than 9m (30ft) with a suitable support – such as a tree – but settle for 1.2m (4ft) if that is the height of a fence, and grow along it instead.

Actinidia kolomikta
Climber for wall or pergola. Dark green heart-shaped leaves tipped with white and pink. Sun or partial shade *3m (10ft)*.

Ceanothus
Wall shrub. Blue flowers in late spring or early summer, or in late summer and into autumn, depending on species. Some are evergreen, others deciduous. Some are of border-line hardiness where winters are cold. Sun *3m (10ft)*.

RIGHT: *Clematis remains one of the most popular climbers. This is 'The President'.*

Clematis
An impressive deciduous climber. Use large-flowered hybrids against a trellis on a wall. Vigorous species such as *C. montana* can be grown along a fence or through a tree. Sun or partial shade. Large-flowered hybrids *3m (10ft)*.

Euonymus fortunei
See *Everbright evergreens*.

LEFT: Actinidia kolomikta.

Garrya elliptica
Evergreen wall shrub. Grown for its long catkins in late winter and early spring. Shade or sun *2.4m (8ft)*.

Hedera
The ivies need no introduction. Choose large-leaved kinds, such as *H. colchica* 'Dentata Variegata', for a pergola or arch, small-leaved varieties of *H. helix* for a wall or fence. Shade or sun *3m (10ft)*.

Humulus lupulus 'Aureus'
Herbaceous perennial climber. Golden leaves. Pergola or arch. Sun or partial shade *3m (10ft)*.

Hydrangea petiolaris
Vigorous climber. Flat heads of white flowers in early summer. Shade or partial shade. Needs tall wall or a tree *6m (20ft)*.

Jasminum nudiflorum
See *Colour for the cold months*. Shade or partial shade. Best against a wall, perhaps secured to a trellis *3m (10ft)*.

Jasminum officinale
Climber. Fragrant white flowers in summer and often into autumn. Pergola or arch *3m (10ft)*.

Lonicera x *japonica*
Evergreen climber. White or pale yellow fragrant flowers from early summer to mid autumn. 'Aureoreticulata' has yellow-veined leaves. Best supported against pergola or fence *6m (20ft)*.

Lonicera periclymenum
Deciduous climber. Very fragrant flowers, pale yellow flushed purple-red, ideal for pergola, arch, or trellis. Some varieties flower in late spring and early summer, others from mid summer to early autumn *3m (10ft)* but can grow much taller up a tree.

Polygonum baldschuanicum
See *Living screens*. Fence or wall.

Pyracantha
Wall shrub. White flowers in early summer, red or orange berries in autumn and into winter. Sun or shade *3m (10ft)*.

Rosa
Climbing and rambling roses need no description or introduction. There are many to choose from, and some are excellent for pergolas, arches, and against the wall around the door. Many are very fragrant. Sun or partial shade *3m (10ft)*.

Vitis coignetiae
Deciduous climber. Large leaves with beautiful autumn colours. Sun or shade. Will grow very tall in a tree but can be contained on a pergola.

ABOVE LEFT: Jasminum nudiflorum.
ABOVE: *Pyracantha – a good wall shrub.*
TOP: Garrya elliptica.

Wisteria
Deciduous climber, with long drooping tassels of blue or white flowers in late spring and early summer. *W. sinesis* and *W. floribunda* are both widely grown, and are suitable for a pergola, or to grow against a house wall. Sun or partial shade *3m (10ft)*, but can be much taller.

PLANTING FOR SCENT

A garden without scent is like a meal without seasoning. All the elements appear to be there, but that extra spice is missing that lifts it from the ordinary and heightens the senses.

You can overdo the seasoning, however, so avoid planting too many fragrant plants of the same kind close together. One scent will compete with another, and the more subtle ones may be lost. Rather, make sure that plants with very fragrant flowers are chosen to flower in succession over a period of months. It will not matter if two fragrant shrubs are planted side by side if one flowers after the other has finished.

Mix plants that flower in the day with those that are scented at night – perhaps a rose that gives off its heady perfume during the day with a honeysuckle or night-flowering nicotiana that comes into its own once dusk falls.

Make use of plants with aromatic leaves that release their fragrance when brushed against or deliberately crushed.

Some of the plants suggested here are ornamental plants in their own right – roses and honeysuckles are highly decorative as well as fragrant – but find space for some plants which flower at night. Although they will add nothing to the daytime display they will certainly make up for lack of visual impact by their wonderful perfume after dark.

Chimonanthus praecox
See *Colour for the cold months*.

Choisya ternata
See *Everbright evergreens*. The green variety is just as good for fragrance.

Cytisus battandieri
Large deciduous shrub. Grey leaves. Pineapple-scented yellow flower in late spring and early summer. Not reliably hardy in cold areas, and best grown as a wall shrub *3 × 2.4m (10 × 8ft)*.

Daphne mezereum
Deciduous shrub. Red, pink, purple or white flowers between late winter and mid spring *1.2 × 1m (4 × 3ft)*.

Hamamelis mollis
See *Colour for the cold months*.

Jasminum officinale
See *Climbers and wall shrubs*.

Lavandula
See *Planting for quick results*.

Lonicera periclymenum
See *Climbers and wall shrubs*.

Mahonia 'Charity'
See *Everbright evergreens*.

Rosa
Roses are among the most fragrant of all shrubs, and you can grow their many forms in beds, borders, and as climbers. Use roses lavishly for a fragrant garden. Heights vary according to species.

ABOVE: *Stocks – varieties of* Matthiola incana – *are worth planting for their fragrance.*
LEFT: *One of the strongest spring fragrances comes from* Daphne mezereum *'rubra'.*

FRAGRANT ANNUALS

If you use a lot of summer bedding plants, be sure to include some fragrant ones such as stocks (*Matthiola incana*), and ornamental tobacco plants (nicotiana hybrids), though bear in mind that many of the compact, day-opening varieties of nicotiana have nothing like the powerful scent of the taller, evening-scented ones.

Night-scented stocks (*Matthiola bicornis*) are totally unattractive by day, so grow these as a gap-filler in a border where their day-time appearance doesn't matter.

Philadelphus
Deciduous shrubs. Several good species and hybrids, all with fragrant white flowers in early summer.

Sarcoccoca hookeriana humilis
See *Plants that prefer shade.*

ABOVE: *Lilacs (varieties of* Syringa vulgaris*) are among the most fragrant shrubs, and although some grow tall they are not too large for a small garden.*

Skimmia japonica
See *Autumn leaves and berries.*

Spartium junceum
Deciduous shrub. Yellow, pea-type flowers in summer *2.4 × 1.8m (8 × 6ft).*

Syringa vulgaris
Deciduous shrub, the popular lilac. The varieties have very fragrant flowers mainly in shades of blue, purple, mauve, and white, in late spring and early summer *2.4 × 1.5m (8 × 5ft).*

Viburnum x bodnantense
See *Colour for the cold months.*

Wisteria
See *Climbers and wall shrubs.*

SCENTED FOLIAGE

Use some of the scented-leaved geraniums (pelargoniums) on the patio. You can even plant some of them at the front of a border. Many herbs, such as pineapple sage, lemon balm, and lemon verbena, make acceptable patio plants in pots.

Among the shrubs with aromatic foliage are *Artemisia arborescens, Choisya ternata, Laurus nobilis, Rosmarinus officinalis,* and *Salvia officinalis.*

Eucalyptus can be grown in a small garden if you prune it back hard each spring to grow like a shrub.

RIGHT: *Wisterias are grown mainly for visual impact, but they are also fragrant.*

ATTRACTING WILDLIFE

You don't have to turn your garden into something that resembles a meadow – some might say overgrown and weedy garden – to attract wildlife.

Lots of shrubs, border and rock plants, and annuals and biennials will attract wildlife of many kinds, from birds, bees and butterflies to wasps and weevils. Not all are welcome, of course, but for the few that you don't want to attract you will certainly gain many beautiful and beneficial animals that will help to control the pests.

You will, of course, need to create particular habitats if you want to encourage particular types of wildlife, such as a pond for aquatic creatures. And there is a lot to be said for leaving an area of grass long – perhaps where bulbs are naturalized if you want a horticultural justification – and if you let a few nettles grow behind the garden shed you will provide food plants for many kinds of caterpillars that will later grace your garden as butterflies.

Attracting wildlife in general often brings the bonus of more beneficial insects such as hoverflies and ladybirds, which will help to keep down pests such as aphids.

LEFT: Aucuba japonica 'Variegata'.

ABOVE: Berberis thunbergii 'Atropurpurea Nana'.

Shrubs

Aucuba (birds)
Berberis (birds, bees, butterflies)
Callicarpa (birds)
Ceanothus (bees)
Cistus (bees)
Cotoneaster (bees, birds)
Cytisus (bees)
Daphne (birds, bees)
Escallonia (bees)
Hebe (butterflies)
Hedera (bees, butterflies)
Hypericum (birds)
Ilex (birds)
Lavandula (bees, butterflies)
Leycesteria formosa (birds)
Ligustrum (bees, butterflies)
Lonicera periclymenum (butterflies)
Mahonia (birds)
Pernettya (birds)
Perovskia (bees)
Potentilla (bees)
Pyracantha (birds, bees)
Rhamnus frangula (bees, butterflies)
Ribes sanguineum (bees)
Skimmia (birds, bees)
Symphoricarpos (birds, bees)
Syringa (bees, butterflies)
Ulex (bees)
Viburnum (birds, bees)
Weigela (bees)

Border and rock plants
Achillea filipendulina (bees, butterflies)
Alyssum saxatile (butterflies)
Armeria maritima (bees, butterflies)
Aster novi-beglii (bees, butterflies)
Erigeron (bees, butterflies)
Nepeta (bees, butterflies)
Scabiosa caucasica (bees, butterflies)
Sedum spectabile (bees, butterflies)
Solidago (birds, bees, butterflies)
Thymus (bees, butterflies)

Annuals and biennials
Centaurea cyanus (bees, butterflies)
Dipsacus spp (birds)
Helianthus annuus (birds)
Hesperis matronalis (bees)
Limanthes douglasii (bees)
Lunaria annua (birds)
Scabious annual (bees, butterflies)

LEFT: Sedum
'Autumn Joy'

BELOW: Solidago.

ABOVE: Alyssum saxatile.

OTHER WAYS TO ATTRACT WILDLIFE

A thick hedge attracts far more wildlife than a fence or wall. A prickly evergreen hedge like holly will provide good nest and roost sites for many birds.

An old log pile provides refuge for many beneficial insects and can make a nest site for small mammals.

SPRING

*This is a time when gardeners need no encouragement.
With lengthening days, the air less chilly, and plump buds and birdsong
to stir the imagination, it is the time when gardeners cannot wait to start
propagating and planting. Early spring is a time for caution, however,
as winter seldom comes to a convenient end as spring approaches.
One of the most common causes of disappointment for novice gardeners is
sowing or planting too early – especially outdoors. Often, plants and
seeds put out several weeks later in the season overtake ones planted
earlier because they are less likely to receive a check to growth.*

OPPOSITE: *Even small spring flowers make a
strong display, like this group of narcissi,
pulmonarias, and Anemone blanda.*

ABOVE: *Tulips are among the most beautiful
spring flowers, but they look even better when
interplanted with forget-me-nots.*

PLANT ONION SETS

The biggest onions are usually grown from seed, but unless you can give them the dedicated care they need the results will be disappointing. Sets (small onion bulbs) are an almost foolproof way to grow onions, and you should be rewarded with a reasonable crop for very little effort.

1 Take out a shallow drill with the corner of a hoe or rake, using a garden line for a straight row. Space the sets about 15cm (6in) apart.

2 Pull the soil back over the drill, but leave the tips of the onions protruding. If birds are a problem – they may try to pull the onions out by the wispy old stems – protect with netting or keep pushing the bulbs back until rooted.

PLANT SHALLOTS

Shallots are useful for pickling, but also store well for use like onions. They are almost always grown from bulbs, bought or saved from last year's crop.

1 Planted in the same way as onion sets, shallots are spaced about 15cm (6in) apart, but the bulbs are larger, so the drill might have to be a little deeper. Push the bulbs into the base of the drill so that the tip is just protruding. Pull the soil back round them with a hoe or rake.

2 Shallots are useful for an early crop, and you can usually plant them outdoors in late winter, except in very cold regions. If you missed the winter planting but still want to get them growing quickly, start them off in individual pots.

3 Keep the pots in a cold frame or greenhouse until the shoots are 3–5cm (1–2in) high. Then plant the sprouted shallots in the garden, spacing them about 15cm (6in) apart.

SOW EARLY VEGETABLES OUTDOORS

Early sowing can be a gamble. If the weather is cold the seeds may rot before they germinate, and some vegetables tend to run to seed if they are subject to very cold conditions after germinating.

Concentrate early sowings on hardy crops like broad beans and early peas. Try a few short rows of a wider range of vegetables, but be prepared to resow if they don't do well.

1 Peas are best sown in multiple rows so that they can support each other, with walking space between the double or triple rows. Broad beans are also often grown in multiple rows. Take out a flat-bottomed drill 5–8cm (2–3in) deep.

2 Space the seeds by hand. Peas are often sown in three staggered rows, spacing the seeds about 4cm (1½in) apart, but you can double this space and still get a good crop. Broad beans are sown in two rows with each seed about 23cm (9in) apart.

3 Pull the soil back over the drill to cover the seeds. If the ground is dry, water well until the seedlings are through. If seed-eaters such as mice are a problem, netting or traps may be necessary.

AN EARLY START

Peas and beans germinate readily in warm soil, but are less reliable in early spring when the soil temperature fluctuates. You can be more sure of

your early peas if you start the seeds off in a greenhouse or cold frame first, then plant them out when they are growing well.

1 A length of old gutter is ideal for starting off the seeds. Block the ends and fill with soil.

2 Sow the seeds about 5–8cm (2–3in) apart, cover, then keep warm and moist.

3 When ready to plant out, take out a shallow drill with a draw hoe, and gradually slide the peas out of the gutter and into the row.

FERTILIZE THE VEGETABLE PLOT

The vegetable plot needs regular feeding if yields are not to suffer. Unlike beds and borders in the ornamental garden, little natural recycling occurs. The crops are removed and leaves do not naturally fall and decay. Bulky organic manures do much to improve soil structure and increase the nutrient-holding capabilities of the soil, but unless you follow an intensive organic approach and apply sufficient manures and garden compost, some chemical fertilizers are necessary if you want a heavy crop.

INDIVIDUAL BOOSTERS

Throughout the growing season, certain vegetables may need boosters from specific fertilizers or quick-acting general fertilizers whenever growth seems to need encouraging. Spring cabbages often benefit from a light dressing of a nitrogenous fertilizer to stimulate the growth of fresh young leaves now that the weather is improving. Fruit crops, such as tomatoes, benefit from a high-potash feed.

1 The quickest way to apply a general fertilizer to your vegetable plot is with a wheeled spreader that you can adjust to deliver the appropriate amount. Calculate and test the delivery rate first.

2 If applying by hand, measure out the amount of fertilizer required for a square metre or yard, so that you can visualize how much you need. Or pour it into a small container as a measure and note how full it is.

3 Mark out metre or yard widths with strings, then use a couple of canes to divide these into metre or yard squares. When one square has been applied, move the back cane forward to mark out the next area.

4 Use your measure to scoop up the appropriate amount of fertilizer (use the application rates advised on the packet as a guide), then scatter it evenly. Hold the hand about 15–23cm (6–9in) above the soil.

5 Always rake the fertilizer into the surface. This spreads it more evenly and helps it to penetrate more rapidly.

HORTICULTURAL FLEECE

Horticultural fleece is a material that a previous generation of gardeners didn't possess, but the fact that it is now widely used commercially is evidence of its usefulness. The fleece will warm up the soil rather like a cloche, and should provide protection from a degree or two of frost. It also offers protection from animals such as rabbits and pests such as butterflies. You can use it just to start off your seeds, or as protection for a growing crop.

1 Sow your seeds then cover the area with the fleece. Anchor it down loosely with bricks or stones initially, while you secure the edges.

FLOATING CLOCHES

Other types of protective covers can also be used successfully. Some are very fine, long-lasting nets (see top), which give little frost protection but effectively keep out most animals and pests, others are perforated plastic films (see above) that let rain through and 'give' enough to rise with the growing crop.

You will have to pull them back to weed and thin. You will find that weeds thrive with the protection as well as the crops!

2 You can secure the edges with soil. Make a slit to tuck the end into, or just heap soil over the edges. Water will flow through the fleece, and it will also stretch a little as the plants grow.

3 You can buy various designs of proprietary pegs to hold the fleece in position, and these are preferable to the soil method as they make it easier to lift and replace the fleece for weeding and other cultivation tasks.

SOW HARDY ANNUALS

Hardy annuals are among the easiest plants to grow – they are undemanding of soil and are simply sown where they are to grow. Provided you thin overcrowded seedlings and give them a sunny position, the results are almost always bright and pleasing.

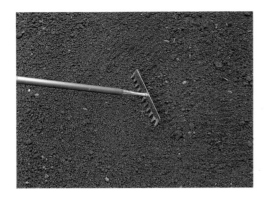

1 It pays to prepare the ground by clearing it of weeds, and raking the surface to a fine, crumbly structure.

2 If you are growing just for cutting, sow in rows in a spare piece of ground, but if you want to make a bright border of hardy annuals, 'draw' your design on the ground with sand and grit.

3 Use the corner of a hoe or rake to draw shallow drills, but change the direction of the drills from one block to the next to avoid a regimented appearance. Check the packet for spacing between rows.

4 Sprinkle the seeds as evenly as possible. If the weather is very dry, run water into the bottom of each drill first and allow it to soak in.

5 Write and insert a label, then cover the seeds by raking the soil back over the drills. Try not to disturb the seeds unnecessarily.

SOWING BROADCAST

Sowing in rows makes thinning and weeding much easier – especially if you don't know what the seedlings look like and find it difficult to distinguish desirable seedlings from weeds. Sometimes, however, the seeds are sown broadcast (scattered randomly) to create a more informal patch of flowers. This is particularly useful for a packet of mixed annuals, for example, where you might want to create the appearance of a wild garden.

Scatter the seeds as evenly as possible (see above), then rake them in – first in one direction and then at right angles.

6 Water thoroughly if the soil is dry and rain is not forecast. Continue to water in dry weather until the seedlings have emerged.

PLANT GLADIOLI

Gladioli are popular, and easy to grow, but their location in the flower garden needs careful thought. Grow them in rows in a spare piece of ground if you want them for cutting, but they look best planted in blocks or clusters when grown among companion plants.

OTHER BULBS TO PLANT

1 If you are growing gladioli for cutting rather than garden display, grow them in rows. Take out a trench as shown deep enough to cover the corms with about 8–10cm (3–4in) of soil. Deep planting reduces the need for staking.

2 Space the corms as recommended on the packet. Planting a double row like this makes supporting easier for tall varieties. Return the soil to the trench to cover them.

Most other summer-flowering bulbs, corms and tubers can be planted in the same way as gladioli, though it is too early to plant any very frost-sensitive plants as the shoots may emerge while frosts are still likely.

As a guide to planting depth, most bulbs should be covered with twice their own depth of soil. If the bulb is 3cm (1in) deep, cover it with 5cm (2in) of soil, though there are a few exceptions.

Some tubers tend to become very dry and shrivelled after a long period in store. You can usually plump them up by soaking in water for a day before you plant, like the anemone tubers shown.

3 If planting in a border among other plants, take out a roughly circular hole, place a group of about five or seven corms in the base, and return the soil. If the ground is heavy, dig in some sand or grit before planting the corms.

4 It is easy to forget where bulbs are planted in a border, so apart from labelling, insert a few small canes around them so that you don't accidentally hoe off the shoots before they emerge.

PLANT SHRUBS

Spring is an ideal time to plant shrubs. You can plant container-grown shrubs in any month provided the ground is not too frozen. However, spring is ideal because the soil is moist and also warm enough for new root growth to help the plant become established quickly.

1 Always clear the area of weeds, and dig out any deep-rooted perennials that will be difficult to eradicate if they grow within the root system of the shrub. Dig in plenty of garden compost or rotted manure.

2 Excavate a large hole, about twice the width of the pot or root-ball. To check the depth, place the plant in position and use a cane or stick across the hole to judge whether the shrub will be at its original depth in the soil.

3 If the roots are dry, water the plant thoroughly then leave for an hour. If roots are wound tightly around the inside of the pot, tease out some of the fine ones to encourage them to grow out into the soil.

4 Place the root-ball in the hole and check that the soil will be level with the potting soil in the root-ball. Return the soil, and firm it well to eliminate large air pockets.

5 To get your shrubs off to a good start, apply a general garden fertilizer at the recommended rate and sprinkle around the plant. Keep away from the stem. Water well.

6 'Balled' or 'root-wrapped' shrubs are sold with their roots wrapped in hessian or a plastic material. Check the depth as before.

7 When the plant is in position, untie the wrapper and slide it out of the hole. Avoid disturbing the ball of soil around the roots.

8 Replace the soil, and firm well to eliminate large pockets of air. Apply fertilizer and water as described for container-grown plants.

9 It is worth mulching the ground after planting. It will conserve moisture and some mulches, such as chipped bark, look attractive too.

PLANT HERBACEOUS PLANTS

Herbaceous border plants can be planted at any time from containers, but most gardeners prefer to get them planted in spring so that they contribute to the summer show.

If you buy plants by mail order they may arrive as small root-wrapped plants, and these should be planted before the new shoots emerge, or are still very short.

ROOT-WRAPPED HERBACEOUS PLANTS

If your herbaceous plants are root-wrapped, keep them in a cool, shady place until you are ready to plant. Make sure that the plants are kept moist at all times.

Remove the wrapping only just before you are ready to plant. Spread the roots out widely within the planting hole before returning the soil.

Root-wrapped plants are more vulnerable than container-grown plants until they become established, so take extra care and keep them well watered.

1 If planting a border, lay the plants out first so that you can visualize the result (don't forget to allow for growth!). It is easier to move them around at this stage, before planting.

2 Water the plants about an hour before you start, and knock them out of their pots only when you are ready to plant.

3 Ensure the ground is clear of weeds before planting, and work methodically from the back of the border or from one end. Most can be planted with a trowel but you may need a spade for large plants.

4 Return the soil, making sure that the plant is at its original depth, and firm well to eliminate any large pockets of air that could cause the roots to dry out.

5 Water the plants thoroughly unless the weather is wet or heavy rain is forecast.

SOW A NEW LAWN

The advantage of a lawn from seed is that it is usually less expensive than turf and you can choose the grass seed mixture. Some turf specialists also offer seed mixtures to suit your specific requirements, but these can be expensive.

Thorough ground preparation is essential for a quality lawn, and this should start several weeks before sowing. If you don't have time to prepare the ground properly this spring, wait and sow in the autumn instead.

1 Dig the ground thoroughly, and make every effort to eliminate difficult or deep-rooted perennial weeds. Then rake the soil level. Use pegs marked with lines drawn 5cm (2in) down from the top as a guide, having checked with a spirit-level on a straight-edge that the pegs are level.

2 Allow the soil to settle for a week, then consolidate it further by treading it evenly to remove large air pockets. The best way to do this is to shuffle your feet over the area, first in one direction then at right angles.

3 Rake the consolidated soil to produce a fine crumbly structure suitable for sowing seeds. If you can, leave the area for a couple of weeks to allow weed seeds to germinate. Hoe them off or use a weedkiller that leaves the ground safe for replanting within days.

4 Use string to divide the area into 1m (1yd) strips, and divide these into 1m (1yd) lengths. Move the canes along the strips as you sow.

5 Use a small container that holds enough seed for a square metre or square yard (make a mark on it if the amount only partly fills the container). Scatter the seeds as evenly as possible with a sweeping motion of the hand.

6 If you have to sow a large area it might be worth hiring a seed/ fertilizer distributor that you can simply wheel over the area. Always check the delivery rate over sheets of paper or plastic first. Lightly rake the seed into the surface. Use a water sprinkler if necessary to keep the soil moist until the seeds germinate.

LAY A LAWN FROM TURF

Turf provides the best method of creating a lawn quickly – you can use it within months – and soil preparation is a little less demanding. You will usually find that it is a more expensive option than seed, but many gardeners are happy to pay a premium for the convenience.

1 Dig and consolidate the soil as described for seed, but there is no need to leave it for a few weeks to allow weed seeds to germinate – the turf will prevent them from germinating. Start by laying the turf along a straight edge.

2 Use a plank to stand on while you lay the next row, as this will help to distribute your weight. Stagger the joints between rows to create a bond like brickwork. If using turf as a long roll there will be fewer joints. Make sure these do not align.

3 Tamp down each row of turf (you can use the head of a rake as shown), then roll the plank forwards to lay the next row.

ABOVE: *A lawn can create a sense of space and is often the central part of the garden. Here an informal shape creates a natural look.*

4 Brush sieved sandy soil, or a mixture of peat and sand, into the joints. This will help to bind the turves together.

5 Shape edges when the lawn is laid. Lay a hose or rope to form the shape for a curved edge, or use a straight-edged piece of wood for a straight edge, and trim with a half-moon edger.

SPRING PRUNE SHRUBS

Only prune shrubs that you know require spring pruning, otherwise you may cut out the shoots that will bear this year's flowers. Advice is given below for some popular shrubs that need spring pruning, but if in doubt about others consult an encyclopedia that gives pruning information.

1 Prune shrubs grown for coloured winter stems shortly before new growth starts. These include *Cornus alba* and *Cornus stolonifera* varieties and *Salix alba* 'Chermesina' (syn. 'Britzensis'). Only prune plants that have been established for a few years.

2 Cut back all the stems to an outward-facing bud about 5cm (2in) from the ground or stump of old, hard wood.

3 Although the pruning seems drastic, new shoots will soon appear and by next winter will make a splendid sight. Prune annually if you feed and mulch the plants, otherwise every second spring.

4 Some popular grey-leaved shrubs, such as *Santolina chamaecyparissus* and *Helichrysum angustifolium*, need regular pruning if they are to remain neat and compact.

5 If you prune the plant regularly from a young age, prune back close to the base to a point where you can see new shoots developing. This may be as low as 10cm (4in) from the ground on some plants, but on old, woody plants you will have to leave a taller framework of woody shoots.

6 The plant will look bare and sparse after pruning, but within a month should be well clothed again.

7 *Buddleia davidii* produces its flowers at the tops of tall, lanky stems if left unpruned. Each spring, cut back all the shoots to within about two buds of the previous year's growth, close to the old stump.

8 Again, this type of pruning looks drastic but it will greatly enhance the look of the plant later in the year.

A few shrubs related to the blackberry are grown for their white winter stems. The shoots arise from ground level like raspberry canes, and these are best cut back every year. Cut all the stems off close to the ground. New shoots will soon grow and the plant will be just as attractive next winter.

PRUNE ROSES

Trials have shown that you can achieve very good results from hybrid tea (large-flowered) and floribunda (cluster-flowered) roses simply by cutting them roughly to an even height with secateurs, or even a hedgetrimmer, without worrying about the detailed pruning shown here. The conventional method is still practised by most rose enthusiasts, however. Don't worry if you make one or two wrong cuts – the roses will probably still bloom prolifically.

1 Moderate pruning is the most appropriate for established hybrid tea roses. Cut back the stems by about half, to an outward-facing bud to keep the centre of the bush open.

2 You can treat floribundas in the same way, but if you prune some shoots severely and others lightly, flowering may be spread over a longer period. Prune the oldest shoots back close to the base, those that grew last year by about a third only.

3 Whichever type of rose you are pruning, cut back any dead or diseased shoots to healthy wood.

START OFF BEGONIA AND GLOXINIA TUBERS

Tuberous-rooted begonias can be grown as pot-plants or in the garden, but wherever they are destined it is well worth starting them into growth now in the greenhouse. This way you will have well-developed plants to put in the garden that will flower much earlier than if the tubers were planted directly into the soil.

Gloxinias, which are suitable only for cultivation in the home or greenhouse, should also be started into growth now.

1 If you are growing your begonias as pot-plants, start them off in small pots to save space in the early stages. Loosely fill the pots with a peat-based or peat-substitute mixture intended for seeds or cuttings.

2 If the tubers have small shoots it will be obvious which is the top, otherwise look for the side with a slight hollow and keep this upwards. Just press the tuber into the compost. Keep in a warm, light place, ideally in a greenhouse.

3 If the begonias are intended for outdoors, perhaps in containers or baskets, start them off in trays instead of pots as this will save space.

LEFT: *'Pin-up' is an outstanding single tuberous-rooted begonia that can be raised from seed to flower in its first year or overwintered as a dry tuber.*

4 Gloxinia tubers are started into growth in the same way, but as they will be grown as pot-plants you may prefer to plant them in their final 13–15cm (5–6in) pots. The 'hairy' side (the remains of old roots) is the one to press into the compost.

POT UP AND POT ON CUTTINGS

Pot up cuttings, such as those of pelargoniums and fuchsias, to ensure that their growth rate is not checked. With warmer temperatures they will now be growing vigorously.

1 Pot up the cuttings as soon as they have formed strong root growth. Use an 8–10cm (3–4in) pot and a potting mixture suitable for young plants. Water thoroughly, then keep out of direct sunlight for a couple of days while they recover from the root disturbance.

2 Cuttings that rooted earlier and have already been potted up for a month or more may need moving into larger pots. Check that the roots have filled the potting mixture before you transfer them. If the mixture has lots of white roots, pot on into a larger size.

3 Use a pot a couple of sizes larger, and trickle the same kind of potting mix around the root-ball. Firm well to remove air pockets, and water thoroughly.

ENCOURAGE BUSHY FUCHSIAS

Bush-shaped fuchsias respond well to early 'pruning' and training. You can start as soon as the cuttings have three pairs of leaves.

1 Pinch out the growing tip of your fuchsia cuttings once three pairs of leaves have formed, if you want a bushy shape.

2 New shoots will form after a few weeks, but for really bushy plants pinch out the tips of these sideshoots too. Repeat this process several times throughout spring to encourage well-shaped bushy plants.

SAVING SPACE IN THE GREENHOUSE

Greenhouse space is often a problem at this time of year. If you are growing cuttings for the garden rather than as pot-plants, keep the young plants in small pots rather than potting them on into larger ones. To avoid a check to growth, however, you must feed the young plants regularly to avoid starvation. Move them to a frost-free cold frame as soon as it is warm enough to do so, and allow plenty of space between the plants so that the leaves are not overcrowded.

PRICK OUT SEEDLINGS

Prick out seedlings as soon as they are large enough to handle. If you leave them in their original trays or pots too long, they will quickly become overcrowded and difficult to separate without damage. Some plants are best pricked out into individual pots (see opposite), but this takes up a lot of space and compost, so most bedding plants are pricked out into trays. Instead of pricking out into trays, you can use a modular or cell system, like the one shown here, where each plant has its own pocket of soil, separated from the others. The benefit of this method is that there will be less root disturbance when the plants are eventually put into the garden.

1 Choose a module that suits the size of plant. A small seedling such as ageratum or fibrous-rooted begonia will not need such a large cell as, say, a dahlia. Fill the individual cells loosely with a potting mixture suitable for seedlings.

2 Strike the compost off level with a straight-edge, but do not compress it. It will settle lower in the cells once the seedlings have been inserted and watered.

3 Loosen the seedlings in the tray or pot you are pricking out from, and if possible lift them one at a time by their seed leaves. These are the first ones to open, and they are usually smaller and a different shape to the true leaves.

4 Use a tool designed for the purpose, or improvise with something like a pencil or plant label, to make a hole large enough to take the roots with as little bending or disturbance as possible.

5 Gently firm the compost around the roots, being careful not to press too hard. Water thoroughly, then keep the plants out of direct sunlight for a couple of days.

ABOVE: *The white alyssum and bright golden annual rudbeckias are among many colourful annuals to be pricked out now.*

PRICK OUT INTO POTS

Some plants, such as bedding pelargoniums and pot-plants for the greenhouse and home, are best pricked out into individual pots rather than trays or even modules.

1 Fill small pots with potting mixture and firm it lightly, using the base of another pot.

2 Loosen the compost with a small dibber or transplanting tool. Hold the seedling by its leaves, not the stem.

3 Make a small hole in the centre of the pot, deep enough to take the roots without damage.

4 While still holding the seedling by a leaf, very gently firm the potting mixture around the roots, using a small dibber or a finger. Don't press too hard as watering will also settle the mixture around the roots.

5 Water carefully so that the potting mixture is settled around the roots without washing the plant out. Keep the seedlings in a warm, humid place out of direct sunlight for a few days.

PRICKING OUT TINY SEEDLINGS

Seedlings are almost always pricked out individually, but there are a few special cases when more than a single seedling is used. Lobelia seedlings are tiny, and individual plants not very substantial, so many gardeners prick out a small group of seedlings together, as shown. Prick out about five or six plants at a time, though the number is not critical. Pricking out tiny seedlings in small groups like this also makes the job much quicker and easier, but it is only recommended for certain plants.

By the time these grow into seedlings large enough to plant out they look like one substantial plant.

6 Writing labels for individual pots is tedious and you probably won't want to do it, yet confusion later is highly probable if you have lots of pots containing different varieties. Group individual varieties into trays, and use just one label.

SOW MAINCROP VEGETABLES OUTDOORS

Vegetable sowing begins in earnest now, with crops like beetroot, spinach beet, summer cabbages, salad and pickling onions, scorzonera and turnips, as well as further sowings of lettuces, peas, radishes, spinach, carrots and cauliflowers. Dwarf beans can be sown in mild areas.

1 Break the soil down into a fine crumbly structure, and level with a rake before sowing.

2 Heavy soils may be difficult to break down into a fine structure with the rake, especially if the soil is dry. Treading on the largest lumps usually helps to break them down.

3 Once the soil is reasonably fine, rake it level, and remove any large stones at the same time.

4 Most vegetables grown in rows, such as beetroots and carrots, are best sown in drills. Always use a garden line to make sure the drills – and therefore the rows – are straight.

5 Take out a shallow drill with the corner of a hoe or rake. Always refer to the seed packet for the recommended depth.

6 Flood the drills with water a few minutes before sowing if the weather is dry. Do it before sowing rather than after so that the seeds are not washed away or into clumps.

7 Sprinkle the seeds thinly and evenly along the drill. Do this carefully now and you will save time later when you would have to thin the seedlings if they come up too quickly.

8 Remove the garden line, then use your feet to shuffle the excavated soil back into the drills as you walk along the row. This technique is easy to master.

9 Use a rake to return soil to the drills if you find it easier, but rake in the direction of the row and not across it, otherwise you might spread the seeds and produce an uneven row.

FLUID SOWING

Fluid sowing is a technique some gardeners use to get the more difficult seeds off to a flying start. Parsnips, early carrots, onions and parsley are among the vegetables sometimes sown this way.

1 Sow the seeds thickly on damp kitchen paper, and keep in a warm place to germinate. Make sure that they remain moist, and check daily to monitor germination.

2 Once the roots emerge, and before the leaves open, wash the seeds into a sieve and mix them into prepared wallpaper paste (no fungicide) or a special sowing gel.

USING PREPARED SOWING STRIPS

From time to time strips of pre-sown seeds, embedded in a degradable material, may be available. These are an expensive way to buy seeds, but save much time and energy normally spent on spacing and thinning.

Take out a drill as advised and place the strip on edge in the drill. Return the soil to the drill, and keep the ground moist.

Because the seeds receive protection from the material in which they are embedded, and this sometimes also contains nutrients to give the seedlings a boost, you may find it an easy way to achieve a row of well-spaced seedlings.

3 Take out the drill in the normal way, and to the usual depth.

BELOW: *Carrots benefit from even sowing. The onions are to deter carrot fly!*

4 Fill a plastic bag with the paste and cut off one corner (rather like an icing bag). Don't make the hole too large. Twist the top of the bag to prevent the paste oozing out, then move along the row as you squeeze out the seeds in the paste.

PLANT POTATOES

It is safe to plant potatoes in most areas, as it will take several weeks before the frost-sensitive shoots emerge from the soil, and these can be protected by earthing up the plants. In cold areas, however, it is best to chit your potatoes (see below) and delay planting for a couple of weeks. The use of cloches, floating cloches or fleece is wise in areas where frost is still likely.

1 Use a draw hoe, spade or a rake head to make wide flat-bottomed or V-shaped drills 10–13cm (4–5in) deep. Space the rows about 43cm (17in) apart for early varieties, 68cm (2¼ft) for second earlies, and 75cm (2½ft) for the maincrop.

2 Space the tubers about 30–45cm (12–18in) apart in the rows. Make sure that the shoots or 'eyes' (buds about to grow into shoots) face upwards. For larger tubers, leave only three sprouts per plant and rub the others off.

CHITTING POTATO TUBERS

Chitting simply means encouraging the potato tubers to sprout before planting. The kind of long shoots that appear when potatoes have been stored in the dark for some time are no use – the shoots must be short and sturdy. Place the tubers in a tray in a light position, perhaps by a window, where there is no risk of frost.

Chitting is useful if you want the tubers to get off to a quick start, as they will usually be through the ground a week or two before unchitted tubers.

3 Cover the tubers by pulling the excavated soil back into the drill.

4 If you don't want the effort of earthing up your potatoes, plant under a black plastic sheet. Bury the edges in slits in the soil and cover with soil to anchor the sheet.

5 Make cross-shaped slits in the plastic with a knife where each tuber is to be planted.

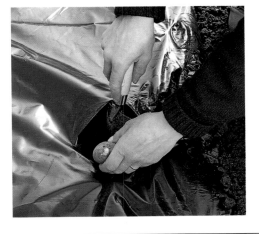

6 Plant through the slit, using a trowel. Make sure that the tuber is covered with 3–5cm (1–2in) of soil. The shoots will find their way through the slits.

PLANT CABBAGES AND CAULIFLOWERS

Cabbages and cauliflowers are not normally sown in their final positions, but started off in seed beds, or sown in late winter and spring in pots or modules in the greenhouse, then transplanted to their growing positions. Buy young plants if you forgot to sow your own.

1 If you have your own seedlings to transplant into the vegetable patch – perhaps growing in a cold frame – water thoroughly an hour before you lift them if the soil is dry.

2 Loosen the soil with a fork or trowel. It is best to lift each one individually with a trowel if possible, but if they have not been thinned sufficiently this may be difficult.

3 Plant with a trowel and firm the soil well. A convenient way to firm soil around the roots is to insert the blade of the trowel about 5cm (2in) away from the plant and press it firmly towards the roots.

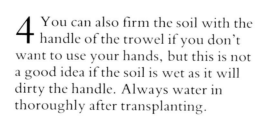

4 You can also firm the soil with the handle of the trowel if you don't want to use your hands, but this is not a good idea if the soil is wet as it will dirty the handle. Always water in thoroughly after transplanting.

5 Cabbage and cauliflower seedlings are often raised in modules so that the plants receive less of a shock when transplanted. Many modules are designed so that you can remove the plant by squeezing the base while gently pulling the plant at the top.

PROTECTION FOR EARLY STRAWBERRIES

Strawberries do not need protection from frost, but cloches will bring the crop on earlier and will also help to keep it clean and protect it from birds and other animals.

Cover the plants as soon as possible, but remember to leave access for pollinating insects when the plants are in flower. Most cloches have a system of ventilation that can be used for this on warm days. With polythene tunnel cloches, lift the material along one side to allow for pollination.

ABOVE: *Space cabbages as advised on the packet, as size varies.*

PLANT WATERLILIES

This is a good time to plant up your pond, whether establishing a new one or just adding new plants to an old one. Waterlilies are likely to be much more expensive than the aquatic plants that you plant around the margins of the pool, so it is worth taking special care.

1 Planting baskets are usually used for plants that grow around the edge of a pond, but for deep-water plants like waterlilies a washing-up bowl is ideal. Use a heavy soil that is not too rich in nutrients, available from aquatic specialists.

2 Never add ordinary fertilizers to the soil, as these are likely to encourage a proliferation of algae that will turn the water green. Use a special slow-release fertilizer, preferably one sold specifically for aquatic plants.

USING OXYGENATING PLANTS

Many oxygenating plants, such as elodea, remain below the surface and have little visual appeal. These are used because they are efficient at releasing oxygen into the water, which helps to keep it healthy for fish and wildlife.

Some oxygenating plants are sold as cuttings bundled together, perhaps weighted so that they sink. Just push these into a container of soil and they will soon root.

Some of the more decorative types, such as myriophyllums, which have a feathery growth above the water, are best planted in baskets like marginal aquatics.

3 Remove the waterlily from its container, and plant in the bowl at its original depth.

4 Add a layer of gravel to reduce the chance of fish disturbing the soil. Gravel also helps to keep the soil in place when the container is lowered into the water.

5 Flood the bowl with water and let it stand for a while. This will reduce the chances of the water becoming muddy when you place the bowl in the pond.

6 Place the bowl in a shallow part of the pond initially, especially if new leaves are just developing. Then push it into deeper water a week or two later.

PLANT MARGINAL AQUATICS

There is nothing marginal about the appeal of most plants that come under this description – the term merely indicates that they are planted in shallower water at the margins of the pool. Most ponds are designed with a shelf on which you can grow marginal plants, most conveniently in baskets sold for the purpose, or you can stand the plants on bricks or slabs.

INTRODUCING FISH

1 Fill a basket sold for marginal plants with garden soil that is not too rich in nutrients, or buy an aquatic compost. Liners are sold to prevent the soil falling through the open sides of the basket.

2 Remove the plant from its container and plant it in the basket at its original depth, using a trowel to add or remove soil as necessary. Firm it in well.

Never place fish directly into the pond. First acclimatize them by floating the plastic bag that you transported them in on the surface of the water for an hour, as shown. This will allow the water temperatures to equalize gradually, after which the fish can be allowed to swim out of the bag.

ABOVE: *Always choose waterlily varieties to suit the size of the pond. Some are suitable for a small pool, others demand a lot of space.*

3 Cover with gravel to help keep the soil in place when you place the container in the pond, and to minimize disturbance by fish.

4 Water first to moisten the soil if it is dry, then carefully place on the shelf at the edge of the pool so that the container is covered by 3–5cm (1–2in) of water.

PLANT OR SOW SWEET PEAS

Sweet peas sown in the autumn and overwintered in a cold frame, or sown in a greenhouse in mid or late winter, will have made sturdy plants ready to be put out, but it is not too late to sow now – indoors or out – for a late summer display. To spread the period over which you can enjoy sweet peas, it is a good idea to sow at different times.

1 Insert the supports before you plant. For the best blooms, on long, straight stems, the cordon system is best, but it is very labour-intensive. Insert T-shaped posts at each end of the double row. Stretch wires between the cross-pieces and secure 2.1m (7ft) canes to these at 23cm (9in) intervals, sloping them slightly inwards.

2 For general garden display and a mass of flowers, a wigwam of canes is more satisfactory. Incline the canes inwards and tie at the top, or use a proprietary cane holder.

3 Wire or plastic netting fixed to canes to form a circular tower is another efficient way to support tall sweet peas for general garden decoration at the back of a border.

4 Remove a hole, large enough to take the root-ball with minimal disturbance, at the base of each cane, or about 23cm (9in) apart.

5 Sweet pea plants are sometimes sold with a cluster of seedlings in one pot. Always separate these and plant individually. Spread the roots out, cover, then water thoroughly.

6 Support the plants from an early stage. They can be wound in and out of netting, or attached to canes with string or metal split rings.

7 If sowing directly into the soil, sow two or three seeds at each position, and thin to one later if more germinate.

STAKE BORDER PLANTS

Some border plants are prone to wind damage, and sometimes a potentially beautiful plant is flattened or broken by the weather. Early staking means that the plants will usually grow through or over the support, which will then become almost invisible.

1 Proprietary supports like this are very efficient at supporting border plants that are not very tall but have a mass of tallish floppy or fragile flowering stems.

2 Proprietary supports that link together as shown are useful where you have clumps of varying sizes to support. They can be linked together to suit the individual plant.

3 Twiggy sticks pushed into the ground among and around the plant can be very effective. They may look a little unsightly initially, but once the plant grows you probably won't notice them.

4 Short canes can be used to support plants such as carnations. If you use a stout cane, loop string or twine around it and the plant. Use thinner split canes to keep individual flower stems or groups of stems upright.

ABOVE: *Tall garden canes are an efficient way to support plants with very tall flowering spikes that are vulnerable to wind damage, such as delphiniums. Insert individual canes at an early stage, and tie the spike to it loosely as it grows.*

TAKE SOFTWOOD CUTTINGS

Softwood cuttings, which are taken from the new shoots produced this year, root quickly and easily, and you can multiply many of your plants this way. The list below suggests a selection of some of the more popular garden plants you can propagate in this way.

1 The exact length of a softwood cutting depends on the plant, and some gardeners prefer variations of the basic technique, but typically the stem is cut off below the third or fourth leaf or pairs of leaves.

2 Trim or pull off the lowest pair of leaves (if the plant has scale-like stipules, such as on a pelargonium, pull off these as well). Trim the base of the stem with a sharp knife, cutting just below a leaf joint.

PLANTS TO GROW FROM SOFTWOOD CUTTINGS

The following are just some of the popular plants that can be propagated from softwood cuttings taken now, but there are many more to try. It is always worth experimenting if there is a plant that you want to propagate but are not sure if softwood cuttings are suitable. The chances are that some will root.
Caryopteris
Clematis
Forsythia
Fuchsia
Helichrysum
Kolkwitzia
Lavandula
Pelargonium
Salvia (shrubby types)

3 Dip the end of the cutting into a rooting hormone for speedier rooting, although many softwood cuttings root easily without this aid. Most rooting powders contain a fungicide, however, and this also helps to prevent rotting.

4 Make a hole with a dibber or pencil, then insert the cutting and firm the rooting mixture gently around it. Do not force the cutting in as this may damage it. If you have a lot of cuttings, insert several around the edge of each pot – but don't let the leaves touch.

5 Water and place in a propagator. If you do not have a propagator, enclose the cuttings in a plastic bag secured with a twist-tie or elastic band. High humidity is very important for softwood cuttings. Make sure that the leaves are not in contact with the bag.

PLANT A HANGING BASKET

The best hanging baskets are those planted with fairly small plants that are then grown on in a light, frost-free place until it is safe to put them outdoors – perhaps in late spring or early summer. A greenhouse is ideal, but you might also be able to use an enclosed or protected porch. Giving the baskets protection for a few weeks enables the plants to recover from the transplanting before they have to contend with the winds and drier soil and air outdoors.

1 Stand the basket on a large pot or a bucket to keep it stable while planting. Use a wire basket if you want a traditional display with plenty of plants cascading from the sides as well as the top.

2 Water-absorbing crystals can be added to the potting compost to act as a buffer if you are occasionally forgetful about watering your plants. However, they are no substitute for regular, daily watering during dry and hot weather.

3 You can use proprietary liners and make slits for planting, but if making a traditional basket, line it with moss to the level of the first row of plants. Fill the basket with potting compost up to that level, then insert the plants.

4 Add more moss and potting mix and repeat until just below the rim. Use a bold plant for the centre. It may be necessary to remove a little of the potting soil from the root-ball if the plant has been in a large pot.

5 Finally, fill in with plants around the edges. Encourage cascading plants to trail quickly and effectively by planting the root-ball at a slight angle so that the plant tilts slightly towards the edge.

6 Water thoroughly and keep in a warm, sheltered place until the plants are well established. If you do not have hanging facilities in the greenhouse, keep the basket on the support used for planting it up.

SOW TENDER VEGETABLES

Mid spring is a good time to sow frost-tender vegetables in most areas. If they are sown too early they may be ready to plant out too soon, and they will start to suffer if they are kept in small containers for too long. Vegetables sown now should be ready for planting outdoors after a few weeks of growth in warmth followed by a week or so of acclimatization in a cold frame. In reasonably warm climates all the vegetables mentioned here can be sown outside once the risk of frost has passed. It is only worth sowing indoors if you want an early crop.

1 Sow runner beans about six to eight weeks before the last frost is likely. Fill a 15–20cm (6–8in) pot with sowing compost to within 3cm (1in) of the rim. put three seeds in the pot, cover with about 5cm (2in) of compost and water.

2 Keep the pots in a warm place, and give them good light as soon as the seeds germinate. If all the seeds germinate, pull out the surplus to leave just one or two seedlings.

3 Outdoor and greenhouse cucumbers can be sown now. Use small pots and fill with a seed-sowing mixture to within 3cm (1in) of the rim. Position two or three seeds in each pot, placing them on their narrow edge, cover with compost and water.

4 Keep the pots moist and warm until the seeds germinate. If more than one germinates, thin them at an early stage to leave just one seedling in each pot.

5 Marrows and courgettes can also be started off in pots. Treat like cucumbers, but as the seeds are larger use a bigger pot and plant about 3cm (1in) deep.

6 Sweet corn is best raised in pots to plant out later, except in very mild regions. You can use ordinary pots, but many gardeners prefer to use peat pots. The roots will grow through these once they are planted out. Peat pots are easier to manage if stood in a seed tray lined with a piece of capillary matting.

TAKE LEAF CUTTINGS

Some houseplants – such as saintpaulias and streptocarpus – root readily from various types of leaf cuttings. Two methods are shown here.

Although you can root them at almost any time of the year, spring is a good time as the young plants will grow quickly.

1 The kind of cuttings taken from saintpaulias are known as a leaf petiole cutting and include a length of stalk. Select young but fully grown, healthy leaves, and cut them off cleanly near the base.

2 Trim the stalks about 3cm (1in) below the leaf blade and insert so that the leaf blade sits just in contact with the cutting mixture. Insert individual cuttings in small pots, or several together in larger ones.

4 Streptocarpus can be propagated from leaf sections. Choose a healthy, mature leaf that is not very old, and with a sharp knife cut it into slices 5–8cm (2–3in) wide.

3 Keep the cuttings moist but not wet, and the air humid. If you do not have a propagator, enclose the pot in a plastic bag, but make sure that it does not touch the leaves. Turn the bag regularly to reduce a build up of condensation. Pot up the young plantlets that form once they are growing vigorously.

5 Push the sections into the rooting mixture so that about one-third is buried. Make sure that the side originally nearest the leaf stalk forms the base. Keep the cuttings in a warm place in good light but out of direct sunlight.

PLANT UP A HERB POT

A herb pot makes an attractive feature, but it is best treated as a short-term home to be replanted annually. If you allow shrubby perennial herbs to become large and established, you will find them extremely difficult to remove when it becomes necessary. Be especially careful of planting a large shrubby plant in the top of a herb pot with a tapering neck. Once the plant has produced a mass of roots, the inward taper makes removal a frustrating task.

1 A herb pot is best filled in stages. Start by adding a good potting compost to the height of the first planting pockets.

2 Using small plants, knock them out of their pots and push the root-balls through the holes in the planting pockets. If necessary, break off some of the root-ball so that you can get it through the hole.

3 Add more potting soil and repeat with the next row of planting holes. Unless the pot is very large, don't try to pack too many herbs into the top. A single well-grown plant often looks much better.

5 In time the shrubby plant may take up all the planting space at the top and you will have an attractive specimen plant, but meanwhile you should be able to fit a collection of smaller herbs around the edge. Avoid mints, which may be difficult to eliminate later.

4 Large earthernware pots can look just as good as herb pots with planting pockets if you plant them imaginatively. If you have an old half-barrel use this instead. Place a bold shrubby herb, such as a sweet bay (*Laurus nobilis*), in the centre.

GROW MINTS

Mints are notoriously difficult to control once they make themselves at home. They send spreading and penetrating shoots beneath the surface which emerge among other plants or even the other side of a path. They are best contained in some way.

1 A growing bag is an ideal home for mints. They will be happy for a couple of seasons, and then are easily removed and replanted for a fresh start. If the mints are in large pots it may be necessary to remove some of the root-ball, but they soon recover.

2 Instead of filling the growing bag with one kind of mint, try planting a collection of perhaps four to six different kinds. This will look good and add to the flavours available for the kitchen.

3 If you want to plant your mint in the border (which avoids the chore of watering frequently), plant it in an old bucket or large pot. Make sure that there are drainage holes in the bottom, and fill with soil or a potting mixture and plant the mint.

4 For a visually pleasing effect, position the rim of the pot just below the level of the surrounding soil, then cover with soil to hide any signs of the pot. Lift, divide and replant annually or every second spring, to maintain vigour.

OTHER HERBS TO RESTRAIN

Although mint is the herb most notorious for being invasive, others can attempt a take-over of the border. Tansy (*Tanacetum vulgare*) and woodruff (*Asperula odorata* syn. *Galium odoratum*) are among the herbs that you may also want to consider planting in a plunged bucket or large pot.

SOW SWEET CORN

Sweet corn is a reliable crop in warm areas, where it can be sown directly into the ground with confidence, but in cold regions with a short growing season, it is best to start the plants off under glass so that they have time to mature before the autumn frosts. In areas where growing conditions are less than favourable, choose a variety specially bred for a cool climate.

1 Sow only when there is no risk of frost and the soil temperature has reached 10°C (50°F). In cold areas, warm up the soil with fleece or cloches for a week or two first.

2 Sow the seeds 3cm (1in) deep and 8cm (3in) apart, and thin to the final recommended spacing later – typically 30cm (12in) apart each way. Sow in blocks rather than single rows.

3 Cover with a fine net floating cloche or horticultural fleece. This can be left on after germination until the plants have pushed the cover up to its limit without damaging the plants.

4 In areas where outdoor sowing is unreliable, raise the plants in modules or peat pots. Plant them out when there is no danger of frost, and after careful hardening off.

PLANT OUTDOOR TOMATOES

Wait until there is little risk of frost before planting your outdoor tomatoes – about the same time as you plant your tender summer bedding. Choose varieties recommended for outdoors.

1 Plant at the spacing recommended for the variety – some grow tall and large, others remain small and compact. Always make sure they have been well hardened off.

2 In cold areas, cover plants with cloches for a few weeks, or use horticultural fleece.

3 Once the fleece or protection has been removed, stake the plants immediately. Some small varieties may not require staking.

RAISING TOMATOES IN GROWING BAGS

Tomatoes do well in growing bags, and this is a practical way to grow them on a patio as well as in a greenhouse or vegetable patch.

Staking is the main problem if you want to grow tomatoes in growing bags on a hard base. There are many proprietary designs of cane supports intended for crops like tomatoes in growing bags, and most should last for several years.

If the growing bag is positioned on soil you can simply push the cane through the bag, as shown.

PLANT RUNNER AND POLE BEANS

In mild areas runner and climbing French beans can be sown in late spring, but in cold areas wait until early summer or start the seeds off indoors. Do not plant out until there is no risk of frost.

1 Sow two seeds 5cm (2in) deep by each cane or support. Thin to one plant later if both germinate. Wait until the soil temperature is at least 12°C (54°F) before sowing.

2 If you raise the plants in pots, plant out once there is no reasonable risk of frost. Use a trowel and plant them just outside the cane. Train them to the cane as soon as they are tall enough.

SUPPORTING RUNNER AND POLE BEANS

Canes and nets are the main methods of supporting runner and pole beans. If you use a net, choose a large-mesh net sold as a pea and bean net, and stretch it taut between well-secured posts. If you use canes, the most popular methods are wigwams (see right) and crossed canes (see far right).

Proprietary supports are also available but, although usually very effective, they can be expensive.

MAKE UP A HALF-BASKET OR WALL POT

Most people love to have a traditional hanging basket, but they can be disappointing unless cared for lovingly. Even though the basket is planted with an all-round view in mind, the side nearest the wall will perform poorly in comparison with the sunny side unless you turn the basket every day or two to even up growth. A half-basket or wall pot fixed against the wall can be just as effective, and because it is planted to look good from the front only, it can be just as bold and striking as a conventional basket. Some wall pots are also decorative in their own right.

1 If the half-basket is small, you may prefer to take it down to plant it. However, drill and plug the holes, fix the hooks or screws and try it out on the wall first.

2 Add a drainage layer, such as broken pots or gravel, then partly fill with a potting mixture.

3 If using a wire half-basket, line it with moss and fill with potting mixture to the height of the first layer of plants.

4 Plant the sides, then add more moss and potting soil.

5 Plant the top of the basket with bold and spectacular plants for an eye-catching display.

6 Choose more restrained plants for a very ornamental wall pot that you want to retain as a feature in its own right.

PUTTING OUT WALL BASKETS

Half-baskets and wall pots are difficult to accommodate in the greenhouse or other sheltered and frost-free position, so it is best to wait until frost is very unlikely before planting. If you can give them a week or two in a greenhouse or cold frame, however, the plants will receive less of a check to growth and the display should be more pleasing.

RIGHT: *A genuine old manger has been used for this lavish display. Well-planted large wall pots can be just as striking.*

HARDEN OFF BEDDING PLANTS

Hardening off is a crucial stage for all plants raised indoors or in a greenhouse. If this is done properly the plants will remain sturdy and healthy, but if you move tender plants straight out into hot, dry conditions or cold biting winds outdoors after a cosseted life on the windowsill or greenhouse, losses could be high.

Plants that you buy from shops and garden centres should have been hardened off before you buy them.

1 Place the plants in a cold frame a week or two before planting-out time. Close the top in the evening and on cold days, otherwise ventilate freely. If frost threatens, cover the frame with insulation material or take the plants into a greenhouse or indoors again.

2 If you don't have a cold frame, cloches can be used instead. Ventilate them whenever possible so that the plants become acclimatized while still receiving protection from the worst winds and cold.

3 If you don't have frames or cloches, group the trays or pots together in a sheltered spot outside and cover them with horticultural fleece or a perforated plastic floating cloche. Take them in again if frost is forecast.

PLANT GREENHOUSE TOMATOES

Greenhouse tomatoes always used to be grown in the greenhouse border, and the soil changed periodically. This was considered risky and ring culture became fashionable. In more recent times growing bags have been in favour. Other methods are used commercially but the three practical and easy methods suitable for amateurs are described here. All three systems have merits and drawbacks, and how well you look after your tomatoes while they are growing can be as important as the system. Choose the one that appeals most or seems the easiest.

1 Always dig in as much rotted manure or garden compost as you can spare and rake in a general garden fertilizer before you plant your tomatoes. Although they can be planted earlier, most amateurs find this is a good time as the greenhouse usually has more space once the bedding plants have been moved out.

2 Most greenhouse varieties grow tall and need support. Tall canes are a convenient method if you have just a few plants, but if you have a lot of plants the string method may be more suitable (see opposite).

3 With ring culture, the water-absorbing roots grow into a moist aggregate and the feeding roots into special bottomless pots filled with a potting compost. Take out a trench about 15–23cm (6–9in) deep in the greenhouse border and line it with a waterproof plastic (this minimizes soil-borne disease contamination).

4 Fill the trench with fine gravel, coarse grit or expanded clay granules. Then place the special bottomless ring culture pots on the aggregate base and fill them with a good potting compost.

5 Plant into the ring and insert a cane or provide an alternative support. Water only into the ring at first. Once the plant is established and some roots have penetrated into the aggregate, water only the aggregate and feed through the pot.

6 Growing bags are less trouble than ring culture to set up, but you still have to feed plants regularly, and watering can be more difficult to control unless you use an automatic system. Insert a cane through the bag or use a string support.

ABOVE: *You can expect crops like this if you plant your greenhouse tomatoes now. For best results, check that the variety is recommended for greenhouse cultivation.*

SUPPORTING TOMATOES ON STRINGS

String is a simple and economical way to support your tomatoes. Fix one wire as high as practical from one end of the greenhouse to the other, aligning it above the border, and another one just above the ground. The lower wire is most conveniently fixed to a stout stake at each end of the row.

Tie lengths of string between the top and bottom wires, in line with each plant.

You don't need to tie the plant to its support, just loop the string around the growing tip so that it forms a spiral.

PLANT AND TRAIN CUCUMBERS

As with tomatoes, there are various ways to plant and train cucumbers.

Try growing cucumbers in growing bags on the greenhouse staging. Insert canes between the growing bags and the eaves, and fix horizontal wires along the length of the roof as shown here. You can then train the growth along the roof and the cucumbers will hang down. A normal growing bag should hold about two cucumbers. Do not over-crowd the plants.

The method shown is easy and convenient, but if you don't want the trouble of ensuring that the growing bags are kept evenly moist, you could plant the cucumbers directly into the border soil and start the horizontal wires on the sides of the greenhouse instead.

SUMMER

*Early summer is a time of intense gardening activity. Everything is
growing rapidly, in many areas tender plants can be put out, and weeds
seem to grow faster than you ever thought possible.
Mid and late summer are times for enjoying the results of your
earlier efforts. There are always jobs to be done, of course,
but you should also make time to relax.
During a dry summer water shortages can be a problem, but always
water thoroughly, as shallow, impatient watering will encourage
surface rooting and make the plants even more vulnerable.*

OPPOSITE: *Roses are part of the summer scene,
but they have even more impact when used
with imagination.*

ABOVE: *By using containers, summer colour
can be brought to even the most unpromising
corner of the garden.*

PROTECT AND EARTH UP POTATOES

Potatoes are earthed up to protect the tubers near the surface from light. If they are exposed, their skins will turn green and the tubers will be completely inedible.

1 Potatoes will usually recover from slight frost damage, but if you know that a frost is forecast once the shoots are through the ground try covering the plants with newspaper or horticultural fleece. Peg into position, then remove the next morning or when the frost has gone.

2 Start earthing up the potatoes when the shoots are about 15cm (6in) high. Use a draw hoe to pull up the soil either side of the row.

3 Continue to earth up in stages, as the potatoes grow, until the soil creates a mound about 15cm (6in) high.

THIN SEEDLINGS

Thinning is a tedious but essential task. The final spacing between plants will determine both the size of the individual vegetables and the total yield. Exact spacing will often depend on whether you are more interested in the total crop or large, well-shaped individual specimens.

1 Follow the spacing advice given on the seed packet when sowing. It should also recommend the ideal final spacing between plants after thinning.

2 Thin in stages, pulling up surplus plants between finger and thumb. The first thinning should leave the plants twice as close as their final spacing, to allow for losses after thinning.

3 Before the plants begin to compete with each other, thin once more to the final spacing.

SOWING MINI-CAULIFLOWERS

Mini-cauliflowers are summer varieties sown in spring or early summer but grown at much closer spacing than normal. Sow several seeds every 15cm (6in) where they are to grow, and thin these to one seedling if more than one germinates. The heads are much smaller than normal, but total yield can still be good.

MULTIPLE SOWING

TRANSPLANTING SEEDLINGS

Do not attempt to transplant spare thinnings of root crops such as carrots and turnips, but other crops – like lettuces and cabbages, for example – can transplant satisfactorily.

The secret of success is to water the row thoroughly an hour before you thin or transplant (check to make sure that moisture has penetrated to root level), and to lift the spare seedlings with as much soil as possible around the roots. Always water well until plants recover, and shade from direct sun for a few days.

Some gardeners grow certain vegetables – such as carrots, beetroot, onions and leeks, in small clusters. Four to six seeds are usually sown in each cell of modular trays (see top), and planted out without any attempt to separate them. These are not normally thinned. The vegetables are usually smaller and less well shaped than those sown in rows and thinned normally, but the overall weight of crop may be good if the spacing recommended for this type of cultivation is followed (see above).

LEFT: *The total yield can sometimes be higher from close spacing, even though individual specimens are smaller.*

SUMMER TROUGHS AND WINDOWBOXES

Frost-tender bedding plants can now be planted in all but the coldest areas, but be guided by local conditions. Tubs and troughs packed with summer bedding plants are a sure-fire way to bring pockets of cheerful colour to parts of the garden that would not otherwise be so colourful. Make the most of windowboxes, too, which will brighten the exterior of any home.

1 Windowboxes and troughs can be planted in the same way – but for a windowbox include more trailers than you would for a trough. Always make sure that there are drainage holes, and add a drainage layer such as broken pots or gravel.

2 Half fill the box or trough with a good potting mix – a loam-based one can be used for troughs, but if the windowbox is to be fixed on brackets choose a lightweight mixture based on peat or a peat substitute.

3 Most people prefer a mixed planting, with some trailers and both flowering and foliage plants. Try arranging the plants before actually planting to help visualize how they will look.

SINGLE-SUBJECT PLANTING

Most people plant mixed groups, but sometimes a single-subject planting can look especially striking. Impatiens and begonia are popular plants suitable for this treatment, but be prepared to experiment with others.

Because single-subject plants have an even height, it is important to choose a container that is in proportion to the plants. For example, compact begonias look lost in a deep trough, but are in keeping with a shallow windowbox.

4 When the positions look right, insert the plants, firming the compost around each root-ball. Plant more closely than in beds or borders, so avoid using plants that will overpower their neighbours.

5 Water thoroughly after planting, and make sure that the compost never dries out. In warm weather this means watering daily, sometimes more than once.

PLANT UP TUBS AND PATIO POTS

Although all the plants suitable for windowboxes and troughs can be used in tubs and large patio pots, the greater depth of potting soil offers scope for larger and often bolder plants, and the circular shape generally demands an eye-catching plant as a centrepiece. Trailers will enhance a plain container, but if you have a very ornate or decorative pot, it may be best to plant trailers with restraint so that the pot itself remains a feature in its own right.

1 Filled tubs and pots can be very heavy to move, so plant them up where they are to be displayed. Cover the drainage holes with a layer of broken pots, gravel or chipped bark.

2 A loam-based potting mixture is best for most plants, but if the pot is to be used where weight is a consideration, such as on a balcony, use a peat-based mixture.

3 Choose a tall or bold plant for the centre, such as *Cordyline australis* or a fuchsia, or one with large flowers such as the osteospermum which has been used here.

4 Fill in around the base with some bushier but lower-growing plants. Choose bright flowers if the centrepiece is a foliage plant, but place the emphasis on foliage effect if the focal-point is a flowering plant.

5 Cover the surface with a decorative mulch such as chipped bark or cocoa shells if much of the surface is visible (this is worth doing anyway to conserve moisture). Water thoroughly.

ABOVE: *Even a simple poppy can make an impact if the container itself is interesting.*

SOW BIENNIALS AND HARDY PERENNIALS

Biennials such as wallflowers and forget-me-nots are very easy to raise from seed, and because they can be sown outdoors they need very little attention. Border perennials such as lupins and aquilegias are also easily raised from seed sown now, and some of them may even flower next summer. Others may take another year or so to establish before flowering.

1 Prepare the ground thoroughly, and eliminate as many weeds as possible. Competition from weeds is often the greatest enemy the seedlings face. Break the soil down into a fine, crumbly structure once it has been cleared of weeds.

2 Take out drills with the corner of a hoe or rake to the recommended depth (this varies with the seed, so check the packet). The drills can be quite close together, because the seedlings will be transplanted as soon as they are large enough.

3 Run water into the drill before sowing if the soil is very dry. Space the seeds thinly, and as evenly as you can. This makes thinning and later transplanting much easier.

4 Cover the seeds by shuffling the soil back with your feet or carefully ease the soil back with the back of a rake. Remember to add a label.

5 Thin the seedlings as soon as they are large enough to handle easily so that they do not become overcrowded.

ABOVE: *Wallflowers are one of the most popular biennials, and really easy to grow from seeds sown now.*

PRUNE SHRUBS

Many shrubs thrive without routine annual pruning, but some that flower in spring or early summer benefit from pruning soon after they have finished flowering. These include *Cytisus* (brooms), *Syringas* (lilacs), philadelphus, and spring-flowering spiraeas.

1 Philadelphus (illustrated) and spring-flowering spiraeas such as *Spiraea × arguta* and *S. thunbergii* become too dense and overcrowded if they are not pruned. Annual pruning keeps them compact and flowering well, and the best time to do this is immediately after flowering.

2 Reduce the shoots by one-third, cutting out the oldest ones. Cut back the old stems to where a new shoot is growing lower down, or to just above the ground if the shoot is very old and the bush very congested.

RENOVATING AN OLD LILAC

Very old *Syringa vulgaris* varieties often become tall and leggy, with the flowers very high up. You may be able to rejuvenate a neglected plant by sawing it down to a height of 30–90cm (12in–3ft). This sounds drastic, and it will not flower for a year or two, but it should shoot from the old wood and produce an attractive compact plant again.

3 Brooms and genistas tend to become woody at the base with age, with the flowers too high up the plants to look attractive. Prune them as soon as the flowers die and the seed pods are beginning to form.

4 Cut back each shoot to about half way along the new green growth. Do not count dark, old wood, and do not cut back into this as new shoots will be reluctant to grow. You will not be able to make an old neglected plant bush from the base – start regular pruning from an early stage.

5 Lilacs benefit from careful dead-heading. As soon as the flowering is over, cut the dead blooms back to the first pair of leaves below the flower head (no further, otherwise you might remove buds from which new flowering shoots will be produced).

FEEDING AND WATERING IN THE GREENHOUSE

Watering is a year-round chore in the greenhouse, but the summer months are even more demanding. Consider an automatic or semi-automatic watering system to make lighter work of the job. Most pot-plants respond readily to regular feeding during the growing season, but underfeeding is not easy to detect until the plants have been starved for some time.

1 Plants should be watered before they show obvious signs of distress such as wilting. With bushy plants it is not possible to judge by the visual appearance of the potting mixture either, and touch is often the only practical guide. However, this is both time-consuming and only reasonably accurate.

2 Moisture indicators for individual pots can be helpful for a beginner, or if there are just a few plants, but they are not a practical solution if you have a whole greenhouse or conservatory full of plants.

3 Capillary matting is an ideal way to water most pot-plants in summer. You can use a proprietary system fed by mains water, or improvise with a system like the one illustrated. This uses a length of gutter for the water supply. You can keep it topped up by hand, with special water bags or from a cistern.

4 If watering by hand, use the can without a rose unless you are watering seedlings. This will enable you to direct water more easily to the roots rather than sprinkling the leaves. Use a finger over the end of the spout to control the flow, or stick a rag in the end to break the force.

5 An overhead spray system operated automatically or when you turn on the tap is useful for a large greenhouse, either for plants on benches or those planted in the border. Water is not so carefully directed to where it is needed, so it is not ideal for pot-plants, but the spray helps to create a humid atmosphere.

6 Use a liquid fertilizer applied with the water if you can remember to do it regularly. There are both soluble powders and liquids that can be diluted to the appropriate strength.

7 Fertilizer sticks and tablets that you push into the potting soil are a convenient way to administer fertilizer if you don't want to apply liquid feeds regularly. Most of these release their nutrients over a period of several months.

Use a general-purpose fertilizer if you want to avoid using different foods for different plants: this is better than not feeding at all.

Some fertilizers are described as being specially formulated for either foliage plants or flowering plants, however, and these will suit the majority of plants within each category. But if you have to feed both flowering and foliage plants with the one fertilizer, these are unlikely to do any harm.

Some enthusiasts prefer to use special feeds for certain types of plant, such as saintpaulias and cacti, but these will also respond to fertilizers used for other pot-plants.

Fertilizers formulated for strong feeders such as tomatoes and chrysanthemums should only be used on other plants with care – they may be too strong.

BIOLOGICAL CONTROLS

The greenhouse or conservatory is an ideal place to practise biological control methods – the predators will thrive in the protected environment, and should multiply rapidly until control is achieved.

1 Various forms of biological controls are available for a number of greenhouse pests. *Encarsia formosa* is a tiny wasp that parasitizes whitefly larvae and eventually kills them. There are other predatory wasps and mites that will attack red spider, soft scale insects and thrips.

2 If weevil grubs destroy your plants by eating the roots, try controlling them in future with a parasitic eelworm. A suspension of the eelworms is simply watered over the potting soil in each pot.

WORKING WITH BIOLOGICAL CONTROLS

Biological controls usually work best when the weather is warm, and some are unsuitable for use outdoors. Use pesticides with care, as they can wipe out your predators as well as the harmful insects and you will destroy the balance between the two.

With biological controls you will always have some pests – they are essential for the predator to be able to continue to breed – but only at a low population level.

AIR LAYER LEGGY PLANTS

Some hardy plants such as magnolias and rhododendrons can be air layered outside, but the technique is most often used for indoor and greenhouse plants that have become tall and bare at the base. Instead of an unattractive 'leggy' plant you can start off again with a reasonably sized specimen that looks good from top to pot. *Ficus elastica* is commonly treated this way, but other plants, such as dracaenas, are worth trying.

Plants can be air layered at almost any time, but early summer is ideal because they are growing vigorously in the increasing light and warmth.

1 Layer the plant above the bare area, just below the leaves. If you are using the technique on a multi-stemmed plant just to increase stock, remove a few leaves from the point where you want to make the layer.

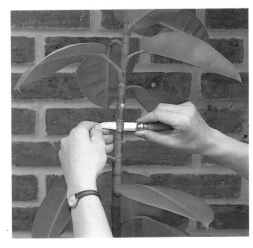

2 Carefully make an upward slit about 3cm (1in) long, below an old leaf joint. Do not cut more than half-way through the stem, otherwise the shoot may break.

3 Make a sleeve out of plastic sheet. It does not have to form a tube as you can wrap it round the stem then make a seal. Fix the bottom of the sleeve a short distance below the cut, using a twist-tie or adhesive tape.

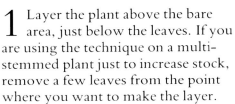

4 Brush a small amount of rooting hormone (powder or gel) into the wound, to speed rooting. Then pack a little sphagnum moss into the wound to keep it open.

5 Pack plenty of damp sphagnum moss around the stem, to enclose the wound, then cover with the sheet of plastic and secure at the top with another twist-tie or tape. Make sure that the moss is kept moist, and carefully check for roots after a month or so. When well rooted, sever from the parent to pot up.

DIVIDE CONGESTED POT-PLANTS

Once a plant has filled its pot and if it is not practical to move it to a larger one, division may revive it and will also give you a number of extra plants. Not all plants respond to division. Those with a fibrous root system, like calatheas and most ferns, are more likely to divide successfully.

A few flowering plants bloom better if kept slightly pot-bound. Check if a particular plant responds well to division in an encyclopedia.

House and greenhouse plants can be divided throughout the year, but late spring and early summer are particularly good times.

1 Water the plant at least half an hour before you divide it. If the plant will not come out of the pot easily, try inverting the pot while you support the plant and tap its rim on a hard surface.

2 Remove any broken pots used to cover the old drainage hole in a clay pot, and pull away a little potting soil to expose some of the roots and make division easier.

3 Most plants can be pulled apart by hand, but if the root-ball is difficult to break open this way use a hand fork.

4 Break the clump into smaller pieces. If you want many plants, divide into quite small pieces, but if you need only one or two, and prefer to start again with larger plants, two or three pieces may be appropriate. It may be necessary to trim off a few of the largest roots to fit the plant in its new pot.

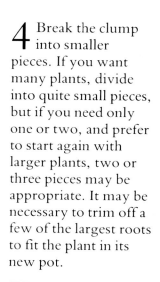

5 Replant sections as soon as possible, trickling potting soil around the roots. If possible, use the same kind of potting material as the plant was in before, and firm it well around the roots. Water and keep out of direct sunlight for a few days.

CONTROL WEEDS

It is never possible to eliminate weeds entirely, but you can control them. Even weeds that are difficult to eradicate can be conquered if you persist, and annual weeds will diminish in numbers if you continue to kill off the seedlings before they can flower and shed more seed.

Once the weed population has been reduced, mulching and prompt action to remove the seedlings that do appear will keep the garden almost weed-free. Be prepared for the battle to be won over a couple of seasons rather than in a few weeks if the garden has been neglected.

1 Deep-rooted perennial weeds that have long, penetrating roots are best forked up. Loosen the roots with a fork, and hold the stem close to its base as you pull up the whole plant. If you don't get all the root out, new pieces may grow.

2 Hoeing is one of the best forms of weed control, but it needs to be done regularly. Slice the weeds off just beneath the soil, preferably when the soil is dry. Keep beds and borders hoed, as well as the vegetable garden.

3 Contact chemical weedkillers are useful if you need to clear an area of ground quickly and easily. Some – which normally only kill the top growth, so are better for annuals than problem perennial weeds – leave the area safe to replant after a day.

4 Some weedkillers kill the whole plant, including the roots. Large areas of ground can be sprayed, but you can paint some formulations onto the leaves to kill the weed without harming neighbouring plants.

5 Mulches are very effective at controlling weeds. In the vegetable and fruit garden various forms of plastic sheeting are a cost-effective method.

6 Where appearance matters, use an organic material such as chipped bark, garden compost or cocoa shells. If the ground is cleared of weeds first, a mulch at least 5cm (2in) thick will suppress most weeds.

SUMMER PRUNE CORDON AND ESPALIER APPLES

Shaped and trained apple trees are normally pruned twice a year – once in summer and again in winter. Summer pruning controls the amount of growth produced each year and maintains the basic shape, winter pruning consists of thinning overcrowded fruiting spurs on old plants. In late spring the new growth at the ends of the main shoots is cut back to its point of origin, but summer pruning is the most crucial in terms of maintaining the trained shape.

ESPALIER

1 Shorten new leafy shoots that have grown directly from the main branches back to three leaves above the basal cluster of leaves. This should only be done once the shoots have dark green leaves and the bark has started to turn brown and is woody at the base. In cold areas it may be early autumn before the shoots are mature enough.

2 If the shoot is growing from a stub left by previous pruning – and not directly from one of the main stems – cut back to just one leaf above the basal cluster of leaves.

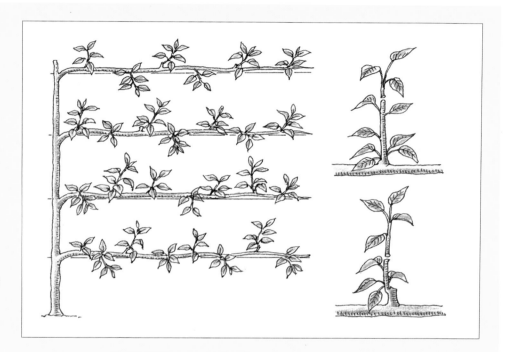

CORDON

1 A cordon is pruned in exactly the same way as an espalier, although, of course, the basic shape of the plant is different. Just cut back shoots growing directly from the main branch to three leaves above the basal cluster of leaves.

2 Cut back shoots growing from stubs left by earlier pruning to one leaf above the basal cluster.

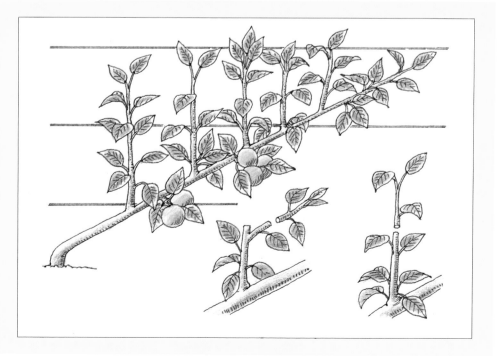

TAKE SEMI-RIPE CUTTINGS

Semi-ripe cuttings – also known as semi-mature cuttings – can be used to propagate a wide range of shrubs, both hardy and tender. If you take them in mid or late summer most will root quickly, and in the case of hardy plants you don't even need a propagator.

1 Choose shoots that are almost fully grown except for the soft tip. The base of the cutting should be hardening, even though the tip may still be soft. Most cuttings are best made 5–10cm (2–4in) long.

2 Strip the lower leaves from each plant to leave a short length of clear stem to insert into the soil.

3 It is well worth using a rooting hormone. Dip the cut end into the powder, liquid or gel, but if using a powder dip the ends into water first so that the powder adheres.

4 Cuttings taken from hardy plants will root outside at this time of year, though they will perform better in a cold frame or propagator.

5 Firm the cuttings to ensure there are no large pockets of air, which might cause the new roots to dry out.

6 Remember to insert a label. This is especially important if you are rooting a number of different kinds of shrubs.

SOME SHRUBS TO PROPAGATE FROM SEMI-RIPE CUTTINGS

Buddleia	*Fuchsia*
Camellia	*Griselinia*
Ceanothus	*Hebe*
Choisya	*Hydrangea*
Cistus	*Philadelphus*
Cotoneaster	*Potentilla*
(illustrated)	*Pyracantha*
Escallonia	*Rosemary*
Forsythia	*Weigela*

7 Water thoroughly. It is worth adding a fungicide to the water initially, to reduce the chance of the cuttings rotting. Make sure that the soil does not dry out at any time.

LAYER SHRUBS

Layering is usually used for shrubby plants that have low branches easily pegged to the ground, but a few border plants can also be layered – carnations and pinks are often raised this way. In comparison with cuttings, layers usually produce fewer but bigger plants.

1 Find a low-growing shoot that can easily be pegged down to the ground. Trim off the leaves just from the area that will be in contact with the soil.

2 Bend the stem down until it touches the ground. Make a hole 10cm (4in) deep, sloping toward the parent plant but with the other side vertical.

3 Twist or slit the stem slightly to injure it. Peg it into the hole with a piece of bent wire or a peg, using the vertical back of the excavation to force the shoot upright.

4 Return the soil and firm it well. If you keep the ground moist, roots should form and within 12–18 months you may be able to sever the new plant from its parent.

DIVIDE FLAG IRISES

Divide flag irises – hybrids derived from *Iris germanica* – after flowering and if the rhizomes have become very congested.

1 Lift the clump with a fork, and cut away and discard the oldest parts. Use only the current season's growth for replanting.

2 Trim the leaves to stumps about 5–8cm (2–3in) long. Replant the pieces of rhizome on a slight ridge of soil, covering the roots but leaving the tops exposed.

LAYERING CARNATIONS

Border carnations and pinks are layered in a similar way to shrubs, but root much more quickly. Select a few well-spaced, non-flowering shoots and remove all but the top four or five leaves on them. Make a small slit in each one with a sharp knife below the lowest pair of leaves, and peg the shoot – slit down – into good soil. Keep moist.

SUMMER CARE FOR GREENHOUSE TOMATOES

The varieties of tomato usually grown in the greenhouse need regular attention, like the removal of sideshoots, feeding, and tying in.

Keep a watch too for early signs of pests and diseases that could otherwise reduce the quantity or quality of the crop.

1 If the plants are supported by strings, simply loop the string around the top of the shoot whenever necessary. It will form a spiral support that holds the stem upright.

2 To secure the plant to a cane, wrap the string twice around the stake and then loop it loosely around the stem before tying the knot.

3 Snap off sideshoots while they are still small. They will snap off cleanly if you pull them sideways. Do not remove sideshoots if you have a low-growing bush variety.

4 If fruits are failing to form, poor pollination may be the problem. Shake the plants each day, or spray the flowers with water, to spread the pollen.

5 The lowest leaves often turn yellow as they age. Remove these, as they will not contribute to feeding the plant, and letting more light reach the fruits can help to ripen them.

6 'Stop' your plants, by removing the growing tip, when they have formed as many trusses of fruit as are likely to ripen. In an unheated greenhouse this may be as few as four in cold areas; six or seven in warmer regions.

7 Tomatoes respond well to feeding. Some tomato feeds are high in nitrogen for early growth, but now that the fruit is developing, a high-potash tomato fertilizer is best.

OTHER GREENHOUSE CROPS

Greenhouse crops like aubergines, cucumbers and melons also need attention at this time of year if you want to ensure a good, healthy crop.

1 Aubergines make bushier plants if the growing tip is pinched out when the plant is about 30cm (12in) high. Allow only one fruit to develop on each shoot. Pinch out the growing tips of these shoots three leaves beyond the developing fruit. Never let the plants dry out, and feed regularly. Regular misting to provide high humidity is beneficial.

2 Many modern cucumbers produce only female flowers, but there are some varieties you might grow in a greenhouse that produce both male and female blooms (the female flowers have a small embryo fruit behind the petals). Pinch out male flowers before they have a chance to pollinate the female ones, as this can make the cucumbers less palatable.

CARING FOR MELONS

Train the sideshoot of melons to horizontal wires, and pinch back the sideshoots to two leaves beyond each fruit that develops. Melons may require pollinating, in which case transfer the pollen from the male to female flowers with a small paintbrush. It may also be necessary to support developing fruits with nets, as shown.

DAMPING DOWN

Splashing or spraying water over the greenhouse path (traditionally known as damping down) helps to create a humid atmosphere. This is especially beneficial for crops such as aubergines and cucumbers, but most plants appreciate a moist atmosphere on a hot day – including the majority of pot-plants. Do it frequently on very hot days, to create the kind of hot and humid atmosphere that most tropical plants prefer.

SUMMER CARE FOR OUTDOOR TOMATOES

Outdoor tomatoes demand less attention than greenhouse varieties, especially if you grow the kinds where you leave on the sideshoots. Feeding and watering is a necessary routine if you want a good crop of quality fruits. Regular watering not only ensures a heavy crop but also reduces the risk of fruit splitting through uneven watering. This sometimes happens if dry weather produces hard skins which then can't cope with a sudden spurt of growth following a wet period. Add a liquid fertilizer to the water, at the rate and frequency recommended by the manufacturer. How well your tomatoes crop outdoors depends on a combination of variety, care and climate. In cold areas, outdoor tomatoes can be a disappointing crop, in warm areas you will almost certainly have more fruit than you can cope with.

1 If growing a cordon variety (one that you grow as a single main stem, supported by a cane), keep removing sideshoots as they develop.

2 Regular tying to the support is even more important outdoors than in the greenhouse, as strong winds can break an untied stem and shorten the productive life of the plant.

3 As soon as the plant has set the number of trusses (sprays) of fruit likely to be ripened in your area, pinch out the top of the plant. In many areas you can only reasonably expect to ripen four trusses, but in warm areas it may be more.

4 Many bush varieties have small but prolific fruits. As it is not practical to support all the sideshoots with canes, some branches bend and come into contact with the soil. Place straw beneath these to keep the fruits off the soil. It will keep them cleaner and reduce the risk of them rotting.

LIFT SHALLOTS

Shallots usually stop growing before onions and, if planted early, can be lifted in mid summer.

But if you planted late it may be late summer before they are ready to ripen and harvest.

1 Loosen the clumps with a fork, but leave them exposed on the surface for a few days. This will give the base of the bulb a chance to dry off before being stored.

2 If the weather is damp, leave the bulbs on trays in a light, warm place so that they are not damp when stored. Or leave them on mesh trays outdoors until dry (see onions, step 3).

RIPEN AND HARVEST ONIONS

Harvest onions when the foliage is straw coloured and brittle dry. They will store better if,

when lifted, they are exposed to the sun to ripen and dry first.

1 Ripening can be hastened once the plants are nearing their maximum size by bending over their tops. Bend them so that the bulbs are exposed to as much sun as possible.

2 As soon as the foliage has turned a straw colour and is brittle, lift them with a fork and leave them on the surface for a few days to dry off. Lay with their roots facing the sun.

3 Finish off the hardening and ripening process by laying the bulbs on netting or wire mesh supported above the ground so that air can circulate freely.

4 If the weather is very damp, cover the bulbs with cloches until you can store them.

TAKE FUCHSIA CUTTINGS

Fuchsias are really easy to root, and by taking cuttings now you will have young plants that can be overwintered in a light position in a cool but frost-free room or in a greenhouse. These will make good plants for next summer, or you can use them to provide more cuttings next spring.

1 Softwood cuttings can be taken for as long as new growth is being produced, but at this time of year semi-ripe (semi-mature) cuttings root easily and are simple to take. Pull off sideshoots about 10cm (4in) long, with a 'heel' of old main stem attached.

2 Trim off the lowest leaves and trim the end of the heel to make a clean cut. If you have taken cuttings without a heel, trim the stem straight across beneath a leaf-joint.

3 Although cuttings will usually root without aid, a hormone rooting powder should speed the process. Insert several cuttings around the edge of an 8–10cm (3–4in) pot filled with a rooting mixture.

4 Label the cuttings, water and place them in a cold frame, greenhouse or on a light windowsill. Keep the compost damp, and pot up individually when well rooted. Protect from frost.

TAKE PELARGONIUM CUTTINGS

Pelargoniums (popularly known as bedding geraniums) can be overwintered in a frost-free place to provide cuttings next spring. Many experts prefer to take cuttings now, however, and to overwinter the young plants in a light, frost-free place.

RIGHT: *Pelargoniums, or bedding geraniums, are one of the most popular of summer plants.*

1 Take cuttings from non-flowering shoots (if you have to use flowering shoots, cut off the blooms). A good guide to length is to cut the shoot off just above the third joint below the growing tip.

2 Remove the lowest pair of leaves with a sharp knife, and remove any flowers or buds. Trim straight across the base of each cutting, just below the lowest leaf joint. You can dip the ends in a rooting hormone, but they usually root readily without.

3 Insert about five cuttings around the edge of a 13cm (5in) pot containing a cuttings mixture and firm gently. Keep in a light, warm position but out of direct sun. Be careful not to overwater, otherwise the cuttings will rot. Pot up individually when rooted.

DAHLIA AND CHRYSANTHEMUM CARE

Dahlias and chrysanthemums come into their true glory at the end of summer and into autumn, just as most flowers have passed their best. Some types are simply left to produce masses of blooms with no intervention, but those grown for large flowers are usually selectively disbudded. This produces fewer but larger blooms. Both types of plant need plenty of feeding and a careful watch has to be kept to prevent pests and diseases marring these plants.

1 To produce larger flowers, pinch out the side buds behind the crown (central) flower bud of dahlias, while they are still small. Many chrysanthemums are also disbudded, but how and when you do it depends on the variety, so be guided by a specialist catalogue or publication.

2 The best way to control pests and diseases is to spray at the first signs. Often it may be possible to prevent spread simply by pinching off and destroying the first few affected leaves. This chrysanthemum shows evidence of leaf miner damage.

3 Chrysanthemums and dahlias benefit from regular feeding. Even if you used a slow-release fertilizer to see them through most of the summer, they will probably respond to a boost now. Use a quick-acting general fertilizer or a high-potash feed, but don't boost with too much nitrogen.

PLANT BULBS FOR SPRING

Spring-flowering bulbs are now widely available, but exactly when you plant them will depend largely on whether the ground has been cleared of summer plants. If planting in beds, it is best to let summer bedding flower for as long as possible, and you may prefer not to disturb the last of the summer colour in herbaceous borders just yet, but in vacant ground it is best to plant as soon as possible. Bulbs are always better in the ground rather than in bags and boxes that are probably stored in less than ideal conditions. Bulbs look good in front of shrubs, and you should be able to plant these as soon as they are obtainable. Indoor bulbs that are specially prepared for early flowering should also be planted as soon as they become available.

1 Fork over the ground before planting, and if the plants are to be left undisturbed for some years, try to incorporate plenty of organic material such as rotted garden compost or manure. Many bulbs like well-drained soil but still benefit from plenty of organic material that will hold moisture and nutrients.

2 Avoid adding quick-acting fertilizers in the autumn. Controlled-release fertilizers that provide nutrients according to the soil temperature can be used, but they are best employed in spring. Instead rake a very slow-acting fertilizer such as bonemeal, which contains mainly phosphate, into the surface, or apply it to the planting holes.

3 Where there is space and the plants will benefit from planting in an informal group or cluster, dig out a hole about three times the depth of the bulbs and wide enough to take the clumps.

4 Space the bulbs so that they look like a natural clump. Use the spacing recommended on the packet as a guide. Wide spacing will allow for future growth and multiplication, but if you intend to lift the bulbs after flowering much closer spacing will create a bolder display.

5 Draw the soil back over the bulbs, being careful not to dislodge them in the process.

6 Firm the soil with the back of the rake rather than treading it, which may damage the bulbs.

7 If you are likely to cultivate the area before the shoots come through, mark out where bulbs have been planted with a few small canes. Always insert a label, as it will be months before the bulbs appear and flower, by which time it is often difficult to remember the variety planted.

RECOGNIZING WHICH WAY UP TO PLANT BULBS

Most bulbs have a very obvious top and bottom and present no problem. Others, especially tubers, can cause confusion because they lack an obvious growing point. If in doubt, just plant them on their side – the shoot will grow upwards and the roots down.

A few bulbs that do have an obvious top are planted on their side because the base tends to rot in wet soil, though these are rare exceptions. *Fritillaria imperialis* is sometimes planted this way, and it is always worth planting vulnerable bulbs on a bed of grit or coarse sand to encourage good drainage around the base, as shown.

PLANTING IN INDIVIDUAL HOLES

If you have a lot of bulbs to plant over a wide area, individual planting holes may be more appropriate than creating larger excavations to take a group of bulbs.

There are special long-handled planting tools, but an ordinary long-handled trowel is just as good. You can use a normal trowel with a handle of conventional length, but it makes planting more tedious if the area is large.

Check periodically to make sure that the holes are being made to the correct depth. After checking a few it will be easy to judge by eye.

Make a hole large enough to take the bulb easily (it must not become wedged in the hole, as the roots will then be exposed to dry air).

Return the excavated soil. If planting a large area, you can shuffle it back in with your feet, then rake the surface level.

ABOVE: *Tulips, wallflowers and forget-me-nots, all ideal for spring bedding.*

SOW SPRING-FLOWERING POT-PLANTS

Provided you can keep your greenhouse frost-free during the winter – ideally at a minimum of 7°C (45°F) – it is worth sowing a few flowering plants to bloom next spring. Some suggestions are given in the box below, and those that are hardy, such as calendulas and limnanthes, can even be grown in an unheated greenhouse provided you do not live in a very cold area.

1 As you are only likely to need relatively few plants, sow in pots rather than seed trays. If you don't have a rounded presser to firm the sowing mixture lightly, use the bottom of a jar.

2 Sprinkle the seeds as thinly and evenly as possible over the surface. Large seeds, such as cyclamens, can be spaced individually. Cover with a sprinkling of the sowing mixture if needed (follow the advice on the packet).

3 Stand the pot in a container of water. Letting the moisture seep up from below like this avoids the risk of seeds being washed away or into clumps were you to water the pot from above.

4 Because the outside air temperature is still warm, most seeds will germinate readily without the need for a propagator, but cover with a sheet of glass, or place in a plastic bag, to reduce water loss through evaporation. Seeds that germinate slowly and erratically, such as cyclamen, benefit from being placed in a heated propagator.

SEEDS TO SOW NOW

Browallia
Calendula (choose a very dwarf variety)★
Cineraria
Cyclamen (for home and greenhouse)★★
Exacum affine
Limnanthes douglasii★
Linaria maroccana★
Primula acaulis (cultivated primroses)★
Primula malacoides
Schizanthus

★ These are tough plants that will tolerate some frost and are suitable for an unheated greenhouse in mild areas
★★ Cyclamen should flower in mid winter the following year (ie after about 16 months)

ABOVE: *The pot marigold (Calendula officinalis), easy and always cheerful.*

PLANT HYACINTHS FOR EARLY FLOWERING

For early flowering indoors or in the greenhouse, you must choose bulbs that have been 'prepared' or 'treated'. The term may vary, but it simply means that before you receive the bulb it has been stored under specially controlled conditions that make it think more of its resting period has elapsed. It looks no different, but it believes winter is more advanced than in reality and that it needs to grow and bloom quickly.

Ordinary, untreated, hyacinths can be planted now in just the same way, but they will flower later in the season. It is a good idea to pot up some bulbs of both kinds, separately, to spread the flowering period.

1 If using a bowl without drainage, use a special bulb mixture based on peat. If you use a container with drainage holes, any ordinary potting mixture can be used.

2 Place a thin layer of the potting mixture in the container, then space the bulbs close together but make sure they are not touching. An odd number will look better than an even number (three or five bulbs are usually planted in a bowl).

3 Pack more potting mixture around the bulbs, but leave their 'noses' exposed. Water, but be careful not to overwater.

4 Keep the planted bulbs in a cold, dark place indoors, perhaps in the garage, or in a special 'plunge bed' outdoors. Simply stand the bowls in a cool, shady position and cover them with several centimetres or inches of grit, peat or coarse sand. If the containers lack drainage holes, protect from rain to prevent water-logging. Check the containers for progress periodically.

AUTUMN

Be watchful and vigilant as the nights become colder. In some areas quite severe frosts are common in early autumn, and in others light frosts may not occur until mid or late autumn, if at all. Listen to the weather forecasts and take in or protect vulnerable plants if frost is expected. Think seriously about winter protection for plants on the borderline of hardiness, and be prepared to give early winter shelter, perhaps in the form of a windbreak, for newly planted evergreens. A little protection can ensure that many plants survive instead of succumbing to winter winds and cold.

OPPOSITE: *The colourful leaves of* Rhus typhina *'Laciniata', with the white plumes of a cortaderia in the background.*

ABOVE: Liriope muscari, *one of the delights of autumn, is fortunately tough and very easy to grow.*

PUT CLOCHES IN PLACE

If you have cloches that you normally use to protect your crops in spring, make the most of them by extending the end of the season as well as the beginning.

Save large barn cloches for large crops such as tomatoes (see opposite), if wished, and use tent and plastic tunnel cloches for low-growing crops such as lettuces.

1 Winter radishes and mooli radishes are frost-hardy, but you can encourage further growth before bad weather sets in by covering them with cloches. If you failed to sow them earlier, you may be able to start them off under cloches now in a mild area, provided you do so while the soil is still warm.

2 Try sowing lamb's lettuce and winter purslane as a cold month crop. They don't need cloche protection except in cold areas, but the cover will ensure a better supply of more succulent leaves.

ABOVE: *Put cloches in place now to warm up the soil for early crops such as lettuces.*

RIGHT: *Beetroot can also be sown earlier if you first warm the soil with cloches.*

3 Put the cloches in position before the cold weather checks growth. With a little protection like this the plants will crop more freely.

PROTECT OUTDOOR TOMATOES

Green tomatoes can be ripened indoors provided they have reached a reasonable stage of maturity, but it makes sense to ripen as many as possible on the plant. As soon as a severe frost is forecast, however, harvest the remaining fruit and ripen as many as possible indoors.

1 Frost will kill tomatoes, but you can often extend their season by a few weeks and ripen a few more fruits on the plant with protection. Bush plants that are already low-growing are best covered with a large cloche. Packing straw beneath the plants first will also provide a little insulation.

2 Cordon-trained tomatoes must be lowered before they can be protected with cloches. Untie the plant and remove the stake.

3 Lay a bed of straw on the ground, then carefully lower the plants onto this. If you lay all the stems in the same direction, you will have a neat row of tomatoes that are easily covered with cloches.

4 Fleece can be used to offer wind protection and enough shelter to keep off a degree or two of frost, though it does not warm the air during the day in the same way as glass or some rigid plastics. Drape several layers over low-growing varieties, and peg it down securely along each side, and at the ends.

5 Fleece can also be used to protect cordon tomatoes while still staked. Sheets of fleece can be wrapped round, or you may be able to buy fleece produced as a tube. Simply cut off the required length, slip it over the plant, and secure at the top and bottom.

PLANT UP A SPRING WINDOWBOX WITH BULBS

Spring bulb displays are less predictable than summer flowers, and it can be especially disappointing when different bulbs planted in the same windowbox flower at different times. The consolation is that this does at least extend the interest. A good alternative is to plant single-subject displays which, although often brief, are frequently bolder.

1 Make sure that there are drainage holes, and add a layer of material to aid quick drainage, such as broken pots or pieces of chipped bark (sold for mulching).

2 Add enough potting soil to cover the bottom couple of centimetres (about an inch). As the bulbs do not need a lot of nutrients during the winter, you can often use some of the potting mixture previously used for summer bedding.

3 You can pack in more bulbs by planting in layers. Place large bulbs such as daffodils or tulips at the lower level.

4 Add more potting soil, then position the smaller bulbs, such as crocuses and scillas. Try to position them so that they lie between the larger bulbs. Be careful about the bulbs that you mix – small crocuses will be swamped by tall daffodils, so choose miniature or dwarf daffodils, to keep a suitable balance.

5 Top up with more potting soil, but leave 2–3cm (¾–1in) of space at the top for watering and perhaps a decorative mulch. As the windowbox will look bare for some months, a few winter pansies will add a touch of interest. Don't worry about the bulbs beneath – they will find their way through the pansies.

BULBS AND SPRING BEDDING

Some of the best container displays for spring combine bulbs with spring-flowering bedding plants such as forget-me-nots (*Myosotis*), double daisies (*Bellis*) and cultivated primroses. This is often more effective than filling the container with bulbs alone. It means that the container looks less bleak after planting, and the period of flowering is greatly extended.

Put the plants in first, then the bulbs between them. If you plant the bulbs first, it will be difficult to remember the positioning and they are likely to be disturbed when you insert the plants.

LEFT: *Even common plants like tulips and pansies can look stunning in the right combination and setting.*

PLANT UP A TUB OR PATIO POT WITH BULBS

Tubs, large pots, and urns can be planted in the same way as windowboxes – with bulbs in multiple layers or combined with spring-flowering plants – but bulbs also make good companions for shrubs and small trees in tubs.

They make the most of space around the edge of the container that is usually wasted, and if the shrubby plant sheds its leaves in winter, the bulbs will complete the important parts of their annual cycle before there is competition for light.

1 If planting an empty container, try placing a small conifer in the centre to provide winter interest. A few ivies positioned so that they trail over the edge will usually improve the appearance in winter.

2 Position the bulbs on the surface first so that they are evenly spaced around the edge. Small plants that multiply freely, such as *Muscari armeniacum*, scillas, chionodoxas, and *Anemone blanda*, are among the plants that can usually be depended upon to improve year by year.

3 Plant with a trowel, being careful to disturb the roots of an established plant as little as possible.

PLANT BEDS AND BORDERS FOR A SPRING DISPLAY

Beds normally used for summer bedding can be replanted with spring bedding – a combination of plants and bulbs will create a better display than bulbs alone. Plants like forget-me-nots and double daisies help to clothe the ground between the bulbs during the winter, and in spring fill in around the base of tall bulbs such as tulips that can otherwise look rather stalky.

It is a good idea to see what your local parks department does for plant combinations. It is better to modify an existing combination that you like, even if you don't want to copy it exactly, rather than experiment if you don't know much about the plants. A failure will mean that you will have to wait another year for the next attempt.

1 Fork over the ground after clearing it of summer bedding plants. Fertilizer is not normally needed, but bonemeal, which is very slow-acting, is worth adding if the soil is impoverished. Apply bonemeal after forking over and rake it in.

2 If you have raised the plants yourself, and have them growing in a nursery bed, water well about an hour before lifting them. Lift with as much soil round the roots as possible.

3 Spring bedding plants bought from garden centres are usually sold in trays or strips. These are usually disposable, so don't be afraid to break them if this allows you to release the root-ball with as little damage as possible.

ABOVE: *Tulips usually look better if underplanted with wallflowers or forget-me-nots.*

4 Space the plants out on the surface, allowing for the bulbs, before planting. Space the bulbs out, then begin planting from the back or one end.

PLANT LILIES FOR SUMMER

Lilies are often planted in spring, but you can also plant them now except in very cold areas. The bulbs are less likely to dry out, which can result in failures. Most lilies prefer a slightly acid soil (pH6–6.5), but some – including *Lilium candidum* – will do well in alkaline soils.

1 Lilies demand a well-prepared site, so dig the soil deeply and work in as much well-rotted manure or garden compost as you can spare. Add plenty of grit to improve drainage if the soil tends to be wet.

2 Lilies look best in groups rather than as isolated specimens, so excavate an area of soil to a depth of about 20cm (8in), large enough to take at least four or five bulbs. Add coarse grit or sand unless the soil is very well drained.

3 Add a sprinkling of bonemeal or a controlled-release fertilizer, as lilies are usually left undisturbed until overcrowded and therefore feeding is more important than with bedding bulbs used for a single season.

4 Space the bulbs about 15cm (6in) apart and make sure that they are deep enough to be covered with about twice their own depth of soil. Sprinkle more grit or coarse sand around the bulbs to deter slugs and reduce the risk of waterlogging.

5 Place small canes or sticks around the planting area before you return the soil. These remind you to avoid damaging the emerging shoots when you hoe. Remember to label.

ABOVE: *Lilies are real eye-catchers, as this drift of the compact 'Little Girl' proves.*

CLEAR SUMMER BEDDING

If frosts have not put an abrupt end to your summer bedding display, the plants will undoubtedly be looking sad and dejected by now.

Even if you do not plan to replant with spring bedding, the garden will look tidier if the old plants are cleared away and the ground dug over.

1 Plants like this will do more good on the compost heap than left on show. Bare soil can look neat and tidy provided you eliminate weeds.

2 Bedding plants generally have shallow roots and are easy to pull up by hand. If some are deep-rooted, just loosen the roots with a fork.

3 Old bedding plants are ideal for the compost heap. Being non-woody they rot down easily.

4 Dig over the ground, and remove any large weeds. Use a spade if the ground is very weedy so that most of them can be buried as the soil is turned, otherwise use a fork.

5 Whether or not you are replanting with spring bedding, rake the ground level so that it looks neat and tidy.

PRESERVE AND STORE GARDEN CANES

Bamboo canes deteriorate after a season or two in use, especially where they have been in the ground. Extend their life by cleaning and preserving them. Store in a dry place, rather than leaving them exposed in the garden.

1 Knock most of the soil off, then scrub the canes with a stiff brush and garden or household disinfectant. Pay special attention to the ends, and make sure any soil is removed.

2 Wipe the scrubbed canes with a cloth to dry them, then stand the ends that have been in the soil in a bucket or container partly filled with a wood preservative. Leave overnight to allow the preservative to penetrate.

3 Bundle the canes to keep them tidy, and store in a dry place until needed next year.

LIFT AND STORE GLADIOLI

Gladioli can only be left in the ground in mild areas where frosts are always light and do not penetrate far into the soil. In cold areas gladioli will be killed if they remain in the soil, so lift them before there are penetrating frosts.

Gladioli flower reliably from year to year, so they are almost always worth saving. The cormels (small corms) that form around the base will reach flowering size within a couple of years if looked after.

1 Loosen the soil with a garden fork before attempting to lift the plants.

2 Trim off most of the foliage, leaving just a stub to dry off. Shake off most of the soil.

3 Leave the lifted plants in a dry place for a few days to dry off. When the remains of the old stems have shrivelled, trim them off, and remove the cormels that have grown around the base. Store these if you want to save them, otherwise discard. Pull off the remains of the old corm to leave just the healthy new corm. Lay the corms in trays and keep in a frost-proof place for a day or two for further drying.

4 Dust with fungicide and store in paper bags away from frost.

REPOT CACTI AND SUCCULENTS

Cacti and succulents can be repotted at any time of the year, though spring or the end of the growing season are convenient times. Many succulents present no special handling problems, but prickly cacti have to be treated with respect.

If possible, choose a soil mix formulated for cacti, as this will be well drained and have the right sort of structure and nutrient level. A soil-based potting mixture is a practical alternative. Some commercial growers use peat-based potting mixtures, but these are best avoided. Apart from the difficulty in keeping the water balance right, peat-based potting mixtures do not have the weight and structure to support large cacti and succulents.

Large specimens do not need regular repotting. Simply remove about 3cm (1in) of soil from the top and replace with fresh cactus soil.

1 To handle a prickly cactus, fold a strip of newspaper, thick paper or thin card to make a flexible band that you can wrap around the plant.

2 Tap the pot on a hard surface to loosen the root-ball. You can then often lift the plant out with the improvised handle. If it refuses to move, try pushing a pencil through the drainage hole to break the bond.

3 If the plant has been in the same soil for a long time, crumble away a little of it from the base and around the sides of the root-ball. But be careful to minimize damage to the roots. Just shake off loose compost.

4 The majority of cacti and succulents are best in pots that are quite small in proportion to the size of the top growth. It is usually best to move the plant into a pot only one size larger. If using a clay pot, cover the drainage hole with pieces of broken pot or other material.

5 While holding the plant with the improvised handle, trickle compost around the old root-ball. With some cacti, their shape makes this difficult to do without your hand touching the spines, in which case you can use a spoon.

6 Tap the bottom of the pot on a hard surface to settle the soil around the roots. This is especially important as it is often difficult to firm the soil with your fingers if the cactus is prickly. Wait for a couple of days before watering.

BRING IN POT-PLANTS FROM THE GARDEN

Many winter and spring-flowering houseplants, such as schulmbergeras, zygocactus, and solanums grown for their winter berries, even orchids, can spend the summer outdoors as they look uninteresting at this stage. Make sure these are brought in before the first frost threatens.

1 Clear away the mulching material if the pots have been plunged into the ground and mulched to reduce the need for regular watering.

2 If the pots do not come up easily, insert a garden fork a little distance away and lever them gently to avoid damaging the pots.

GREENHOUSE SHADING

3 Remove leaves and debris from the surface of the potting soil, which will almost certainly have become contaminated. Wipe the pot clean with a damp cloth, and be especially careful to clean the bottom of the pot so that it does not make a mess indoors.

4 Always check for pests and diseases before taking the plant indoors or into the greenhouse. Look on the backs of the leaves too, which is where snails will often be found. Even a small snail can do a lot of damage if left undetected. If the plant has thick or glossy leaves, wipe them over with a proprietary leaf shine to improve their appearance. Plants left outdoors almost always become splashed with mud and dirt.

Plants now need all the light they can get, so remove greenhouse shading as soon as possible. If you applied a shading wash earlier in the year, clean it off now. Most can be rubbed off with a duster when the glass is dry. Internal or external shading material such as blinds or nets can also be removed now, as shown here. You may be able to use the same internal fixings to secure winter insulation.

LIFT AND STORE POTATOES

Early and mid-season varieties are best eaten soon after harvesting, but the late varieties are grown mainly for storing for winter use. If you grow a small quantity they are best stored in paper sacks kept indoors, but if you grow a lot and indoor storage space is limited, try using the traditional clamping method. It looks primitive but works except where winters are very severe.

1 Lift the tubers with a fork once the foliage has died down. You can leave them in the ground for longer if penetrating frosts are not likely to be a problem, but lift promptly if pests like slugs appear.

2 Leave the potatoes on the surface for a couple of hours so that the skins dry off and harden.

3 Sort the potatoes before storing. It is sufficient to grade them into four sizes: very small, small, medium and large. Discard or use up very small ones immediately, keep small ones for use soon, and only store the medium and largest.

RIGHT: *Potatoes are best left to dry off for a couple of hours before sorting and storing.*

4 Place the largest potatoes in sacks to store in a cool but frost-proof place. Paper sacks are best, but if you can't obtain them, use plastic sacks in which case make slits with a knife to provide some ventilation.

5 If you have too many potatoes to store in sacks, or don't have space indoors, make a clamp in the garden. Excavate a shallow depression and line it with a thick layer of straw.

6 Pile the potatoes on to the bed of straw, as shown.

7 Heap a thick layer of straw over the top. It must be thick enough to provide good insulation.

8 Mound earth over the straw, but leave a few tufts of straw sticking out of the top for ventilation.

PROLONGING HERBS

Parsley is one of the herbs that will continue to provide leaves for harvesting throughout the winter if you protect the plants with cloches. Make sure that the end pieces are tightly secured.

STRAW PROTECTION

Vegetables such as celery (shown here) and beetroot benefit in cold areas if you protect the stems with straw. Pack the straw among and between the plants in the blocks or rows. It does not matter if the tops of the leaves are exposed – you are only protecting the edible part.

Mature celery will usually survive some frost, but the protection is useful if it turns very cold before you are ready to lift it. In mild areas you can leave beetroot unprotected, but the straw does help to keep plants in better condition for longer in cold areas.

NATURALIZE BULBS IN GRASS

Naturalizing bulbs is a good way to enjoy a trouble-free display each spring, and one that should improve each year. You will need an area of grass that you don't mind leaving unmown until early summer, to allow bulb foliage to die back naturally.

1 If you have a lot of small bulbs, such as crocuses and eranthis, to plant in a limited area, try lifting an area of turf. Use a spade or half-moon edger to make an H-shaped cut.

2 Slice beneath the grass with a spade until you can fold the turf back for planting.

3 Loosen the ground first, as it will be very compacted. If you want to apply a slow-acting fertilizer such as bonemeal, work it into the soil at the same time.

4 Avoid planting in rows or regimented patterns. You want them to look natural and informal, so scatter them and plant where they fall.

5 If you plant large bulbs this way, you will have to make deeper holes with a trowel. Plant them so that they are covered with about twice their own depth of soil.

6 Firm the soil then return the grass. Firm again if necessary to make sure it is flat, and water if the weather is dry to ensure that the grass grows again quickly.

7 Large bulbs such as daffodils are easier to plant using a bulb planter that takes out a core of soil. Scatter the bulbs randomly so that the display will look natural.

8 Push the bulb planter into the soil, twisting it a little if the ground is hard, then pull it out with the core of soil. Release the core of soil and place the bulb at the bottom of the hole.

9 First pull off a little soil from the base of the core (to allow for the depth of the bulb), then replace the core in the hole. Firm gently.

RIGHT: *Try naturalizing bulbs, like these anemones, at the edge of the lawn, where you can leave the grass long until the plants die down.*

LIFT AND STORE DAHLIAS

Do not discard your dahlias – lift the tubers before frosts penetrate the ground, and store them for next year. Even seed-raised plants will have formed tubers that you can store.

1 Lift the dahlia tubers once the first frosts have blackened the foliage. Use a fork to lift the tubers, to minimize the risk of damaging them. Cut off the old stem to leave a stump about 5cm (2in) long.

2 Stand the tubers upside down so that moisture drains easily from the hollow stems. Using a mesh support is a convenient way to allow them to dry off. Keep in a dry, frost-free place.

3 After a few days the tubers should be dry enough to store. Remove surplus soil, trim off loose bits of old roots and shorten the stem to leave a short stump. Label each plant.

4 Pack the tubers in a well-insulated box with peat, vermiculite, wood shavings, or crumpled newspaper placed between them. Keep in a frost-free location.

WINTER QUARTERS

A spare bedroom or cool but frost-free garage are sensible places to store overwintering bulbs, corms and tubers such as dahlias. Avoid a very warm place, as roots will spread more rapidly if they become established, and the bulbs or tubers are more likely to dry out. Keep bulbs, corms and tubers where you can easily check them about once a month, to ensure they are all still sound. Any that start to rot must be removed immediately.

PREPARE THE POND FOR WINTER

Although ponds need little routine maintenance, there are a few end-of-season tasks that are essential if you want to keep your plants and fish in good condition.

1 Protect the pond from the worst of the leaf fall with a fine-mesh net. Anchor it just above the surface of the pond. This is not practical for a large pond, but it is useful for a small one. Remove the leaves regularly, and eventually take the netting off.

2 If you are not able to cover your pond with a net, or don't like the appearance of one, use a fish net or rake to remove leaves regularly – not only from the surface, but also from below the surface as well. Too many leaves in the water can pollute the pond.

3 Submerged oxygenating plants, such as elodea and rampant growers like myriophyllum, will eventually clog the pond unless you net or rake them out periodically. This is a good time to thin them simply by raking out the excess.

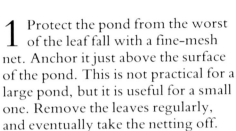

4 Trim back dead or dying plants from around the edge of the pond, especially where the vegetation is likely to fall into the water.

5 To divide overgrown water plants, first remove the plants from their containers. It may be necessary to cut some roots to do so.

6 Some plants can simply be pulled apart by hand, but others will have such a tight mass of entangled roots that you need to chop them into smaller pieces with a spade.

7 Discard any pieces you don't want for replanting, then pot up the others in planting baskets. Cover the top of the baskets with gravel to prevent soil disturbance.

TAKE IN TENDER AQUATICS

Some aquatic plants, such as the water lettuce (*Pistia stratiotes*) and *Salvinia auriculata*, will be killed by frost, even though they can multiply rapidly outdoors in summer. The fairy moss (*Azolla caroliniana*) sometimes survives a mild winter in favourable areas, but as an insurance policy a few plants should be overwintered in a frost-proof place.

1 Net a few plants in good condition. They may already be deteriorating in the cooler weather, so don't save any that appear to be rotting or badly damaged.

LEFT: *A pond can look perfect in summer, but if you have tender pond plants, now is the time to take them in.*

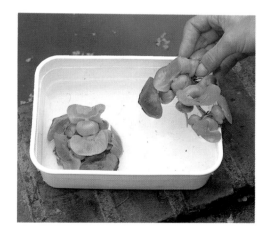

2 Put a handful of the plants into a plastic container – such as a lunch box or ice cream container. Don't cram them in so that they are overcrowded. Use extra containers rather than have them all touching. Some gardeners put a little soil in the bottom to provide nutrients.

3 Keep the plants in a warm, light place, such as a greenhouse. You might also be able to keep them on a light windowsill. Top up or change the water occasionally to prevent the water becoming stagnant.

CARING FOR MINIATURE WATERLILIES

With the exception of tropical waterlilies, which are usually only grown by enthusiasts with heated pools, waterlilies are very hardy and are usually planted deep enough not to come to any harm.

Miniature waterlilies are sometimes used for raised miniature pools, in a half barrel or shrub tub for example, and these are vulnerable. Because the container is raised above the ground, in very severe weather the water can freeze solid throughout. This can lead to winter losses. Try wrapping your raised miniature pool in several layers of bubble insulation material, or move it into a cool greenhouse for the winter.

AUTUMN LAWNCARE

Autumn is a good time to prepare your lawn for the year ahead, and the best time to tackle any long-term improvements. Tasks, such as raking out lawn debris, eradicating moss, feeding and aerating, will improve the quality of your lawn greatly if carried out on a yearly basis.

1 Over the years, grass clippings and debris form a 'thatch' on the surface of your lawn. This affects growth of the grass and should be removed with a lawn rake. Raking also removes moss.

2 If grass growth is poor, aerate the lawn. You can do this by pushing the prongs of a fork about 15cm (6in) into the ground.

3 Brush a soil improver into the holes made by the fork. Use sand or a mixture of fine soil and sand if the ground is poorly drained. Alternatively, use peat, a peat-substitute or very fine, well-rotted compost if the ground is sandy.

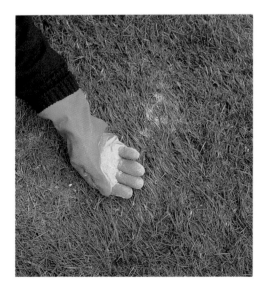

4 If your lawn is in poor condition and needs reviving, apply an autumn lawn feed. It is essential that you use one formulated for autumn use, as spring and summer feeds will contain too much nitrogen.

5 If the grass contains a lot of moss, apply a moss killer. Use one recommended for autumn use – the mixture known as lawn sand, sometimes used to kill moss, contains too much nitrogen.

6 You can tidy an uneven edge at any time, but doing it in autumn will relieve the pressure at busier times of year. Hold a half-moon edger against a board held in position with your feet. This is not an annual job.

COLLECT AND COMPOST LEAVES

Never waste leaves: they will make excellent garden compost if you rot them down; and, if left on the ground, they can damage areas of grass and smother small plants.

1 Don't let leaves lie for long on your lawn. The grass beneath will turn yellow and be prone to disease. On a small lawn, rake them up with a lawn rake.

2 Leaves on paths and drives are best brushed up with a broom or besom.

4 Leaves can be added to the compost heap or bin, but some leaves rot down slowly, so it is best to compost a large amount on their own. Rotted leaves are a useful addition to potting soils.

3 You can buy special tools to lift the leaves without too much bending, but two pieces of wood are also an effective way to lift them once they have been brushed into a heap.

MECHANICAL AIDS

Raking out thatch and moss from your lawn by hand is tiring. If you have a large lawn, invest in a powered lawn rake. This will do the job rapidly and efficiently. Take the drudgery out of aerating your lawn by using a hollow-tined aerator that removes a core of soil effortlessly and efficiently. Equally, you could invest in a powered lawn rake or a special leaf sweeper to clear large lawns of leaves.

DON'T LET LEAVES SMOTHER SMALL PLANTS

If you let leaves lie for long on small plants, such as alpines, they may begin to rot due to the lack of light and free movement of air. The leaves will also provide a haven for slugs and other pests that may eat your plants. Wait until most of the leaves have fallen from the trees, then go round and pick them off vulnerable plants, as shown.

PROTECT VULNERABLE SHRUBS

Many shrubs on the borderline of hardiness can be coaxed through the winter with a little protection. There are several methods you can use to provide shelter.

1 A little protection from cold winds and snow is all that many cold-sensitive shrubs require in areas where they are of borderline hardiness. Push cut branches of evergreens, such as conifers, into the soil around the plant.

2 If the shrub is tall, you may also need to tie cut branches of evergreens, or bracken, so that they remain in position.

3 If you don't have a supply of evergreen shoots or bracken, use horticultural fleece or a woven mesh for protection. For extra protection, fold these over to give more than one thickness before tying into position.

4 Some shrubs are damaged by cold winds as much as low temperatures, and for these a windbreak will prevent wind scorch. Insert canes or stakes around the plant, then fix several layers of wind-break netting or plastic sheeting to these.

RIGHT: *Always knock heavy falls of snow off your conifers before the weight can damage the branches and spoil the shape of the tree.*

PROTECT NEWLY PLANTED EVERGREENS

An evergreen planted in late summer or the autumn may not have grown new roots out into the soil, and if not watered regularly, it will not be able to absorb water as rapidly as it is lost. A windbreak for the first winter will reduce moisture loss and help a vulnerable plant to survive.

2 If you don't want to erect a shield, perhaps on aesthetic grounds, water in very dry spells to keep the roots moist, and cover the plant with a large plastic bag, pegged to the ground, when very severe weather is forecast. Remove it afterwards.

1 Insert three stout canes or stakes around the plant, then wrap a plastic sheet or several layers of horticultural fleece around the edge. Peg down the bottom.

PROTECT DELICATE ALPINES

Some alpines with hairy leaves are likely to rot if they become too wet and waterlogged during the cold months.

SNOW PROTECTION

1 If you know that a particular alpine needs winter wet protection, cover it with a sheet of glass or rigid plastic substitute supported on special wires.

2 You can also use bricks to support and weight the pane. If you have a spare cloche, perhaps not needed until spring, you might be able to use this to protect alpines. Leave the ends open, but make sure that the cloche is firmly anchored and not likely to be lifted by strong winds.

Conifers with an attractive or formal shape can be disfigured by a heavy fall of snow that pulls down or breaks the branches. If you live in an area of heavy snowfall, tie the branches, as shown. Green or brown twine is less conspicuous than string.

PLANT A HEDGE

Shrubs can be planted at almost any time of the year if you buy them in containers, but this is an expensive way to plant a hedge as you need so many plants. Most garden centres stock bundles of bare-root hedging plants at this time, so plant now if you want to create a hedge economically.

1 Prepare the ground thoroughly, as a hedge will be there for a long time and this is your only opportunity to improve the soil. Clear it of weeds, and dig deeply, especially if the soil is shallow or compacted.

2 Take out a trench about 25cm (10in) deep, using a garden line to ensure that the row will be straight.

3 Add as much garden compost or rotted manure as you can spare, then fork it into the base of the trench to improve the soil and encourage deep rooting.

4 Return the soil to the trench, adding more organic material as you do so. Then apply bonemeal and rake it in. Don't apply fast-acting fertilizers at this time of year.

5 You may find bare-root hedging simply bundled together, with their roots in a bed of peat or soil. If not, and if you will not be planting it out immediately, dig the hedging into a spare piece of ground.

6 Dig large holes at the appropriate spacing. A typical spacing is 38–45cm (15–18in), but it may be different for some plants, so always check the recommended spacing first.

7 Firm the plants in well, treading around them to remove any large air pockets that may cause the roots to dry out.

8 Water thoroughly, and be prepared to water regularly in dry spells for the first year.

PLANT A ROSE

Nowadays roses get planted throughout the year because most are grown in containers. Those ordered from specialist nurseries by mail order may arrive bare-root, however, and some garden centres and other shops also sell them like this in the autumn, perhaps with their roots wrapped in moss and a protective sleeve. These are plants that have been lifted from the field; they are often less expensive than those grown in containers, and can be just as good if planted promptly.

PLANTING A CLIMBING ROSE

Never plant a climbing rose too close to a wall or fence. Try to position the root-ball about 35cm (15in) away, and angle the stem slightly towards the support. In this way, the shoots can be trained normally, yet the roots will not be in the driest area of soil.

LEFT: *Roses always add charm to a garden, and now is a good time to plant.*

1 Dig a hole large enough to spread all the roots out, and fork in as much garden compost or rotted manure as you can spare. It is especially important to break up any compacted soil.

2 Trim off any broken or damaged roots, and if they appear dry, soak the roots in a bucket of water for an hour or two.

3 Trickle soil back around the roots, remembering to give the plant a shake occasionally to settle the soil around them.

4 To ensure the rose is planted firmly, with no large pockets of air, and that the bush cannot be rocked by wind, firm the soil with your feet. Rake over and water thoroughly.

5 If the plant was unpruned when bought, cut back all the shoots to about 15–20cm (6–8in) above the ground. This will also reduce the risk of winds loosening the rose.

INSULATE THE GREENHOUSE

Insulation will cut down heating costs. Even if you don't heat your greenhouse during the winter, insulation will afford extra protection for those not-quite-hardy plants.

1 There are many ready-made fasteners for securing polyethylene to the inside of a metal greenhouse. They usually slot into the groove in the metal molding and can be secured in position with a twisting motion.

2 With the main part of the clip in place, the top is pushed or twisted into position, clamping the polyethylene liner. If using thick bubble polyethylene, you may need clips designed for the extra thickness.

3 You may find it easier to line the sides and roof separately. If you decide to do this, be prepared to use a draught proofing strip if there is a gap at the eaves.

4 You can fix the insulation to a timber-framed greenhouse with drawing pins, or special pins sold for the purpose.

5 If you don't want to fix the insulation directly to the wooden frame, suction fixers can be attached to the glass. These can also be used for metal-framed greenhouses. Moisten the plastic before pressing into place.

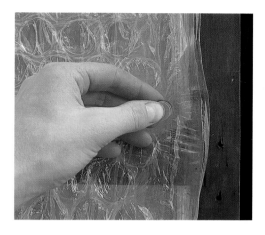

7 Whichever method of fixing you choose, you should always insulate the ventilators separately. Although you need to conserve heat as much as possible, some ventilation is essential when it's warm enough. You must be able to open at least one ventilator if necessary.

6 Secure the liner to the cup with the special pin provided (or use a drawing pin).

8 To avoid too much warmth being lost between the sheets where they join, seal joins with a transparent tape.

RIGHT: *Bubble insulation will keep the temperature up and your bills down.*

SCREENS AND DIVIDERS

Thermal screens made of clear plastic or special translucent fabrics are widely used commercially to conserve heat. Fixed horizontally over the plants, they seal off the space at the top of the greenhouse. They are usually pulled across at night, and drawn back during the day. A similar technique can be used in your own greenhouse by stretching supporting wires along each side of the greenhouse, over which the fabric can be draped or pulled (see below left).

If you have a large greenhouse, it may be more economic to heat just part of it. Use a vertical screen to partition off the end (see below right) to reduce the area to be heated.

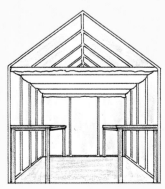

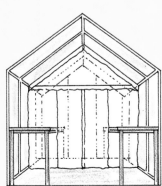

INSULATION MATERIALS

Proper double glazing is not very practical or cost-effective for most amateur greenhouses where very high temperatures are not normally maintained. Polyethylene sheeting is the most practical choice as it can be taken down at the end of the heating season and used again if stored carefully for the summer.

Single thickness, heavy-duty polyethylene lets through plenty of light, and is cheap to buy, but it is not the most effective material for conserving heat.

Bubble polyethylene is more efficient because air trapped in the bubbles cuts down heat loss. If possible, choose bubble polyethylene that is thick, with large pockets of air. It lets through less light, but is more efficient at reducing heat loss.

OVERWINTER TENDER FUCHSIAS

Most fuchsias are killed by frost, so unless you know that a particular variety is hardy enough to be left outdoors for the winter in your area, overwinter them in a frost-proof place.

1 If your fuchsias have been grown in pots during the summer, lift them to take into the greenhouse. If planted in the open soil, lift with a fork and remove excess soil.

2 Pot up the plants individually, or in large boxes if you have a lot of plants, then put them in a frost-free place, such as in the greenhouse or on a light windowsill indoors.

3 Tidy up the plants by removing old leaves and pinching out any soft green tips. You must keep the plants cool but frost-free, with the soil almost dry.

OVERWINTERING FUCHSIAS OUTDOORS

If you don't have a greenhouse or space indoors, try this method instead of throwing the plants away. Dig a trench about 30cm (12in) deep, line with straw, then lay the plants on this, as shown above. Cover the plants with more straw and then return the soil.

Dig them up in spring, pot them up and keep in warmth and good light to start into growth again. If the winters are not too harsh, many of the plants should survive.

PROTECTING HARDY FUCHSIAS

Hardy is a relative term, and although some fuchsias are tough enough for the roots not to be killed by frost where winters are not too severe, in cold areas they may succumb without a little extra protection.

Leave the old stems on, even though these will be killed, as this may afford the plant some additional shelter. To reduce the depth to which severe frosts penetrate, cover the crown with a thick layer of bracken, straw or peat, as shown here. Remove the protection in spring when the new shoots appear.

In mild areas, extra protection is not necessary for tough species such as *Fuchsia magellanica*.

OVERWINTER PELARGONIUMS

Pelargoniums, otherwise known as bedding geraniums, should be overwintered in a light and frost-free environment. If you have a lot of plants, a greenhouse is the best place to keep them, but if you do not have a greenhouse you may have space for a few plants indoors.

1 Lift the plants before the first frost if possible, though they will often survive a light frost if you take them in promptly afterwards.

2 Shake as much of the soil off the roots as possible, to reduce the size of the plant.

3 Trim the longest roots back to about 5–8cm (2–3in) long, to make potting up easier.

4 Shorten the shoots to about 10cm (4in), and trim off any remaining leaves. Although this looks drastic, new shoots will grow in spring, which you can use for cuttings if you want more plants.

5 The most effective way to store pelargoniums for the winter is in large trays at least 15cm (6in) deep. Half fill with soil or sowing compost, position the plants and add more compost to cover the roots. Water well initially, then only when the soil becomes almost dry.

6 If you want to overwinter your pelargoniums on a windowsill indoors, you may find it more convenient to use large pots instead of trays.

DEALING WITH YOUNG PLANTS

Fuchsias and pelargoniums can be rooted from cuttings taken in spring or autumn. If you are overwintering old plants, you can use them to provide plenty of cuttings in spring.

If you took cuttings in late summer or the autumn, however, your young plants will still be growing actively. Make sure that you keep these plants in good light and reasonably warm, in which case they will probably retain their foliage. If conditions are favourable, pelargoniums may even flower during the winter months.

PRUNE BLACK CURRANTS

Black currants fruit best on year-old branches, so in pruning an established bush the aim is to remove the oldest shoots and encourage new ones. Prune while the plant is dormant.

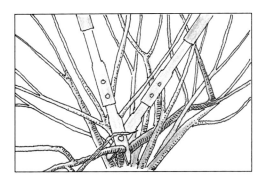

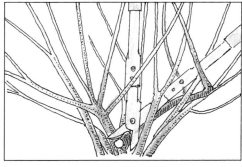

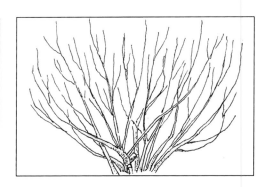

1 Only start pruning once they are old enough to fruit reliably. Cut back one-third of the shoots close to the base, choosing the oldest.

2 Cut back to their point of origin any diseased, damaged or badly placed shoots.

3 This is what the bush should look like after pruning, with plenty of well-spaced young shoots.

PRUNE RED AND WHITE CURRANTS

Unlike black currants, these fruit on shoots that are at least two years old. They are usually grown on a 'leg' (a short length of clear stem) as shown, but can be grown as a bush or trained as cordons.

1 If it was not done in the summer, start by removing any crossing or over-crowded shoots, to allow plenty of light into the centre of the bush.

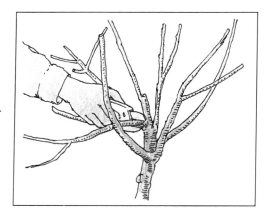

2 When badly placed shoots have been removed, shorten last summer's growth at the tip of each main shoot by half.

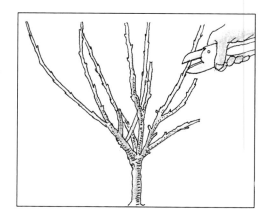

3 Finally, cut back the side-shoots to within one or two buds of the main stems. This will encourage fruiting.

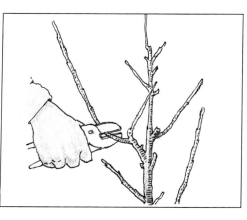

4 On an old bush it may be necessary to cut out a few very old shoots that no longer fruit well, but try to leave a vigorous young sideshoot to replace each one.

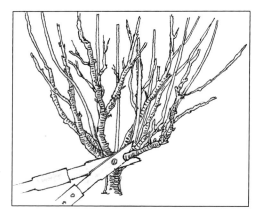

PRUNE RASPBERRIES

Autumn-fruiting raspberries bear fruit on canes grown that year, so pruning is easy. Summer-fruiting raspberries fruit on shoots that are a year old, so be careful not to prune last summer's shoots.

 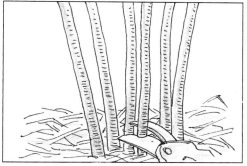 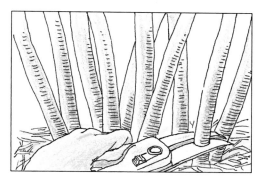

1 Provided you are sure the variety is autumn-fruiting, simply cut all the canes down to ground level while they are dormant.

2 On summer-fruiting raspberries cut the old canes (dark stems) that fruited this summer to just above the ground. Tie in the remaining shoots to support wires if necessary.

3 If the raspberries have been growing undisturbed for several years, the clumps may have become congested. Thin out surplus canes to leave them about 8cm (3in) apart.

PRUNE GOOSEBERRIES

Gooseberries fruit on shoots that are a year or more old, and continue to fruit quite well even if you neglect pruning. But with spiny stems, the fruit is difficult to harvest if not pruned annually.

 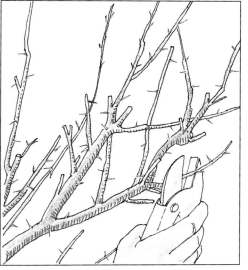 

1 If the job was not done after harvesting, cut out any low branches near the soil to an upward-pointing bud, and also eliminate any badly placed and crossing branches. Try to ensure that the centre of the bush is left open.

2 While the bush is dormant, reduce the length of new summer growth at the tips of the main shoots by about half. Then go along each main branch and prune back the sideshoots to two buds from the old wood.

3 If the plant is old, cut out one or two of the oldest shoots, to a point where there is a younger replacement to take over.

PLANT SOFT FRUIT

Nowadays most soft fruits – with the exception of cane plants such as raspberries – are usually sold in containers. They can be planted at almost any time, but late autumn is ideal when there is a good choice of plants in garden centres. Bare-root plants must be planted while dormant.

1 Excavate the soil for an area at least twice the size of the root-ball or container so that you can improve the soil over an area that the roots are likely to explore later.

2 Although it is not essential, your fruit will do much better if you can add plenty of humus-making material to the soil. Dig in as much rotten manure or garden compost as you can spare.

3 Soak the roots of bare-root plants in water for an hour before planting, and water container-grown plants for at least half an hour before planting. Place a plant in the hole and use a cane to make sure that it will be at its original depth.

4 Firm the plant in well, pressing with the heel of the foot to remove any large pockets of air around the roots.

5 After firming the soil, hoe and rake the ground to remove footprints, then water thoroughly.

6 Although it seems drastic, most bushes grown on stems that sprout from the base, such as black currants and raspberries, are best cut back to about 23–30cm (9–12in) after planting. This will stimulate new shoots to grow from the base.

POT UP HERBS FOR WINTER USE

You don't have to make do with dried or frozen herbs just because it is winter. Some herbs, such as mint, chives, parsley and marjoram, can be potted up to grow indoors or in the greenhouse for a fresh supply of winter leaves. The supply will be modest, but no less welcome.

1 Mint is an easy plant to force indoors, or in a cold frame or greenhouse. Lift an established clump to provide a supply of roots to pot up.

2 Be careful to select only pieces with healthy leaves (diseased leaves are common by the end of the season). You can pull pieces off by hand or cut through them with a knife.

3 Plant the roots in a pot if you want to try to keep the plant growing indoors for a month or so longer. Three-quarters fill a 20–25cm (8–10in) pot with soil or potting soil, then spread the roots out and cover with more soil.

4 If you want a supply of tender fresh leaves early next spring, cut off the tops and put the roots in seed trays or deeper boxes, then cover them with soil. If you keep them in a greenhouse (or even a protected cold frame) you will be able to harvest new mint much earlier.

5 Chives also respond favourably to lifting for an extended season. Lift a small clump to pot up. If it's too large, you should be able to pull it apart into smaller pieces.

6 Place the clump in a pot of ordinary garden soil or potting soil, firm well, and water thoroughly. It should continue to provide leaves after those outdoors have died back, and will produce new ones earlier next spring.

PARSLEY AND MARJORAM

If you cut down and pot up marjoram, it will usually spring into new growth provided warmth and light are right.

Parsley is always a dependable winter herb if grown from a late summer or autumn sowing and kept on a windowsill.

LIFT AND PROTECT CHRYSANTHEMUMS

Not all autumn-flowering chrysanthemums have to be lifted (see box), but many do. The roots are potted into boxes, which means that you can start them off in warmth in spring.

1 Lift the roots after the plants have finished flowering and before severe frosts arrive.

2 Shake surplus soil off the roots before removing from the garden.

3 Trim the tops off and cut any long, straggly roots back to keep the root-ball compact.

4 Place a layer of soil or potting soil in a box or tray about 10cm (4in) deep. Position the roots and cover them with about 3cm (1in) of soil, firming lightly. Don't forget to label the plants. Keep the box in a cool, light place, such as a cool greenhouse, light garage windowsill, or a cold frame. For most types of chrysanthemum it does not matter if they receive a touch of frost. Keep the soil slightly damp but not wet.

BELOW: Chrysanthemum *'Countryman'*, is a reflexed early-flowering outdoor variety.

OVERWINTERING CHRYSANTHEMUMS

There are many kinds of chrysanthemum, but it is only the autumn-flowering chrysanthemums that are likely to cause confusion regarding overwintering.

In mild, frost-free climates they can all be left in the ground, and many of the species like *Chrysanthemum rubellum*, are hardy even in cold areas.

But in temperate climates the highly bred early-flowering autumn chrysanthemums are best lifted and stored, and even those outdoor ones that flower later are best treated this way. Even those that tolerate some frost are more likely to survive if kept fairly dry. Wet and cold is the combination to avoid.

PROTECT POND PUMPS

If you leave a pump in your pond over winter, ice may damage it. Don't just take it out of the pond and leave it where moisture can enter – store it in a dry place.

1 Remove submersible pumps from the water before penetrating frosts cause the water to freeze deeply.

2 Clean the pump before you put it away. It will probably be covered with algae which can be scrubbed off.

3 Remove the filter and either replace it or clean it. Follow the manufacturer's instructions.

4 Make sure all the water is drained from the pump. If your pump is an external one, make sure the system is drained.

5 Read the manufacturer's instructions, and carry out any other servicing that is necessary before storing the pump in a dry place. It may be necessary to send it away for a service, in which case do it now instead of waiting until spring.

DISPOSE OF YOUR RUBBISH . . . WISELY

Gardeners always acquire a lot of rubbish and debris in the autumn, but there is no one simple way to deal with it all. Be environmentally friendly and recycle as much as possible through composting.

To improve the chances of good compost, add a layer of manure or a proprietary compost activator after every 15cm (6in) of kitchen and garden refuse. Woody material such as hedge clippings and pruning will rot down too slowly to put straight on to the compost heap. These are best put through a shredder, then composted or used as a mulch. Some things are best burnt – diseased material and pernicious perennial weeds for instance, as well as woody material if you don't have a shredder. An incinerator that will burn the rubbish quickly is preferable to a traditional smoky bonfire.

A large quantity of leaves is better composted separately. Some leaves rot down slowly, but the end product is particularly useful for adding to potting mixtures.

TAKE HARDWOOD CUTTINGS

Hardwood cuttings root more slowly than most of the softwood or semi-ripe cuttings that you can take during the spring and summer, but they need much less attention. They don't need heat, and because you plant them in the open ground (or in a cold frame), watering won't be an onerous chore.

Many shrubs, and even trees, can be raised from hardwood cuttings. Some of them are suggested in the box below.

1 Choose stems that are firm and hard but not old and thick (pencil thickness is about right). With shrubs like this dogwood you should be able to make several cuttings from one shoot. The length of the cutting will depend on the plant, but about 15cm (6in) is appropriate for most. Make a cut straight across the stem, just below a node.

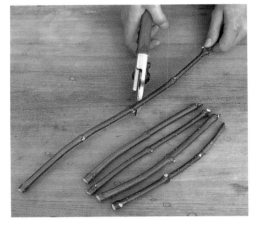

2 Make the second cut about 15cm (6in) above the first, and above a node, but this time at an angle so that you will know which is the top and which the bottom of the cutting.

3 Although a rooting hormone is not essential, it should increase the success rate, especially with plants that are difficult to root. Moisten the bases of the cuttings in water.

4 Dip the moistened ends into a rooting powder. You can also use liquid and gel rooting hormones, in which case you should not dip the end in water first. Treat only the base end of each cutting.

SHRUBS TO PROPAGATE

The list below is just a selection of the shrubs that usually root easily from hardwood cuttings, but there are many others. Be prepared to experiment, or consult a specialist book to see which plants are normally rooted by this method.
Aucuba japonica (spotted laurel)
Buddleia (butterfly bush)
Cornus alba (dogwood)
Cornus stolonifera (dogwood) – illustrated
Forsythia
Ligustrum ovalifolium (privet)
Philadelphus (mock orange)
Ribes sanguineum (flowering currant)

Roses (species and hybrids)
Salix (willow)
Spiraea
Viburnum (deciduous species)

5 Make a slit trench with a spade, a little shallower than the length of the cuttings. Choose a position where the cuttings can be left undisturbed for a year.

6 Sprinkle some grit or coarse sand in the base of the slit if the ground is poorly drained. This will help to prevent water-logging around the cuttings.

7 Insert the cuttings 8–10cm (3–4in) apart, upright against the back of the slit, leaving about 3–5cm (1–2in) above the ground.

8 Firm the soil around the cuttings, to eliminate the pockets of air that would cause the cutting to dry out.

9 Water the cuttings and label. Remember to water them in dry weather.

TREES FROM HARDWOOD CUTTINGS

Some trees can also be propagated from hardwood cuttings, and those below are particularly easy.

If propagating trees, decide whether you want a multi-stemmed tree or one with a single main stem. If the latter, set the cuttings deeper in the trench so that the top bud is just below the surface of the soil.

Platanus (plane)
Populus (poplar) – illustrated
Salix (willow)

AUTUMN CLEAN THE GREENHOUSE

Autumn is an ideal time to clean the greenhouse. It is likely to be less full than in spring, and it is important to start the season of cold, dull days with clean glass to allow in all available light, and an environment as free as possible of pests and diseases.

1 If you have not already removed the remains of summer shading, do it as soon as possible. Shading washes like this are easy to wipe off with a duster if dry.

2 Whether or not summer shading has been used, clean the glass. The easiest way to clean the outside is with a brush or cleaning head on a long handle. Spray with water, adding a little detergent if necessary, and rub clean. Rinse with clean water.

LEFT: *Even if the greenhouse is still filled with colour, autumn is a good time to give the structure, shelves and benches a thorough clean.*

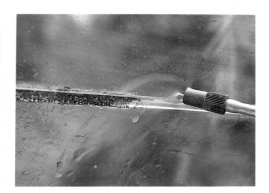

3 A proprietary glass cleaner will be very effective in removing dirt and grime, but is usually only practical for a small greenhouse where you can easily reach the glass. Clean the glass inside as well as out.

4 Algae often grow where the panes of glass overlap, an area that also traps dirt. Try squirting a jet of water between the panes, then dislodge the dirt with a thin strip of rigid plastic (a plastic plant label usually works well).

5 Finally, squirt another jet of water between the panes to move the loosened dirt and algae.

7 Fumigation is a good way to control a number of pests and diseases that may be lurking in nooks and crannies around the greenhouse. You may be able to keep some or all of the plants in, or you can fumigate an empty greenhouse. Check the label.

6 Dirt and soil also accumulates where the glass joins the base, and this can be a breeding ground for pests and diseases. Use a label or a small tool to lift the soil out of the crevice, then douse with a garden disinfectant (keep away from plants).

9 Diseases are easily carried over from one plant to another on old pots and seed trays. When you have a moment between now and spring, wash them all in a garden disinfectant, scrubbing them well. The inside is as important as the outside.

8 It is worth disinfecting the frame and staging, whether or not you fumigate the greenhouse. Rather than use a household disinfectant, use one sold for the garden and greenhouse.

WINTER

A well-planned garden will not be devoid of colour or interest in the winter months, and working outdoors can be a real pleasure. There are always jobs to be done, and tackling them now relieves the pressure in spring.

Sometimes there is no choice but to become an armchair gardener. This is the time to scan your gardening books and plant encyclopedias for ideas, perhaps plan minor improvements or even totally redesign your garden, and of course fill in your seed order – perhaps one of the most pleasurable jobs of all.

OPPOSITE: *The red-stemmed* Cornus alba *remain bright and interesting throughout the winter.*

ABOVE: *Focal points like this ornament can help to compensate for the lack of colour during the cold months.*

WINTER DIG THE VEGETABLE PLOT

If you have a vegetable plot, or other large area of ground that requires digging, this is a good time to do it. If the soil is a heavy clay, leaving it rough-dug over the winter will allow frost and the weather to help break down large clods. This will make it easier to rake level and to produce a seedbed of fine, crumbly soil in spring. You may prefer to leave digging a light, sandy soil until spring, as this type of soil tends to become flattened and compacted by winter rain if dug too early. New weed growth may also be a problem by spring and can be dealt with at the same time.

1 Divide the space to be dug in half lengthways, marking the area with string. Dividing the plot like this avoids moving excavated soil from one end of the plot to the other.

2 Take out a trench the depth and width of a spade blade. Pile the soil at the end of the other half of the plot, as shown.

3 When you remove the next trench, throw the soil forward into the space left by the first. Digging is easier if you first 'cut' a slice the width of the bite of soil to be dug.

4 Push the spade in parallel to the trench, taking a slice of soil about 15–20cm (6–8in) deep. Larger bites may be too heavy to lift comfortably.

5 Loosen the soil by pulling back on the handle, while trying to keep the bite of soil on the spade.

6 Flick the soil over with the wrist, inverting the clod of earth so that the top is buried. Lift with your knees, not your back.

7 When the end of the plot is reached, fill the trench with soil taken from the first row of the return strip.

8 Finally, fill the trench left when digging has been completed with the soil put on one side from the initial excavation.

DOUBLE DIGGING

Single digging is adequate for most plants, and adding manure or garden compost in this top layer is likely to do more good for short-rooted plants like lettuces and cabbages than burying it deeply. However, for certain deep-rooted crops, such as runner beans, or to break up neglected ground, double digging can be useful. Bear in mind that it also doubles the effort!

1 Divide the plot up in the same way as described for single digging, and deal with the soil from the end of each strip in the same way. But this time make the trenches about 40cm (16in) wide and 25cm (10in) deep.

2 Spread a generous layer of well-rotted manure or garden compost – or other bulky organic material that will retain moisture and add humus – over the bottom of the trench.

3 Fork this thick layer of manure or organic material into the bottom of the trench. A fork is better than a spade because it will penetrate the harder lower layer more easily and will mix the material into the soil better.

4 Move the garden line to the next position, maintaining the same 40cm (16in) spacing, or thereabouts. Cut and slice the soil and throw it forward as before, but take several bites per strip, otherwise the soil will be too heavy.

TEST YOUR SOIL

Many people garden successfully without ever testing their soil, but they are probably fortunate in gardening on ground that is not deficient in nutrients, is neither too acid nor too alkaline, and receives plenty of nutrients anyway as part of normal cultivation. If things don't seem to be growing well, a soil test is the best starting point for putting things right, and keen growers test their soil routinely once a year.

Professional soil testing is the most accurate for nutrients, but you can get a reasonable idea of the major nutrients in your soil with simple indicator kits. Testing for pH (see the box opposite) is quick and effective.

Bear in mind that kits vary from one manufacturer to another, so always follow the manufacturer's instructions if they vary from the advice given here.

1 Collect the soil sample from about 5–8cm (2–3in) below the surface. This gives a more typical reading of nutrient levels in the root area. Take a number of samples from around the garden, but test each one separately.

2 With this kit one part of soil is mixed with five parts of water. Shake together vigorously in a clean jar, then allow the water to settle. This can take between half an hour and a day, depending on the soil.

3 Draw off some settled liquid from the top few centimetres (about an inch) for your test.

4 Carefully transfer the solution to the test and reference chambers in the plastic container, using the pipette provided.

5 Select the appropriate colour-coded capsule (different ones are used for each major nutrient) and empty the powder it contains into the test chamber. Replace the cap, then shake vigorously.

6 After a few minutes, compare the colour of the liquid with the shade panel that forms part of the container. The kit contains an explanation of the significance of each reading, and what – if anything – to do.

WHAT IS pH?

The term pH is a scientific way of stating how acid or alkaline something is. Soils vary in their degree of acidity or alkalinity. The scale runs from 0 (most acid) to 14 (most alkaline), with 7 as neutral. Soils never reach these extremes, and horticulturally, 6.5 can be considered neutral in that it is the pH at which most plants will grow happily. Acid-loving plants, such as rhododendrons, camellias, peonies (see above) and heathers, need a lower pH and may develop chlorosis – a yellowing of the leaves – if grown on chalky soil. Chalk-loving plants like dianthus and lilacs prefer a pH of 7 or above.

These differences may sound small, but on the pH scale 1 point represents a ten-fold increase in acidity or alkalinity.

TESTING THE pH

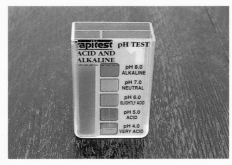

Collect your samples and mix with water as described for nutrient testing, but for the pH test you don't have to wait for the mixture to settle, and only the test chamber is filled with the solution. Clean tap water is used for the reference chamber. Add the indicator chemical provided with the kit, then put the top on and shake vigorously. Compare the colour with the shade panel on the container for the nearest pH value.

USING PROBE METERS

Probes that measure the pH on a dial are very quick and easy to use, but some people consider them less accurate than colour indicator tests. To ensure an accurate reading, follow the instructions and keep the tip clean.

Push the probe into the soil, and take the reading once the needle seems to have settled. Take several readings from the same area to check results, then move on to another part of the garden.

ADDING LIME TO THE SOIL

Never add lime unless you have tested your soil first and know that it is necessary. Too much lime applied regularly can be harmful for your plants. Always check that you are applying the right sort of lime at the appropriate application rate. Your testing kit should contain advice about how much lime (which will vary with type) to apply to your soil to adjust the pH.

1 Hydrated lime, often used for gardens, should not be handled unnecessarily. Always use gloves, and goggles to protect your eyes. Ground limestone is safer to handle.

2 Rake the lime into the surface, whichever kind of lime you use.

PROTECT WINTER HELLEBORE FLOWERS

Winter-flowering hellebores such as *Helleborus niger* (Christmas rose) are frost-hardy, but their pale blooms are often only just above soil level.

If you want to cut the flowers to take indoors, covering the plants will reduce mud splashes and keep the blooms clean and in good condition.

1 Protect low-growing winter-flowering plants such as *H. niger* with a cloche if you want perfect blooms to cut for indoors. Though frost-hardy, the flowers tend to become splashed with mud and damaged by the weather.

2 If you don't have a cloche, improvise with a piece of polythene over wire hoops, or a pane of glass supported on bricks.

ABOVE RIGHT: Helleborus argutifolius *is a tall species that will not need protection.*

RIGHT: Helleborus orientalis *may benefit from protection for early cut blooms.*

CHECK BULBS AND CORMS IN STORE

Don't wait until it is time to plant your tender overwintering bulbs before checking them for rot. Storage rots are common, and easily spread from affected bulbs or corms to healthy ones.

1 Bulbs, corms and tubers being over-wintered in a frost-free place should be checked once a month. By eliminating diseased or soft bulbs or corms, you will prevent the rot spreading to others.

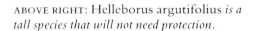

2 If you discover soft or diseased bulbs in store, it's worth dusting the others with a fungicide. Check with the label to ensure that it is suitable for the purpose, and be careful not to inhale the dust.

SERVICING YOUR MOWER

Winter is the best time to have your mower serviced. The chances are you won't bother once it is in regular use during the summer. You may prefer to have the servicing done professionally, which is often cheaper at this time than in spring, but you can do some of the simple tasks yourself. The advice below should be followed in conjunction with your handbook.

1 Remove accumulated clippings and dirt from around the blade housing of a rotary mower, being certain that any power supply is disconnected. Use an abrasive paper to clean metal blades.

2 Wipe the blade with an oily rag or spray with an anti-rust aerosol. If the blade is in poor condition, replace it with a new one. On appropriate models you may consider replacing it with a plastic blade for safety.

3 If you have a petrol mower, drain the fuel and oil before storing the machine for the winter.

4 Remove the spark plug, clean it and reset the gap if necessary. If the plug is in poor condition, replace with a new one.

5 Pour a table-spoonful of oil into the cylinder and pull the starter to turn the engine over half a dozen times before you return the spark plug, thus coating the engine.

6 Brush or wipe away accumulated clippings from a cylinder mower. If the mower is electric, disconnect the power supply before you start.

7 Wipe the mower with an oily rag, or spray with an anti-rust aerosol, before you store it.

8 Oil the chain if your mower is fitted with one. You may have to remove the chain guard to reach it.

BRING ON FORCED BULBS

Whether your bulbs flower at Christmas, or on any particular date, depends partly on whether you used prepared bulbs in the first place. However, timing also depends on how cold you have kept the bulbs and at what point you bring them out from their resting place into light and warmth.

ABOVE: *Moss provides a more instant way of improving the appearance of a bowl or basket of bulbs. Lift clumps of moss, with roots intact, from your garden and cover the surface.*

1 Check bowls of bulbs plunged outdoors beneath sand, peat or grit used to keep them cool and dark while roots develop. If the shoots are about 3cm (1in) high, it is time to bring them indoors.

2 If you have kept bulbs in a cool, dark place indoors, in a cupboard or loft, check these periodically too. Bring them into the light when the shoots are 3–5cm (1–2in) tall.

3 Wipe the container clean if it has been plunged outdoors, then place in a light but cool position indoors or in a conservatory. Only put in a warm place once the buds have emerged and are beginning to show colour, else the stems may be too long and weak.

4 If you sow grass seed on the surface as soon as you bring the bulbs into the light, you should have an attractive carpet of grass by the time they flower.

5 Just before the bulbs come into full flower, cut the grass to a height of about 3–5cm (1–2in), to make it look even and neat.

WHEN FLOWERING IS OVER

Never attempt to grow the same bulbs indoors for a second year, with the exception of indoor plants like amaryllis (*Hippeastrum*) – see the box below for more information. Forcing hardy bulbs to flower indoors drains their reserves and results are almost always disappointing a second time. But there is no need to discard them. Plant them in the garden where they should gradually recover over a few seasons.

1 If you plan to keep your bulbs to grow in the garden, dead-head them as soon as the display is over. This will avoid energy being wasted on seed production.

3 In spring, plant the bulbs out in a border or other spot where they can be left undisturbed to grow as a natural group. Some types of bulb may not produce flowers the following season, but probably will do so in subsequent years.

KEEPING AMARYLLIS TO FLOWER AGAIN

The houseplant popularly known as amaryllis is really a *Hippeastrum*. Many are sold in flower during the winter, or as bulbs that grow with phenomenal speed once started. You should be able to keep them so that they flower another year if you follow this advice.

- Cut the flower stalks close to their point of origin once the flowers fade.
- Keep watered, and feed occasionally.
- From late spring onwards keep in a greenhouse or conservatory if possible.
- If you don't have a greenhouse or conservatory, stand the plant outside for the summer.
- Let the foliage die down in late summer or the autumn.
- Start into growth again in late autumn or early winter.

2 Do not plant directly into the garden, but acclimatize them gradually by placing in a cold frame or other cool but protected place. Regular watering and a dose of liquid feed will help them recover.

ABOVE: *Amaryllis should flower the following year – the box, left, tells you how.*

FORCE RHUBARB

Rhubarb is one of those crops that almost looks after itself, and if you have an established clump, forcing tender young stems is very easy. There are many methods of forcing rhubarb, and they all seem to work well. Just choose a technique that you find convenient.

ABOVE: *Rhubarb is a useful early crop that you can start forcing now. A terracotta forcing pot is shown in the background.*

1 Choose a method of excluding light. Special pots were once used for this, but now most people improvise. An old tea chest, bucket, or barrel are simple but effective alternatives. If you don't have these, make a frame from wire-netting and canes as shown here.

2 Pile straw into the wire-netting cage, pressing it well down, to provide warmth and protection.

3 Another simple way to make a rhubarb forcer is with a plastic dustbin. If you don't mind cutting the bottom out of it, use it the right way up with a lid on, otherwise use it inverted without a lid.

4 For really early crops many gardeners lift a well-established root to leave on the surface for a few weeks. This gives the root a cold spell that makes it think winter is more advanced than it is.

5 Replant your chilled crown for outdoor forcing, or bring it into the greenhouse. If you have a warm greenhouse, place it under the bench, screened with black plastic. Alternatively, pot it up and put in a plastic bag to take indoors. Make sure there is plenty of air in the bag by keeping it loose and making a few small air holes, then place the bag in a warm yet convenient place – under the stairs or in a kitchen cupboard. Check progress periodically.

FORCE CHICORY

Chicons, the forced and blanched new shoots produced from chicory roots, are an enjoyable winter vegetable when fresh produce is scarce. It is best if you grow your own roots from plants sown in late spring or early summer, but you may be able to buy roots for forcing.

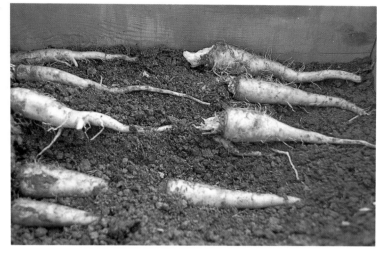

1 To produce chicons, you should choose a variety of chicory recommended for the purpose – 'Witloof' is an old and traditional variety. Lift the root from mid autumn onwards, and leave on the surface for a few days.

2 When the roots have been exposed for a few days, which helps to retard growth, trim the tops off to leave a 3–5cm (1–2in) stump of growth. You can pot them up now or store them in a box of sand, peat or dry soil for use later.

3 To force, place three roots in a 23cm (9in) pot, using a moist potting soil or ordinary garden soil. You may have to trim the ends of the roots to fit them in the pot. Leave the crowns exposed.

   Cover the pot with a second pot with the drainage holes blocked (use a piece of kitchen foil for this), and keep in a temperature of 10–18°C (50–65°F). Keep the compost just moist. The chicons will be ready in about three weeks.

WRITING LABELS IN ADVANCE

It makes sense to do as many jobs as you can in winter that will save time later when you are busy sowing and planting. Instead of waiting, write your labels on a day when you can't get into the garden. You will probably make a neater job of it by doing it more leisurely, and it will take pressure off the time when you're busy in the garden.

TAKE ROOT CUTTINGS

Nearly everyone takes stem cuttings at some time, but surprisingly few gardeners bother with root cuttings. Some useful plants can be propagated this way (see the box opposite for examples), and it is an interesting and relatively simple winter job, because root cuttings are only likely to be successful if taken during the dormant season.

1 Lift a young but well-established plant to provide the cuttings. If you don't want to use the whole plant for cuttings, and prefer to leave the parent plant largely undisturbed, just remove soil from one side to gain access to the roots.

2 If the plant has large, fleshy roots, cut some off close to the main stem or root. You should be able to make several cuttings from one root by cutting it into sections later.

3 Cut each root into lengths about 5cm (2in) long. To help you remember which way up they are, cut them horizontally at the top and diagonally at the bottom.

4 Fill a pot with a gritty potting mixture and insert the cuttings using a dibber or pencil to make the hole. The top of the cutting should be flush with the top of the potting soil.

5 Sprinkle a thin layer of grit over the surface. Label, as nothing will be visible for a few months, and it's easy to forget what the pot contains. Place in a cold frame or greenhouse and keep the potting soil just moist.

6 Some plants, such as border phlox and rock plants like *Primula denticulata*, have thin roots. These can be laid horizontally, so don't make sloping cuts to indicate the bottom. Just cut into 3–5cm (1–2in) lengths.

7 Fill a seed tray with a gritty compost and firm it level.

8 Space the cuttings out evenly over the surface, then cover them with a layer of the gritty potting mix. Keep moist but not too wet, in a cold frame or greenhouse.

SOME PLANTS TO GROW FROM ROOT CUTTINGS

Acanthus
Echinops
Gaillardia
Phlox (border)
Primula denticulata
Pulsatilla vulgaris
Romneya coulteri

LEFT: *Border phlox can be propagated from root cuttings. This one is* Phlox paniculata *'Flamingo'.*

INSULATE COLD FRAMES

Old-fashioned cold frames with brick or timber sides were not as light as modern aluminium and glass or plastic cold frames, but they were warmer. Glass sides let in more light, but also lose heat rapidly. Have the best of both worlds by insulating your glass-sided cold frame during the coldest weather, while taking full advantage of the glass sides in spring and summer.

COVERING COLD FRAMES

Cold frames of any kind benefit from a warm blanket thrown over them on very cold nights. A piece of old carpet is an ideal alternative (see above). Put it in place *before* the temperature drops, and remember to remove it the next morning unless it remains exceptionally cold. Your plants need light and warmth.

1 Sometimes there are small gaps between the glass and an aluminium frame. This does not matter in hot weather, but for winter warmth it's worth sealing the gaps with draught-proofing strip sold for windows and doors.

2 Insulate the glass sides with sheets of expanded polystyrene. Cut it with a knife or saw. Measure accurately, allowing for the thickness of the material where sheets join at the ends. Push sheets into place so that they fit tightly.

TAKE CHRYSANTHEMUM CUTTINGS

Chrysanthemums that are overwintered in a greenhouse or cold frame are usually propagated from cuttings once the old stool (clump of roots) starts to produce shoots. It is better to raise vigorous young plants from cuttings than simply to replant the old clump. Chrysanthemums that have been boxed or potted up in the autumn, and kept frost-free and just moist, will soon start producing new shoots. Stimulate growth now with plenty of light and warmth.

1 When your boxes or pots of chrysanthemum stools have produced shoots about 5cm (2in) long, it is time to take cuttings.

2 If possible, choose shoots coming directly from the base of the plant. Cut them off close to the base.

3 Pull off the lowest leaves and trim the ends of the cuttings straight across with a sharp knife.

4 Dip the ends in a rooting hormone. If using a powder, dip the end in water first so that it adheres. Hormone treatment usually improves the rate and speed of rooting.

5 Insert the cuttings around the edge of a pot containing a mixture suitable for cuttings.

6 If you don't have a propagator, cover the pot with a plastic bag, but inflate it to ensure it is not in contact with the leaves. Turn the bag regularly to avoid condensation dripping onto the leaves. Remove when the plants have rooted.

RIGHT: *Many chrysanthemums can make colourful garden plants for the autumn, and they are easily propagated from cuttings taken at this time of year.*

SOW SEEDS FOR SUMMER FLOWERS

It is too early to sow seeds outdoors, and it is likely to be too soon to sow most tender bedding plants in the greenhouse or on a windowsill. But it is not too soon to sow summer flowers that need a long growing period before they flower, such as fibrous rooted begonias (*Begonia semperflorens*). If in doubt, check the seed packet to see whether a particular flower needs early sowing or not.

Because it is difficult to provide the necessary warmth economically at this time of year, especially in a greenhouse, it is best to start the seeds off in a propagator, and move them out once they have germinated. By sowing in pots you will be able to germinate more kinds of seeds in your propagator at the same time. Sowing in pots is also sensible for seeds where only a few plants are needed, such as for trees and shrubs.

1 Fill the pot with a seed sowing compost, and gently firm and level it. Using the base or top of a jar is a convenient way of doing this.

2 Sow thinly, and as evenly as possible. Bear in mind that you have to handle the seedlings later, and very close spacing will make this difficult. Most can be sprinkled easily between finger and thumb, like salt.

3 Large seeds are best spaced individually. If they are very large, you can insert them into small holes made with a dibber.

4 Most seeds should be covered with a light sprinkling of the same soil mix. Use a sieve to spread the soil evenly. Some seeds germinate best in light and should not be covered – check the sowing instructions.

5 To avoid disturbing the evenly distributed seeds, water the pot initially by standing it in shallow water. Remove the pot and let it drain when the surface looks moist.

6 If you don't have a propagator, cover the pot with a sheet of glass or plastic until the seeds germinate. Turn the covering periodically if condensation is heavy. Don't forget the label!

SOW EARLY CROPS IN YOUR COLD FRAME

If your cold frame is not packed with over-wintering plants, make use of it for early vegetable crops. Radishes and turnips are among the crops that grow quickly and mature early in a cold frame, but you can also try forcing varieties of carrot. Suitable varieties of lettuce also do well.

1 Dig over the ground in the frame, working in as much organic material as possible. Farmyard manure is useful for enriching the soil for these early crops. Do not apply powerful artificial fertilizers at this time.

2 Rake the soil level, and make shallow drills with the rake or a hoe. You can sow the seeds broadcast (scattered randomly), but this makes weeding and thinning more difficult.

3 Sow the seeds thinly, then rake the soil back over the drills. Water thoroughly, then keep the frame closed until the seeds germinate. Once they are through, ventilate on mild days, but keep closed, and if possible insulated, at night.

WARM UP THE SOIL

If you have a kitchen garden, start warming up the soil with cloches to get your vegetables off to an early start. Although most early vegetables are not sown until early spring, you need to have your cloches in position several weeks before you plan to sow.

1 Cloche designs vary considerably, but most can easily be made into long runs the length of the row. Make sure that they are butted close together and that plastic cloches are well anchored to the ground.

2 End pieces are essential, otherwise the cloches will just become a wind tunnel. Make sure they are fixed firmly in place.

3 Polythene tunnel cloches are inexpensive to buy, and although they need to be re-covered after a few seasons, a replacement sheet is inexpensive. Fix the hoops first, then stretch the sheet over them.

4 Use the special fixing wires to hold the sheet in position.

5 Secure the ends with sticks or pegs, pulling the plastic taut.

6 Heap a little soil over the edges to anchor the cloches.

PREPARE BEAN AND CELERY TRENCHES

You can grow a satisfactory crop of beans without special soil preparation, and achieve a respectable crop of self-blanching celery by planting on ground that has not been specially enriched. But if you want an especially heavy and impressive crop, it is worth preparing the trench.

1 Take out a trench 25–30cm (10–12in) deep and 60cm (2ft) wide for runner beans, 38cm (15in) wide for celery. Heap the soil to one or both sides of the trench.

2 Add as much rotted manure or garden compost as you can spare. This will add some nutrients and benefit the structure and moisture-holding capacity of the soil.

3 Fork the manure or garden compost into the soil at the bottom of the trench – don't leave it as a layer. Finally, rake the soil back into the trench.

APPLY SLOW-ACTING FERTILIZERS

Apply slow-acting fertilizers such as bonemeal and proprietary controlled-release fertilizers when the vegetable plot has been dug and levelled, ready for sowing from early spring onwards. Controlled-release fertilizers release their nutrients only when the soil is warm enough for the plants to use them. Fertilizers should always be applied evenly and at the recommended rate.

1 Divide the area into strips 1m or 1yd wide with string, and space canes at the same interval to form a square. Scatter the measured dose, then move the canes. Rake into the soil.

TAKE DAHLIA CUTTINGS

If you require just one or two more dahlia plants, you can simply divide the tubers before planting them in late spring, making sure that each piece has an 'eye' or bud. For more plants, it is best to take cuttings after starting the tubers into growth early in the greenhouse.

1 Plant the tubers in deep boxes of compost. You will not be able to bury the tubers, but that does not matter so long as you trickle as much soil as possible around them. Keep the boxes in a light, warm place.

2 Take the cuttings when they have two or three pairs of leaves. If you take a tiny piece of the parent tuber, they should root quickly without a rooting hormone.

3 You can take larger cuttings if you miss the earlier stage, but try not to let them become longer than 8cm (3in). Cut off with a sharp knife just above the tuber.

4 Remove the lowest pair of leaves to leave a clear stem. Pull the leaves off carefully or cut them off with a sharp knife. If some of the leaves have grown large, cut these in half and discard the tips. This will reduce the area of leaf through which moisture can be lost while the cutting is rooting.

5 To increase the number of cuttings likely to root successfully, dip the cut ends into a rooting hormone. Insert the cuttings around the edge of a pot, label, then place in a propagator to root.

6 If you don't have a propagator, enclose the pot and cuttings in a plastic bag. Try to keep the leaves out of contact with the bag. They should root in a matter of weeks if you keep them in a warm, light position.

PLANT CLIMBERS

You can plant container-grown climbers at almost any time of the year provided the ground is not frozen or waterlogged. However, it is much easier to train in new shoots as they grow than it is to untangle them from their temporary support and attempt to retrain them.

1 Excavate a hole about twice the diameter of the root-ball. The centre of the plant should be at least 30cm (12in) away from the wall or fence, otherwise the roots will be too dry.

2 Dig in a generous amount of rotted manure or garden compost. This is particularly important when planting a climber near a wall or fence, as you need material that will hold moisture around the roots.

3 Tease out some of the fine roots from around the edge of the rootball, to encourage the plant to root out into the surrounding soil. Return and firm the soil around the plant, and apply a slow or controlled-release fertilizer.

4 Loosen the stems first if they have been tied to a cane, then tie them to the support. Spread them out evenly, and don't be afraid to spread them wide and low – new shoots will grow upwards to fill the space.

5 Water thoroughly after planting, and be prepared to water regularly in dry weather for the first year. Climbers are usually planted where walls or other plants shield them from most of the rain.

6 Apply a mulch at least 5cm (2in) thick around the plant after the ground has been soaked thoroughly. This will reduce water loss as well as suppress weeds.

SOW BEDDING PLANTS

Late winter is a good time to sow the majority of frost-tender plants used for summer bedding if you have a heated greenhouse, although a few such as pelargonium (bedding geraniums) and *Begonia semperflorens* are best sown earlier to give them a long period of growth before planting out in late spring or early summer. Quick-growers, such as alyssum and French marigolds (*Tagetes*

patula), will soon catch up even if you sow in early or mid spring.

Because you usually need quite a lot of each kind for bedding, it is normally best to sow the seeds in trays rather than pots. However, you may prefer to use pots for the more difficult seeds that need to be germinated in a propagator, as you can pack more in.

1 Fill a seed tray with a sterilized compost suitable for seeds and seedlings. A potting mix could inhibit germination or harm some seedlings. Strike the compost off level with the rim of the tray.

2 Use a presser board (a scrap of wood cut to the right size will usually do the job) and press the compost gently until it is firmed about 1cm (½in) below the rim.

3 Water the tray now, before you sow. This should provide enough moisture for the seeds initially, and won't wash fine seeds away or to one side of the tray.

4 Very large seeds can be spaced by hand, but most medium-sized seeds are easily scattered with a folded piece of stiff paper. Tap it with a finger as you move it over the surface.

5 Unless the packet advises not to cover the seeds (a few germinate better if exposed to light), cover them by sifting more of the sowing mixture over the top.

6 Unless you are placing the tray in a propagator, cover it with a sheet of glass, or place it in a plastic bag. Turn the glass over or the bag inside out regularly (it may be necessary to do this every day) to prevent condensation drips.

7 Remove any covering when the first seeds start to germinate. If you don't, the seedlings may succumb to diseases. It may be possible to reduce the amount of warmth needed once the seeds have germinated, but good light is essential.

SOWING FINE SEEDS

Very tiny seeds, like lobelia and begonia, are difficult to handle and to spread evenly. Mix them with a small quantity of silver sand to provide greater bulk, then sprinkle the sand and seed mix between finger and thumb as you move your hand over the surface of the tray.

PRICK OUT BEDDING PLANTS

Seeds sown in mid winter may be ready for pricking out, and even those sown in late winter may be ready to move on soon. Never let seedlings become overcrowded after germination.

1 Fill seed trays with a potting mixture recommended for seedlings. Strike the compost off level, then firm it with fingers or a pressing board.

2 Prick out a seedling by loosening the soil and lifting up the plant by its seed leaves (the first ones that open, which usually look very different from the proper leaves).

3 Make a hole in the potting mix, deep enough to take most of the roots without curling them. Gently firm the compost round the roots.

4 To help produce an evenly spaced box of plants, first prick out a row along the end and one side. When you have this spacing right, fill in the rest of the tray.

5 Exact spacing will depend on the type of plant you are pricking out. Large ones need more space than small ones. You are unlikely to fit more than 40 plants in a seed tray.

6 If you find it more convenient, use a modular tray system. This makes spacing easier, and there is less root disturbance when the plants are put in the garden later.

INDEX

ACKNOWLEDGEMENTS

Specially commissioned photography © Anness Publishing Limited. All photography by Peter Anderson and John Freeman except as listed below.

Key: t = top; b = bottom; l = left; c = centre; r = right.

Derek Fell: pages 15b; 27t; 35t, b; 63tr; 87. Paul Forrester: pages 1; 140tr; 176tr, br; 237bl, cb, br. Michelle Garrett: page 239tr. Robert Harding: page 24. Jacqui Hurst: pages 14; 65t; 78t; 79t, bl; 89t, b; 91t; 94tl; 194cr; 240tl.

Additional Picture Credits

The publishers would like to thank the following for permission to reproduce images in this book:

The Garden Picture Library: pages 12t (Marijke Heuff); 34 (Ron Sutherland); 48 (John Duane); 68 (Jane Legate).
The Harput Garden Library: pages 2 (Count and Countess Labia, Cape Town); 6 (designed by Maggie Geiger, NYC); 7t (Exbury Gardens, Hants), c, b; 11t (a garden in Canterbury), b (designed by Michael Balston); 13b (designed by Arabella Lennox-Boyd); 15t (Nooroo Mt. Wilson, NSW); 17b (designed by Trevor Frankland), t (designed by John Patrick, Vic); 20b (designed by Antony Noel, London); 24t (designed by Berry's Garden Co., Golders Green); 25b (designed by Christopher Masson); 26t (designed by Malcolm Hillier, London); 36 (designed by Christopher Masson, London); 38b (designed by Wayne Winterrowd & Joe Eck, London); 39b (designed by Anne Alexander-Sinclair); 40t (designed by Ernie Taylor, Great Barr), b (a garden in Tayside); 42t (designed by Berry's Garden Co., Golders Green); 46t, b (designed by Hilary McMahon for Costin's Nursery, RHS Chelsea); 53b (designed by Antony Noel, London); t (Fudler's Hall, Mashbury); 56t (designed by Jan Martinez, Kent); 61b (designed by Bruce Kelly, NYC); 67br (designed by Arabella Lennox-Boyd); 72b (designed by Anne Alexander-Sinclair); 74br (designed by Lalitte Scott, NYC); 76br (designed by Phillip Watson, Fredericksburg, Va); 78b (designed by Simon Fraser, London); 82t (Joe Elliot, Broadwell, Gloucs); 86 (designed by Beth Chatto); 87 (designed by Ernie Taylor, Great Barr); 90 (Bank House, Borwick); 128 (designed by Susan Whittington); 129; 166 (Fudler's Hall, Mashbury); 192 (The Dingle, Welshpool); 193; 197t (Penny Crawshaw); 230 (designed by Beth Chatto); 231 (designed by Brian Daley & Allan Charman).

Peter McHoy: pages 4; 12b; 32t; 33t; 42t; 47bl; 51br; 54t, b; 55bl; 56b; 57t, b; 61t; 69; 76bl; 83b; 84t, bl, br; 85t; 96t, c, b; 97t, c, b; 98t, b; 99t, c, b; 100t, b; 101t, c, b; 102t, b; 103t, bl, br; 104t, b; 105tl, tr, bl, br; 106t, b; 107tl, tr, b; 108t, b; 109; 110tc, b; 111t, m, b; 112tr, tl, b; 113t, b; 114t, b; 115tr, br, l; 116t, b; 117tl, tr, b; 118l, r; 119t, b; 120t, c, b; 121; 122t, b; 123t, bl, br; 124t, b; 125t, b; 126; 127t, c, b; 133tr, cr; 139bl; 142br; 144br; 147br; 149br; 151bl; 153br; 154br; 163tr; 165tl; 169cl, bl, br; 171br; 172bl; 173tl, ct, tr, bl, cb; 180bl; 183tr; 184tr; 186br; 189br; 190br; 195br; 198bl; 199br; 201cl, cr, bl, br; 204br; 205br; 207t, cl; 209tr; 212tl, ct, tr, br; 213bl; 215t; 217cr; 224br; 226bl; 227br; 228b; 235tl; 236tr, c; 238tl, ct, bl, cb, br; 241tl, tr, bl, cb; 243c; 244br.

The publishers would like to thank the following for their generous help in the production of this book:

Mr and Mrs Blackadder, Judith Blacklock, Nick and Jenny Brunt, Mr and Mrs Richard Chilton, Mrs Eadie, Brand and Sheila Inglis, Mr and Mrs Norman Moore, Joan Parkinson, Vera Quick, Jean Rankin, Peggy Robinson, Audrey Simons, Mrs Shacklock, Chris Sharp, Derek Waring and Dorothy Tutin, Steven Woodhams, Ginny Worsley and Helen Yemm for allowing us to photograph their gardens; Anthony Gardiner of Gardiner's Herbs, 35 Victoria Road, Mortlake, London, for his help with sourcing locations; Andy and Neil Sturgeon of The Fitted Garden and Acorn Landscaping, Garson Farm Garden Centre, Winterdown Road, Esher, Surrey, KT10 8LS for providing the locations, materials and equipment for the step-by-step photography.